Suriname

WORLD BIBLIOGRAPHICAL SERIES
General Editors:
Robert G. Neville (Executive Editor)
John J. Horton

Robert A. Myers   Ian Wallace
Hans H. Wellisch   Ralph Lee Woodward, Jr.

John J. Horton is Deputy Librarian of the University of Bradford and currently Chairman of its Academic Board of Studies in Social Sciences. He has maintained a longstanding interest in the discipline of area studies and its associated bibliographical problems, with special reference to European Studies. In particular he has published in the field of Icelandic and of Yugoslav studies, including the two relevant volumes in the World Bibliographical Series.

Robert A. Myers is Associate Professor of Anthropology in the Division of Social Sciences and Director of Study Abroad Programs at Alfred University, Alfred, New York. He has studied post-colonial island nations of the Caribbean and has spent two years in Nigeria on a Fulbright Lectureship. His interests include international public health, historical anthropology and developing societies. In addition to *Amerindians of the Lesser Antilles: a bibliography* (1981), *A Resource Guide to Dominica, 1493-1986* (1987) and numerous articles, he has compiled the World Bibliographical Series volumes on *Dominica* (1987) and *Nigeria* (1989).

Ian Wallace is Professor of Modern Languages at Loughborough University of Technology. A graduate of Oxford in French and German, he also studied in Tübingen, Heidelberg and Lausanne before taking teaching posts at universities in the USA, Scotland and England. He specializes in East German affairs, especially literature and culture, on which he has published numerous articles and books. In 1979 he founded the journal *GDR Monitor*, which he continues to edit.

Hans H. Wellisch is Professor emeritus at the College of Library and Information Services, University of Maryland. He was President of the American Society of Indexers and was a member of the International Federation for Documentation. He is the author of numerous articles and several books on indexing and abstracting, and has published *The Conversion of Scripts* and *Indexing and Abstracting: an International Bibliography*. He also contributes frequently to *Journal of the American Society for Information Science, The Indexer* and other professional journals.

Ralph Lee Woodward, Jr. is Chairman of the Department of History at Tulane University, New Orleans, where he has been Professor of History since 1970. He is the author of *Central America, a Nation Divided*, 2nd ed. (1985), as well as several monographs and more than sixty scholarly articles on modern Latin America. He has also compiled volumes in the World Bibliographical Series on *Belize* (1980), *Nicaragua* (1983), and *El Salvador* (1988). Dr. Woodward edited the Central American section of the *Research Guide to Central America and the Caribbean* (1985) and is currently editor of the Central American history section of the *Handbook of Latin American Studies*.

VOLUME 117

Suriname

Rosemarijn Hoefte

Compiler

CLIO PRESS

OXFORD, ENGLAND · SANTA BARBARA, CALIFORNIA
DENVER, COLORADO

British Library Cataloguing in Publication Data

Hoefte, Rosemarijn, 1959 –
Suriname. — (World bibliographical series, V. 117).
1. Suriname – Bibliographies
I. Title   II. Series
016. 9883

ISBN 1-85109-103-3

Clio Press Ltd.,
55 St. Thomas' Street,
Oxford OX1 1JG, England.

ABC-CLIO,
130 Cremona Drive,
Santa Barbara,
CA 93117, USA.

Designed by Bernard Crossland.
Typeset by Columns Design and Production Services, Reading, England.
Printed and bound in Great Britain by
Billing and Sons Ltd., Worcester.

THE WORLD BIBLIOGRAPHICAL SERIES

This series, which is principally designed for the English speaker, will eventually cover every country in the world, each in a separate volume comprising annotated entries on works dealing with its history, geography, economy and politics; and with its people, their culture, customs, religion and social organization. Attention will also be paid to current living conditions – housing, education, newspapers, clothing, etc.– that are all too often ignored in standard bibliographies; and to those particular aspects relevant to individual countries. Each volume seeks to achieve, by use of careful selectivity and critical assessment of the literature, an expression of the country and an appreciation of its nature and national aspirations, to guide the reader towards an understanding of its importance. The keynote of the series is to provide, in a uniform format, an interpretation of each country that will express its culture, its place in the world, and the qualities and background that make it unique. The views expressed in individual volumes, however, are not necessarily those of the publisher.

VOLUMES IN THE SERIES

Contents

Contents

Contents

Introduction

Geography

Geography and climate

Suriname is located in the shoulder of South America, sharing borders with the Atlantic Ocean to the north, Guyana to the east, Brazil to the south, and French Guiana to the west. Its surface area of 163,820 square km – this figure includes the two disputed territories with French Guiana and Guyana respectively – makes it one of the smaller states within the continent. The majority of the 400,000 inhabitants live in the small coastal area, which is about 350 km long. The rest of the country, which constitutes more than ninety per cent of the area, is covered by rainforest.

Climatologically Suriname is a tropical country: it is sunny, hot and humid. The average monthly temperature varies between twenty-five and twenty-nine degrees Celsius and the average rainfall per year is 1,500 mm in the coastal area and up to 3,000 mm in the mountainous interior. Three types of climate may be distinguished: the main part of the country has a monsoon climate; the shoreline and the southeast are wet; while a variable wet/dry climate prevails in the inhabited coastal area. There are four distinct seasons: the short dry season starting at the beginning of February and ending in late April; followed by the long rainy period from late April to mid-August; the long dry period lasting from mid-August to early December; and a short rainy period from early December to early February. Suriname does not, however, experience the extreme weather conditions common in the Caribbean such as hurricanes.

Geology

Suriname forms part of the Guyana Shell, one of the earth's oldest pre-Cambrian massifs, which began its formation some 1.9 billion years ago. In the north, the Guyana Shell is covered by sedimentary rock and the landscape rises south of this belt which causes the large rivers to run in a south-north direction. The country can be divided into several geological and topographical zones. The coastal zone consists of sandbanks and mudbanks. The New Coastal Plain, consisting mainly of clay, begins behind the narrow coastal zone and is the most important agricultural area, particularly because the formation of peat has created fertile soil. The Plain was formed during the Weichsel Ice Age and measures 17,000 square km. To the south the smaller Old Coastal Plain consists of swamps as well as dry grounds formed during the last interglacial period. This coastal plain is covered by various types of vegetation depending on the topography: swamps, old ridges, or clay flats. Further south there is an irregular zone of savannas – the Zanderij formation, formed in the Pliocene era – and tropical rainforest. The major part of Suriname is mountainous – Juliana Peak in the Wilhelmina Mountains is the highest summit (1,280 m) – and covered with dense rainforest.

Urbanization

Strategically located along the Suriname River, Paramaribo is the hub of Suriname. As the capital, this town is the centre of government but it also overwhelmingly dominates the social, cultural, and economic life of the country. Although the plantations historically formed the economic and population centres, Paramaribo has always been the seat of government and has an important service sector. Migration to the city increased appreciably after the abolition of slavery, although to this day, there is not much industry of importance in Paramaribo. The majority of the population works for the government or in the service sector – banking, insurance, educational and medical institutions, and company headquarters are all concentrated in the city. The district of Paramaribo houses forty-eight per cent of the total population (195,029 persons).

The second largest population centre is located in the district of Nickerie. Almost ten per cent of the Surinamese population lives in the area between Wageningen and Nieuw Nickerie in the west. Wageningen (3,500 inhabitants) is a company-town in which most of the population is employed in the production of rice, while Nieuw Nickerie is the district capital with an agrarian character, although some administrative services and educational and medical institutions are also based there.

Population

The population of Suriname is characterized by ethnic diversity. Colonists and slaves from Europe and Africa soon outnumbered the original Amerindian inhabitants, while in the 19th century indentured labourers from Asia came to the country to work on the plantations. It is important to note, however, that no one group clearly dominates the other population groups.

Archaeological studies suggest that the first Amerindians reached the Guianas in 3000 BC. These paleo-Amerindians were the forefathers of the Arawaks. A thousand years later the Caribs migrated to the area and evicted most of the Arawaks, although both Arawaks and Caribs experienced a tremendous demographic decline with the arrival of European adventurers and settlers. These Europeans soon started to import African slaves to work on the plantations, and the resultant Surinamese population of African descent is divided into two groups: the Maroons and the Creoles.

The Maroons are the descendants of runaway slaves who escaped the plantations to form their own communities in the rainforest. After a protracted guerrilla war against the colonial authorities in the 18th century, they established viable and independent societies. In the 19th and 20th centuries the contacts between the Maroons and the outside world increased. The Maroons started to participate in the colonial economy: first they were involved in the lumber industry, and later they engaged in the production of gold and became involved in the river transport facilities used by the gold prospectors. Missionaries and government officials visited the Maroons and established schools, medical facilities, and later, airstrips. The Maroons have managed, however, to keep their African-based cultures (including their languages) intact, a fact that has attracted many researchers. They are divided into six groups or tribes, each under its own leader or Granman: the Ndjuka, Saramaka, Paramaka, Matawai, Aluku or Boni, and Kwinti.

The second group comprises the Creoles, also known as town Creoles, descendants of non-fugitive slaves, who often mixed with other ethnic groups.

The British Indians, or Hindustanis, first arrived in Suriname in 1873 as contract labourers for the plantations. In total 34,000 British Indians migrated to Suriname between 1873 and 1917. The Javanese, or Indonesians, too, were indentured labourers, 33,000 Javanese arrived in Suriname between 1890 and 1939. They remained at the plantations and colonization settlements longer than British Indians. Numerically, the British Indians had become the largest ethnic group by the 1960s and by 1989, thirty-five per cent of the population was

British Indian. Their growing economic and political power challenged the position of the Creoles, and in the 1980s they overtook this group. Although numerically only the second largest population in the country (thirty-two per cent) the Creoles have long dominated economic and political life. The third largest ethnic group (fifteen per cent) are the Javanese. The Maroons form approximately ten and a half per cent of the population and in the 1980s became heavily involved in Surinamese politics and initiated a civil war. The 1980 census counted approximately 6,300 Amerindians living in tribes along the interior rivers. These tribes are usually divided into Amerindians of the interior, including the Wayana and the Trio, and the Amerindians of the littoral: the Caribs, the Arawaks, and the Warrao. Those who are not part of tribal organizations and live in the urban areas are often treated as second-class citizens. The Chinese and the Lebanese (often called Syrian) populations, while forming small minorities, possess great economic influence. The rest of the population is formed by Europeans – mainly Dutch – and Americans, as well as (often illegal) migrants from Guyana and Haiti.

Since 1870 the population of Suriname has increased but because of immigration and later emigration this growth shows many fluctuations. In 1870, 50,000 people lived in the coastal areas, in the 1920s the 100,000 mark was passed, mainly because of the immigration of contract labourers from Asia. Even when this migration slowed down, the population growth continued because of a decrease in the death rate. After the Second World War the death rate kept going down, while the number of births increased and in 1960, Suriname had 256,000 inhabitants. From 1972 to 1975 the population decreased as a result of mass emigration to the Netherlands. Subsequently the population gradually recovered and in 1980 360,000 people lived in Suriname. This figure increased to 416,839 by 1 January 1989 and by the year 2000 Suriname's population is expected to number 698,000.

Emigration to the Netherlands is a centuries-old phenomenon in Suriname. The élite families traditionally sent their sons to Dutch schools and universities to receive an education. Since the 1950s members of the Creole middle-class have also left for the Netherlands and in the 1970s, a true mass migration of all ethnic groups and all classes took place in reaction to the deteriorating economy and political developments. The independence of Suriname, widely seen as a Creole plan, was expected by many to lead to racial unrest, so in 1975 approximately 40,000 Surinamese boarded planes to Amsterdam. The following years saw the number of migrants decrease to less than 10,000 as the expected racial problems did not materialize but in 1979, however, it reached 18,000. Despite the fact that since 1980

Surinamese nationals have needed a visa to enter the Netherlands, the number of Surinamese migrants has continued to increase, with some 200,000 Surinamese (one third of the total population) presently living overseas, many of them in Amsterdam and The Hague.

Culture

Language

The cultural diversity of Suriname may be best expressed by the number of languages spoken: there are twenty-two languages of which Dutch, Surinamese-Dutch, Sranan Tongo, Surinamese-Javanese, High-Javanese, Hindi, Sarnami, Saramaccan, Ndjuka, Hakka (Chinese), English, and Spanish all have written forms. The languages of Suriname can be divided into four groups according to their origin: Amerindian languages, Creole languages, Asian languages, and European languages.

Five Amerindian languages are spoken: Carib (or Kalinha) is spoken by 2,500 people; Arawak (or Lokono) is the native language of some 1,000 Amerindians; Wayana (also spoken in Brazil) is spoken by 1,000 Amerindians living along the Litani River and more westward near the Tapanahoni and Palumeu Rivers. Trio consists of two languages: the actual Trio as well as Akuryo (or Wama). The Warrao language is nearly extinct.

Two of the Creole languages spoken in Suriname are influenced by Portuguese: Saramaccan and Matawai. The other Creole languages have their origins in African languages and in English: Paramakan, Ndjuka, Aluku, Kwinti and Sranan (Sranan Tongo). The latter is the lingua franca, not only based on English, but including African, Portuguese, and Dutch elements as well. Sranan, also called Negro-English, was developed at the plantations where it served as the language between masters and slaves and between the slaves themselves.

The Asian languages can be divided into four groups: Sarnami, Javanese, Chinese, and Lebanese. Sarnami Hindi is a generic term for a number of languages and dialects from India which underwent many changes in Suriname due to the influence of other languages. At religious functions Urdu and Hindi are used. Surinamese-Javanese distinguishes two social dialects: Ngoko (low Javanese) and Kromo (high Javanese). The Chinese population speaks Hakka, a southern Chinese language and a dialect of Arabic is spoken by the Lebanese.

Of the European languages six have had an influence in Suriname: English and Portuguese are the basis of several Creole languages; the

Introduction

Huguenots, who arrived in Suriname in the second half of the 17th century, have contributed French words to Sranan; German was spoken by the Moravian Brethren, and had but a negligible influence on any of the languages of Suriname; the Spanish language is important because of the integration with other countries in Latin America; while Dutch is the official language, used exclusively in the educational system. Attempts to make Sranan the official language have met resistance from the non-Creole population in general and the British Indians in particular.

Religion

As can be expected, there exists a strong correlation between ethnicity and religion in Suriname. The principal religions are Christianity, Hinduism, and Islam. The majority of the Creole population is Christian; Roman Catholicism being the largest denomination, followed by the Moravian Brethren (EBG-Evangelische Broeder Gemeente). As elsewhere in the Caribbean and Latin America, the evangelical sects are becoming increasingly popular among Christians.

Approximately eighty per cent of the British Indians are Hindu. The Sanathan Dharm represents the orthodox direction, while the Arya Samaj is more liberal. Both organizations are involved in religious activities such as the building of temples and the education of priests as well as in social work. Religious customs and rites are still very important pillars of British-Indian cultural life and traditions.

The rest of the British Indian population, as well as the Javanese, are Moslems. The majority of the British Indians belong to a more orthodox school than the Javanese traditionalists. The latter group often incorporates pre-Islamic cultural elements in its religious rites.

The Christian missions (Roman Catholic and Moravian Brethren) have not been very successful among the Asian immigrant groups, except for the Chinese. The Maroon and Amerindian populations responded more enthusiastically to Christian teachings. However, Afro-American religious traditions continue to be of great importance to the Maroons and to the Creoles, who still perform Afro-American religious rites, such as *winti* services.

Winti (literally wind) is a traditional polytheistic and largely secret religion of West African origin. The word *winti* encompasses several meanings: all supernatural beings created by God (Anana); the condition, or behaviour, of an individual who believes he is possessed by these beings; diseases, illnesses and other problems caused by the gods, ghosts or magical forces. Thus *winti* recognizes a multitude of gods and ghosts, including their own myths, rites, offerings, taboos, and magical forces. The phenomenon of *obia* (healer-god; supernatural force; amulet) plays a central role: *obia* can bring on illnesses and other calamities. A diviner or *lukuman* (literally seer) can trace the origin of these problems, while a *bonuman* or *obiaman* (often the same person as the *lukuman*) functions as a healer.

An ever-diminishing group of Jews still belongs to the Dutch Jewish and Dutch-Portuguese Jewish Congregations. The majority of the Jewish population, however, has been assimilated into the Creole group.

History

First settlements

The Spanish sighted the coast of Guyana in 1499, but did not show much interest in the area. Rumours about gold in Eldorado, however, attracted other European adventurers, like Sir Walter Raleigh. Eldorado was never found, but the Europeans colonized the coast, despite Amerindian resistance to these intrusions which caused many of the colonization attempts to be abandoned.

The English established the first permanent settlement in 1650 when the Governor of Barbados, Francis Lord Willoughby, sent an expedition to the Guianas. Within a year one hundred planters and their slaves had settled the country between the Coppename and Marowijne Rivers. They were later joined by Portuguese-Jewish planters who had fled the Spanish Inquisition. The sugar plantations prospered and grew in number with African slaves providing the labour force for the estates. The Dutch, meanwhile, had established trading posts on the Essequibo and Corantijn Rivers and were gradually extending their control to the Berbice River.

Sixteen years after the English had settled the area near Torarica, upstream from present-day Paramaribo, a squadron from the Dutch province of Zeeland, led by Abraham Crijnssen, invaded the English possession. As a result of this conflict, England ceded Suriname to the Dutch Republic under the Treaty of Breda (1667), by which England gained control of Nieuw Amsterdam (present-day New York). The majority of the English planters left Suriname for Barbados and Jamaica taking with them capital goods, slaves, and their technical know-how. This, coupled with raids by Amerindians and runaway slaves, turned Suriname's prosperity into an economic malaise. The province of Zeeland was not optimistic about the future of Suriname and sold this possession to the West India Company

Introduction

(WIC), the city of Amsterdam, and the Van Aerssen van Sommelsdijck family. Cornelis van Aerssen soon left for Suriname to restore order. He subdued the Amerindians and initiated a new economic boom by promoting new large estates and setting up the regular importation of slaves from Africa. Despite the murder of Van Aerssen in 1688, the colony started to prosper again. The number of plantations grew as well as the size of single plantations. Instead of the more family-based plantations of the English, now a large slave labour force toiled on extensive estates directed by a white manager.

Plantation Colony

Despite occasional intrusions by the French, the number of plantations continued to increase, as did the production of sugar, coffee, cacao, and later cotton. In the mid-18th century the colony had 500 plantations and in 1787, approximately 50,000 inhabitants, of whom ninety per cent were slaves. The prosperity of the plantations, however, was largely based on credit. The estates served as security and in most cases the value of these securities was lower than the amount of the loans. Moreover, this 'easy money' was often spent on luxury goods rather than on the plantation itself. This illusion of prosperity was quickly shattered by a major slave revolt in Berbice (1763) and by continuing problems with Maroons, who depleted the labour force and pillaged the plantations in their search for food, tools, and women. Two opposing tactics were employed by the planters to eliminate the threat posed by the Maroons: a resort to arms as well as the ratification of peace treaties with the Ndjukas and the Saramakas in 1761 and 1762, respectively. The Maroon attacks had shocked economic confidence in Suriname, while a financial crisis at the Amsterdam stock-market, which stopped the money flow to the colony, did the rest. Most of the plantations now fell into the possession of creditors who left the daily management of the estates to administrators in Paramaribo. This absentee ownership had further negative influences on the plantation economy: short-term interests led to the exhaustion of the soil, machinery, and the labour force. Calm was restored finally in 1790 and new plantations were founded to the west of Paramaribo, along the Saramacca, Nickerie, and Coronie Rivers. These plantations were often owned by colonists of English and Scottish descent. The (false) prosperity in the last decades of the 18th century led to a brief flourishing in the cultural life in Paramaribo. A leisure class had the time and money to spend on literature, theatre, and science. The first newspaper began publication, a communal theatre was built and the Hortus Surinamensis briefly enjoyed public attention.

As a result of the Napoleonic wars in Europe, Suriname was 'offered protection' by Britain in 1799. However, with the Peace of Amiens (1802), Suriname returned briefly into the possession of the Dutch, only to be occupied for the third time in its history by the English in 1804. The years of the English Interim Government (1804-16) led to economic deterioration: the disruption of trade made it virtually impossible to sell products in Europe or to import slaves. In this respect, one of the most important developments under the British was the abolition of the slave trade in 1808. When Suriname returned to the Dutch, the number of plantations had been reduced drastically and an economic recovery did not materialize. The situation worsened even further: in 1821 and 1832 fires burnt down large parts of Paramaribo; from 1844 the government in The Hague had to make up the budget deficits in the colony; and new slaves were no longer imported after the abolition of the slave trade. The planters were forced to treat their slaves better in order to improve their productivity, stimulate the birth rate, and lower the death rate. The abolition of slavery itself was not seriously considered, however, until 1853. In the British colonies the slaves were freed in 1833, and the French followed in 1848, after a long and technical debate a law was passed in the Dutch parliament proclaiming the abolition of slavery on 1 July 1863. The planters received 300 guilders from the Dutch treasury in compensation for every slave released by them. Although more than 33,000 slaves were free now, there was a ten-year period of state supervision, which included mandatory contract work by the former slaves for a planter of their choice. State supervision provided a means of peaceful transition from slavery to free labour and guaranteed the planters an adequate supply of labour for some years.

Contract labour and economic changes

In 1873 the first British-Indian indentured labourers arrived in Suriname. Even though the planters greeted these new labourers with a sigh of relief, problems soon began to surface. The colony's plantation labour supply was now dependent on a foreign nation which was entitled to stop the migration, furthermore, the British Indians remained subjects of Great Britain and could appeal against any decisions made by the highest Dutch authority and had the right to request the assistance of the British consul. Finally, political developments in India suggested that contract migration might become illegal. This did indeed happen; 1914 saw the last British Indians arrive in Suriname. Of the 34,000 British Indian labourers who came to Suriname on a contract basis, one-third returned to India after the expiry of their contracts. Meanwhile, however, the

Introduction

Surinamese plantations had tapped a new supply of labour in the Dutch East Indies and the island of Java in particular. In 1890, the first group of Javanese indentured labourers set foot on Surinamese soil. Until the outbreak of the Second World War some 33,000 Javanese migrated to Suriname and approximately one quarter of them opted for repatriation to the East Indies on completion of their contracts.

Following the abolition of slavery, Suriname also experienced some major economic changes. During the period of state supervision of labour (1863-73) sugar and its byproducts represented eighty per cent of the total value of exports, in the following decade this fell to fifty per cent. The value of sugar exports continued to decline up until the First World War when it represented approximately twenty to thirty per cent of the total value of all exports. The Great Depression caused another sharp downfall, and by 1939 only six per cent of the total value of exports was derived from sugar products. The deteriorating position of Suriname in the world sugar market was caused mainly by factors outside its control such as the opening of the Suez Canal which facilitated trade with East Asia; the imposition of preferential tariffs in Europe; and competition from beet sugar. The production of sugar was now confined to large estates. Of eighty-seven sugar plantations registered in 1860, eighty had disappeared by the turn of the century and in 1940 only four remained in operation. These estates had managed to keep production going at the pre-Emancipation level despite the severe problems posed by the rapidly declining price of the product.

Economic crises within the sugar industry had a disastrous effect on the economy as a whole because of the overwhelming predominance of that commodity. Yet, total collapse was always avoided by (temporary) resort to alternatives such as tropical products, gold and bauxite, although only the latter of these could replace sugar as the mainstay of the economy. In an agricultural colony like Suriname the search for alternatives to sugar focused on products that could be produced by smallholders. However, the cultivation of coffee, cacao, citrus fruits and bananas could not remedy the situation; severe competition from other Latin American countries and crop diseases rendered these alternatives almost unviable.

Nonagricultural alternatives to sugar included balata (rubber), gold, timber, and bauxite. For a short time balata tapping was a lucrative enterprise, it was short-lived, however, because of competition from other areas along with inexpert tapping and the increasing inaccessibility of productive trees. Gold-mining started in the 1870s in the Lawa area, and the colonial administration fostered this activity by granting favourable concessions and by promoting the building of a railway from Paramaribo to Lawa. When construction was finished in 1912, however, the production of gold was already on the decline. Its exploitation never lived up to the initial high expectations; the small amounts found locally did not turn out to be very profitable because of the high production costs. Timber of good quality was found deep in the interior, but exploitation was haphazard and the Maroons mostly cut, transported, and sold the timber locally.

In 1915, bauxite deposits were found by an American geologist. This discovery gained particular importance during the First World War and in 1917, the Suriname Bauxite Company, an American enterprise, started production. By the 1930s bauxite had become the country's primary export. The industry also became the major employer, paying higher wages and providing better fringe benefits than other enterprises. It should be noted that bauxite has continued to be the most valuable export in Suriname.

Not surprisingly, Suriname did not escape the effects of the Great Depression of the 1930s, and the result was unemployment, social unrest, and political resistance. In 1931 Paramaribo was the scene of riots, which were violently suppressed by the police. The arrival of Anton de Kom, a Creole activist fighting imperialism and colonialism proved to be a major catalyst. De Kom was regarded as a hero by all population groups and in January 1933, the government arrested De Kom in an attempt to curb his influence. A crowd of his supporters assembled to demand his release, and despite warnings, the police killed two demonstrators and wounded several others. This tragedy put an end to the active protest against the administration and De Kom was ultimately deported. The Second World War brought a brief economic boom to Suriname. The stationing of US army troops there to defend the bauxite mines and transport routes, as well as the growing importance of bauxite in the world economy led to an increase in employment and migration from the rural districts to Paramaribo and the mining centres. It is important to recognize that Suriname produced two-thirds of the bauxite used by the Allied Forces during the war.

Autonomy

The Second World War was also an important phase in the political emancipation of the colony. The growing anti-colonialist feeling, as expressed in the Atlantic Charter for example, did not bypass Suriname. In 1866 a new colonial constitution had already provided for a certain measure of autonomy and the *Koloniale Staten* (Colonial Estates) were established. Yet, this assembly had a merely supervisory function. After the war meetings between the Netherlands, Suriname, and the Netherlands Antilles, resulted in a new legal order. In 1954 the *Charter of the Kingdom of the Netherlands* came into existence. It was intended to lead eventually to the independence of the overseas territories. From then on the Kingdom of the Netherlands comprised three equal and autonomous partners: the Netherlands, Suriname, and the Netherlands Antilles. Only defence, foreign affairs, the determination of nationality rights and status, and the guarantee of fundamental human rights remained the exclusive domain of the government in The Hague.

Since 1950 the *Staten* have held full parliamentary powers and their members have been elected on the basis of universal suffrage. The political parties are organized on an ethnic basis, the three most important parties being the Creole NPS (National Party Suriname), the British-Indian VHP (Progressive Reformational Party, Vooruitstrevende Hervormingspartij) and the Javanese KTPI (Party of Unity and Higher Order, Kaum Tani Persatuan Indonesia).

Independence

The enthusiasm for the *Charter* as an ingenious and progressive arrangement of post-colonial affairs soon waned. The NPS in particular desired an autonomous foreign policy for Suriname, while the VHP objected to such a modification of the *Charter*. This conflict between the Creoles and British Indians on the political development of Suriname continued until 1975. The Creoles called for political independence by arguing that it was a prerequisite for economic independence. In the opinion of British Indians, however, economic stability was the precondition for political sovereignty. Yet, because the coalition-cabinets of Creoles and British Indians governed Suriname from 1958 to 1973, relations with the Netherlands did not change. Meanwhile, in the Netherlands support for the independence of the overseas territories was growing. In 1969 riots in both Suriname and Curaçao revealed great social and political tensions. In the latter case, the *Charter* compelled the Dutch military to intervene in the conflict, which not only damaged relations within the Kingdom, but also seemed to shatter the liberal Dutch image abroad. A final, and more practical motive for the Dutch to amend the *Charter* was the mass migration of Surinamese to the Netherlands. Thousands of Surinamese fled the unstable socioeconomic situation in their country. However, on arrival in the Netherlands, they found a declining Dutch economy caused by the growing competition for housing and jobs. These migrants had the same rights as Dutch citizens and thus put a strain on the Dutch social security system.

Both the Dutch and the Surinamese governments concluded that the independence of Suriname would be the only solution to halt the migration and rebuild the reputation of the Netherlands abroad. In 1973, the Creole-dominated government headed by Henck Arron declared that Suriname would withdraw from the Kingdom of the Netherlands before 1976. Despite the fact that Prime Minister Arron's cabinet enjoyed only the smallest majority in parliament and that the largest opposition party, the British-Indian VHP rejected sovereignty, on 25 November 1975 Suriname celebrated its independence. Even though the country was now a sovereign republic, ties with the Netherlands remained close: in foreign affairs and defence matters the two countries collaborated a great deal, and economically the Dutch influence was extensive. Development aid worth 35 billion guilders was to be spent within ten to fifteen years on the basis of the Multi Annual Development Plan (Meerjarenontwikkelingsplan, MOP). The treaty concerning development cooperation stipulated that Paramaribo and The Hague would consult each other and that both governments would share responsibility for the disbursement of the monies. In short, although Suriname had become an independent republic, the assistance of the Netherlands remained instrumental in determining the development of the country.

The military régime

The Arron administration did not live up to its promises of political, social, and economic reform. The solidarity apparent at the festivities celebrating independence soon vanished and ethnic interests prevailed over national interests. A lack of planning, as well as nepotism, patronage, and corruption characterized Surinamese society. Not surprisingly, the emigration of Surinamese continued unabated. Meanwhile, Dutch-Surinamese relations came under severe pressure as the spending of development aid caused much friction. Suriname opted for investments in large-scale projects, mainly to promote the bauxite industry in west Suriname. The Netherlands warned against relying solely on one industry and their increasing economic dependence on the United States and the Netherlands. Yet, Suriname prefered ambitious infrastructural projects over diverse small-scale plans. This irritation over the projects chosen, as well as inefficiency and fraud, led to repeated delays and cancellations in the transfer of money to Suriname. Furthermore, the role of the Netherlands was rather ambiguous as the country acted simultaneously as donor, spender, and receiver. An appreciable percentage of the huge amounts of money were returned to the Netherlands because of the obligation to employ Dutch personnel and capital goods for the implementation of the projects. The Dutch not only decided if projects fitted within the framework of the MOP, but also if they corresponded to the interests of the Dutch economy. Needless to say, charges of neo-colonialism were often heard.

In this atmosphere of stagnation and dejection, a relatively minor incident would have sufficed to light the fuse of the powder keg. Unrest among the Non-Commissioned Officers (NCOs) in the Surinamese Army proved to be such an incident. Their most important grievance was that their union had not been acknowledged by their superiors. On 25 February 1980, sixteen NCOs executed a *coup d'état*. The most prominent figure turned out to be Sergeant Desi Bouterse. Both the Arron cabinet and the parliament were discharged of their duties. The military allowed President Johan Ferrier to remain in office and declared that the constitution and all treaties remained in force. Furthermore, a swift return to civilian government was promised. In May 1980, a civilian government headed by Henk Chin A Sen was indeed appointed, but this did not bring about the stability that was hoped for. In the following August Bouterse claimed that a leftist *coup d'état* had been thwarted. At the same time that the left was being discredited, the right was rendered bereft of leadership when President Ferrier resigned and left for the Netherlands; Prime Minister Chin A Sen became Ferrier's successor. To complete this redistribution of power the constitution was suspended, leaving the military, and Bouterse in particular, to wield executive power.

Within a year the military was calling their 'intervention' a 'revolution'. This change in terminology signalled another political transformation. From 1981 to 1984, Bouterse closely cooperated with the PALU (Progressive Labourers and Farmers Union, Progressieve Arbeiders en Landbouwers Unie) and the RVP (Revolutionary People's Party, Revolutionaire Volks Partij) and embarked on a socialist course. The main result was that a wedge was driven between the military and the civilian politicians. The military, PALU, and RVP organized a Revolutionary Front to create a sovereign socialist state. Chin A Sen meanwhile, drafted a new constitution and prepared for free elections. In February 1982, Chin A Sen concluded that his mission was hopeless and resigned. Once more Bouterse seized the opportunity to restructure the power of state and once more the military was the beneficiary. The civilian politicians and the new president, Fred Ramdat Misier, were completely subordinate to the military. The revolution had by then reached its most radical stage. The formation of a people's militia, the establishment of close relations with Cuba and Grenada, the standardization of the university, the Judiciary, and public enterprises, all resulted in an increasing polarization between revolutionaries and democrats. The opposition finally managed to organize itself and under the leadership of the largest trade union federation, the *Moederbond*, churches, journalists, professionals, scholars, and employers all protested against the ideological betrayal by the military and called for the restoration of democracy. During the night of 8 December 1982, the military brutally silenced this opposition by torturing and murdering fifteen of their carefully selected opponents, burning down a newspaper office, two radio-stations, the office of the *Moederbond*, and closing five daily and weekly newspapers, as well as two press agencies. Although violations of human rights had occurred before, the magnitude of the 'December murders' sent an enormous shock wave through Suriname and many citizens went underground, or fled the country.

For nearly three years, the Netherlands had given the benefit of the doubt to Suriname. In December 1982 this scepticism turned into sharp denunciation of the 'power hungry' military. All treaties were suspended and it was declared that development cooperation would only resume when fundamental human rights were guaranteed and the country became a parliamentary democracy again. The events of December 1982 not only proved to be traumatic in Suriname, they also put Surinamese-Dutch relations under extreme tension. Even though the suspension of Dutch aid, constituting more than one-fifth of Suriname's national budget, wreaked havoc on an already weak economy, Bouterse continued on the same revolutionary path. Yet, closer ties to Cuba, Grenada, and Libya as well as Brazil could not compensate for the loss of funds from The Hague. In addition, the demand for Suriname's only major export product, bauxite, fell. As a result of these crises, unemployment, inflation, and the budget deficit continued to increase. Limits on imports, a shortage of foreign currencies, and a lack of raw materials forced many businesses to cease their activities. Bouterse made the best of a deteriorating situation and decided to change course. He dropped his revolutionary friends in PALU and RVP and allowed the return to the political arena of the 'old order' trade unions and employers' organizations. This cautious retreat from a socialist experiment heralded the beginning of the process of redemocratization. A National Assembly, which included representatives of the military, trade unions and employers, was to prepare a new constitution. The essential change, however, came when the military allowed the traditional political parties (NPS, VHP, KTPI) to become (legally) active again and within a year they formed part of a new cabinet.

Introduction

Return to democracy

The process of redemocratization did not mean the end of Bouterse's problems, however. Rumours about drugs trafficking by the military seemed to be corroborated by the arrest of Etienne Boerenveen, a high military official, in an FBI sting operation in Miami. Moreover, since the summer of 1986 the army had been plagued by a guerrilla war in east Suriname. Under the leadership of the Ndjuka Ronnie Brunswijk, a former body-guard of Bouterse, the Jungle Commando demanded the resignation of Bouterse, the restoration of democracy, and the emancipation of the Maroons. The Jungle Commando, though small and poorly equipped, rapidly conquered east Suriname. The war continues to cause an enormous upheaval in the interior. The National Army, in particular, is accused of gross violations of human rights, causing thousands to flee to Paramaribo, the Netherlands, and French Guiana.

Nevertheless, in a referendum in September 1987 a new constitution was approved by ninety-five per cent of the electorate. This constitution provided for an elected National Assembly as the highest legislative institution, as well as a Privy Council consisting of representatives of political parties, interest groups, and the military, and which acts as a supervisory body. The army not only has the task of defending the country's sovereignty, but also has to liberate the country and to improve its development.

In the elections in November 1987 the NPS, VHP, and KTPI united in a Front for Democracy and Development (Front voor Democratie en Ontwikkeling) and scored a clear victory by winning forty of the fifty-one seats in the National Assembly. In January 1988 Ramsewak Shankar was inaugurated as President of Suriname, while Henck Arron returned as Prime Minister and Vice-President. Although the old political parties may officially be back in control, the hand of the military is still clearly evident. Despite its initial optimism, the Dutch government is reluctant to release funds for Suriname except for humanitarian assistance. The Hague is worried about the lack of economic planning, the numerous incidents involving the military, and the persistant civil war, now involving Amerindian groups as well as Maroons. Even though the black market is flourishing, the return of democracy has not led to the revival of the official economy. As a result, the future of Suriname is bleak and the number of emigrants continues to grow.

Economy

Prior to the 20th century Suriname was a plantation colony producing sugar, coffee, cotton and cacao for the European market. The decline of plantation agriculture in the 19th century seemed to lead to the complete economic ruin of Suriname. However, the exploitation of bauxite saved the colony from bankruptcy and for many years Suriname has been the world's leading producer of bauxite.

The period 1955-65 saw the implementation of Suriname's first Ten-Year Development Plan. The focus was on the improvement of the infrastructure, including the construction of the international airport, Zanderij, near Paramaribo. The most spectacular as well as far-reaching project was the construction of a dam and hydro-electric plant on the Suriname River. Besides the economic impact, this plan had tremendous ecological and human consequences. The flooding of 1,350 square km of land to create Lake Brokopondo forced the migration of 5,000 to 6,000 Saramakas and Ndjukas during the period 1958-64. The second Ten-Year Plan involved industrialization on the basis of hydro-electric power. The following MOP plan concentrated on west Suriname in order to exploit the bauxite deposits there. It called for the construction of a railway from the town of Apoera to the Bakhuis Mountains; the Corantijn canal linking Wageningen to Wakay; and a dam and two hydro-electric power stations in the Kabalebo River. Only the first phase of the project has been realized to date, although the railway is not in use at present.

Bauxite and its derivatives (alumina and aluminium) account for approximately eighty per cent of the total value of exports and about eighteen per cent of the Gross Domestic Product (GDP). However, the bauxite-mining industry employs only four per cent of the working population, making bauxite revenues critically important in the financing of other activities, such as the sizeable civil service, which employs more than forty per cent of the working population.

Mining began in 1915, but only in 1922 did the first shipment of bauxite leave Suriname. The most important bauxite company is Suralco (Suriname Aluminum Company), a fully owned subsidiary of Alcoa (Aluminum Company of America), with Shell/Billiton as the second-largest company. In the 1970s Suriname lost its traditional North American market for bauxite due to internal political changes, increased international competition, and the world economic recession. The 1980s also saw the production of bauxite fall. Consequently, aluminium smelting and the production of primary metal has declined drastically. The crisis in the bauxite industry has led to a loss of employment in the industry itself and has also had repercussions for the economy as a whole. Problems increased even further when the guerrilla war focused on the area near Moengo. The refinery there, and the hydro-electric plant in Brokopondo, were both damaged. At the moment, however, there is some optimism about the chances of survival of the industry. However, the plans to exploit bauxite deposits in the Bakhuis Mountains in west Suriname, as well as the projected construction of a hydro-electric power station on the Kabalebo River, have been (temporarily) abandoned.

However, Suriname does have other mineral resources including gold, diamonds, iron, platinum, and manganese and the exploitation of oil in the Saramacca district also looks promising. The Suriname State Oil Company (Staatsolie) announced in 1986 that proven reserves were in excess of 450 million barrels.

Agriculture, fishing, and forestry contribute approximately ten per cent of the GDP and employ seventeen per cent of the working population. Rice is the most important crop and is grown by smallholders of Javanese and British-Indian descent on plots of less than one hectare, as well as by large corporations. In the district of Nickerie production is largely mechanized; the rice farm at Wageningen is the largest and the show-piece of the agricultural sector. Rice is used for domestic consumption and export, but since 1986 output has declined dramatically. Sugar, bananas, coconuts, coffee, fruit, and vegetables are all grown in small quantities, and the production of oil palm was one of the country's most valuable crops. However, a guerrilla attack in 1986 on one of the largest plantations resulted in a sharp drop in the production of palm oil. Livestock makes an insignificant contribution to the economy; efforts to breed a herd of cattle for the production of milk and meat have not been very successful to date. Fishery is becoming increasingly important, especially shrimps which represent ten per cent of the total value of exports. Even though Suriname is largely covered by forest, this resource has been underexploited and timber only forms three per cent of annual exports. Foodstuffs and consumer goods dominate the manufacturing sector, which employs approximately ten per cent of the working population and accounts for ten to fifteen per cent of the GDP. This sector has been hit hard by the economic crisis which has limited the purchasing power of the population and has severely curtailed the importation of raw materials and machinery.

In its 1989 annual report, the Central Bank of Suriname (De Surinaamsche Bank) expressed great concern over the country's economy and the ever-increasing dependency on bauxite. The main reasons for the 'deplorable financial and economic situation' are, according to the Central Bank, the huge budget deficit, in relative terms one of the highest in the world, and the financial methods used to cover this deficit, as well as the small quantity of official currency.

The alarming situation is disguised somewhat by the sending of money, food; and other products by relatives and friends abroad. It is estimated that this unofficial importation corresponds to more than half of Suriname's official imports. In 1986, the official unemployment rate was twenty-five per cent, but unofficially it was estimated to be at least thirty per cent. Guerrilla attacks, and foreign exchange shortages, in particular continue to cause the loss of thousands of jobs.

About the bibliography

Suriname is a fascinating country. Various aspects of this socially and culturally diverse country continue to intrigue researchers and this is reflected by the content of this selective bibliography. Two areas which hold a particular attraction for academics are firstly, the society and culture of the Maroons, and secondly, the study of Suriname's languages, with particular focus on the seven Creole languages. More general trends in Caribbean historiography, such as the importance of the plantation economy and the forms of forced labour used therein are also considered, Another important field of study concerns the large number of Surinamese emigrants living in the Netherlands. The chapter on politics reflects the sad irony that only negative news from the Third World arouses any interest in the West and presents a selection of the flood of publications which followed the *coup d'état* of 1980. The inclusion of many recent publications (from the late 1980s) has resulted in a selection which to a certain extent reflects the current state of research in Suriname.

This selective bibliography intended for an international audience covers important English-language publications as well as significant and recent studies in other languages such as Spanish, German, French, and Dutch. Many of the latter publications, however, contain summaries in English and are thus readily accessible to English speakers. Publications on the Caribbean in general are not included, unless they contain chapters or specific information on Suriname. The same applies to periodicals. Only periodicals on the Caribbean which regularly contain articles on Suriname are mentioned.

All publications are entered only once, although many could be cited under several chapter headings. The index, however, provides a valuable reference to the literature and directs the reader to information on subjects, names, titles and places.

Introduction

Acknowledgements

The compilation of this bibliography leaves a trail of debt. The Ministry of Education and Science in the Netherlands subsidized the project. Assistant editor Milica Djuradjević saved me from many a pitfall. I am grateful to the staff of the library and the respository of the Royal Institute of Linguistics and Anthropology in Leiden whose friendliness and efficiency are unmatched. I want to thank Jo Derkx, Ineke Deurwaarder, Juliette Henket, Marcel Hoefte, Ingrid Loeffen, Peter Meel, Gert Oostindie, and Maarten Smit for their assistance in the project and I am especially beholden to Marlies Heeger and Irene Rolfes, who spent so much time helping me in the last phases of this undertaking.

The Country and its People

1 **Suriname; places and peoples of the world.**
Noëlle Blackmer Beatty.   New York, Philadelphia: Chelsea House,
1988. 96p. map.
A short introduction to Suriname, covering the natural environment, its history, the
population, government and education, the economy, urbanization, and the arts. The
book includes a glossary, an index, a list of basic statistical facts, and an historical
chronology.

2 **The Dutch Caribbean: foto's uit Suriname en de Nederlandse Antillen.**
(The Dutch Caribbean: photographs from Suriname and the Netherlands
Antilles.)
Willem Diepraam, Gerard van Westerloo.   Amsterdam: De
Arbeiderspers, 1978. 112p.
Following an introductory text in English and Dutch by journalist Van Westerloo,
photographer Diepraam presents pictures of Suriname and the Netherlands Antilles.
Approximately fifty of the photographs were taken in Suriname.

3 **The land and people of the Guianas.**
Alan Mark Fletcher.   Philadelphia, New York: J. B. Lippincott, 1966.
map. (Portraits of the Nations Series).
An introduction to Guyana, Suriname, and French Guiana. The first three chapters
sketch the common characteristics of these three countries, such as their geography
and early history. Four chapters are dedicated to Suriname. One chapter discusses the
Maroons, here erroneously called Ndjukas. This chapter contains other errors and
should be read carefully. Although some of the information on the economy and on
the governmental structure is dated, the book provides a rather useful overview for the
general reader.

1

The Country and its People

4   **Les Guyanes. (Guyana, Surinam, Guyane française).** (The Guyanas.
    Guyana, Suriname, French Guiana.)
    Jean-Claude Giacottini.   Paris: Presses Universitaires de France, 1984.
    127p. map. bibliog. (Que Sais-Je? 1315).
A booklet covering the three Guianas. The first three chapters discuss some common characteristics of these countries: the natural environment; history; and population. In the next three chapters, the author deals with each country separately. In the section on Suriname, he treats the mining economy; agriculture, fishing and forestry; small-scale industries; and the social and economic problems of the country.

5   **Cultureel mozaiek van Suriname. Bijdrage tot onderling begrip.** (Cultural
    mosaic of Suriname. Contribution to mutual understanding.)
    Edited by Albert Helman.   Zutphen, The Netherlands: De Walburg
    Pers, 1977. 448p. maps. bibliog.
An indispensable introduction to Suriname and its inhabitants. The twenty-eight contributors discuss anthropological, sociological, political, economic, and cultural aspects, such as costume; sport and games; language and oral literature; religion and education; architecture; the media; and the arts.

6   **Netherlands America. The Dutch territories in the West.**
    Philip Hanson Hiss.   New York: Duell, Sloan & Pearce, 1943. 225p.
    maps.
An introduction to Suriname and the Netherlands Antilles intended for an American audience. This book was written when these territories were increasing in strategic importance for the United States and provides a general overview of the history of the Dutch colonies in the West. The author pays much attention to the economic sectors important to the Allied war effort, which in the case of Suriname was the bauxite industry. Twenty-one appendices list data on topics varying from statistics on emancipated slaves to rainfall.

7   **Holländisch-Guiana: Erlebnisse und Erfahrungen während eines
    43jährigen Aufenthalts in der Kolonie Surinam.** (Dutch Guiana: events
    and experiences during a 43-year residence in the colony of Suriname.)
    A. Kappler.   Stuttgart, FRG: (no publisher), 1881. 495p. map.
A document relating the experiences of Kappler, a German who came to Suriname as a soldier (1836-41) and later became a collector of plants and animals, which he sold in Europe. Later he settled along the Marowijne River (1846-79), where he founded the town of Albina, in order to facilitate the exploration of the jungle and to establish trading links with the Amerindians and Maroons. The book includes extensive descriptions of expeditions into the interior, as well as of the population and flora and fauna there.

8   **Suriname.**
J. Moerland.   Zutphen, The Netherlands: Terra, 1984. 80p. maps.
bibliog. (Koninklijk Instituut voor de Tropen, Landendocumentatie
1984, 1).

A good Dutch-language introduction to Suriname. The author successively describes
the physical geography; history; spatial structure; population; administration and
politics; society; the economy; and, finally, the developmental policy of the country.

9   **Surinam in pictures.**
Martha Murray Sumwalt.   New York: Sterling Publishing, 1971. 64p.
map. (Visual Geography Series).

A general illustrated introduction to Suriname. The book gives the reader a quick
overview of the geography; history and administration; people and culture; and the
economy of the country. Published in 1971, this volume is in places rather dated.

10   **Kijk op Suriname.** (A look at Suriname.)
J. Tj. Wassink.   Amsterdam, Brussels: Elsevier, 1980. 128p. bibliog.

A colourful introduction to Suriname by a Dutchman who has lived in Suriname for
many years. He pays much attention to the population, the economy, architecture, and
the interior. The book is illustrated with over 200 colour photographs.

11   **Frimangron. Suriname: reportages uit een Zuidamerikaanse republiek.**
(Free men's land. Suriname: reportage from a South American
republic.)
Gerard van Westerloo, Willem Diepraam.   Amsterdam: De
Arbeiderspers, 1975. 224p. maps.

A wonderful collection of photographs taken in 1973 and 1975, with accompanying
texts by journalist Van Westerloo, this book shows life in Paramaribo, the regions
outside the capital and the interior. The texts are historical and socio-economic in
character. Both photographs and text emphasize the cultural diversity of Suriname.
Diepraam and Van Westerloo call Suriname 'a construction, not a country'.

12   **Suriname, de schele onafhankelijkheid.** (Suriname, the one-eyed
independence.)
Edited by Glenn Willemsen.   Amsterdam: De Arbeiderspers, 1983.
257p. maps. bibliog.

This volume's supposed leitmotiv is domination and resistance, yet not all of the eight
contributions focus on this theme. Topics discussed include colonial society; Maroons
and their religions; nationalism and ethnicity; migration; independence; economic
development; and Suriname during the Second World War.

Geography and Geology

Geography

13 **Landforms and soils in eastern Surinam (South America).**
M. H. W. de Boer. Wageningen, The Netherlands: Centre for
Agricultural Publishing and Documentation, 1972. 169p. maps.
(Agricultural Research Reports, 771).

A dissertation (Landbouwhogeschool Wageningen, the Netherlands, 1972) on the
quaternary geogenesis in eastern Suriname based on fieldwork and sedimentary-
petrographic research. The development of the river valleys is explained in terms of
changes in sea level, tectonic movements, and changes in climate. A detailed study of
pedogenesis is based on eight soil profiles. This publication also includes a classification
of twenty-seven soil profiles according to US, French, and Brazilian classification
systems as well as summaries in French and Spanish.

14 **Global radiation at Paramaribo.**
K. J. Lenselink, R. van der Weert. *De Surinaamse Landbouw*, vol. 21,
no. 1 (1973), p. 21-27. bibliog.

Starting in 1971 global radiation was measured daily and the duration of bright
sunshine was determined with a sunshine recorder. The authors discuss the use of
regression analysis to calculate monthly variations in global radiation throughout the
year.

15 **Geomorphology and soils of Sipaliwini savanna, south Suriname.**
Hans Theo Riezebos. Utrecht, The Netherlands: Geografisch Instituut
Rijksuniversiteit Utrecht, 1979. 168p. maps. bibliog. (Utrechtse
Geografische Studies, 12).

This thesis (Rijksuniversiteit Utrecht, the Netherlands, 1979) describes the landscape
of the Sipaliwini savanna. The author emphasizes the relation between geomorphology
and soil development and notes the presence of three planation levels which

characterize the geomorphology of the savanna. The lowest level comprises the actual valley floors and flood plains; the other two levels constitute the so-called summit levels. The study of soil profiles from the three geomorphic units reveals the presence of a soil toposequence. The author developed a model to describe the evolution of the area in connection with tectonic, hydrologic, climatic, and vegetation conditions. From this model it appears that changes in vegetation from tropical rainforest to savanna may be induced by changes in relief which follow river incision and planation. Riezebos implies that climatic changes may play a less important role in changing the vegetation than is generally understood.

16 **The Emma Range in Surinam; a study of physical geographical problems, including the morpho-tectonical evolution, and weathering phenomena.**
Johan Jacob Wensink. PhD dissertation, Universiteit van Amsterdam, 1968. 159p. maps. bibliog.

An investigation of the physical geography of the Emma Range in central Suriname and the processes of weathering under humid tropical conditions. In this part of Suriname, which had not been investigated before, the author surveyed the climate, the landforms, the geology in relation to weathering, and geomorphological problems. In addition, measurements were made for the determination of geographically important altitudes. Wensink analyses and describes the profiles of a number of weathering products from various types of parent rock. A morphoscopic analysis was used to compare the degree of rounding of quartz grains in this area with those in northern Suriname.

Geology

17 **The changing shoreline of Surinam (South America).**
P. G. E. F. Augustinus. Utrecht, The Netherlands: Natuurwetenschappelijke Studiekring voor Suriname en de Nederlandse Antillen, 1978. 232p. maps. bibliog. (Uitgave, 95).

The aim of this publication is to obtain an insight into the origin of Suriname's Young Coastal Plain, particularly into the processes which contributed to its development. The Young Coastal Plain is the Holocene part of the coastal lowland, extending along the entire coast between the mouths of the Marowijne and Corantijn Rivers over a distance of approximately 350 kilometres. Its width varies from 30 kilometres in the east to 140 kilometres in the west. The volume contains sixty-nine text illustrations and seventeen plates.

18 **Über den Einfluss von Klima, jüngerer Sedimentation und Bodenprofilentwickelung auf die Savannen nord-Surinams (Mittelguyana).** (On the influence of climate, recent sedimentation and soil profile development in the savannas of northern Suriname, Central Guiana.)
J. P. Bakker. *Erdkunde,* vol. 8, no. 2 (April. 1954), p. 89-112. maps. bibliog.

A paper discussing the influence of climate, recent deposition, and the development of soil profiles on the formation of savannas in northern Suriname. These savannas are not only the result of climate, and the author considers the other causes responsible for their formation. He also questions whether perhaps edaphic and human factors have played a more important role in these regions than hitherto assumed. The article includes a summary in English.

19   **Gravitational and geomagnetic investigations in Surinam and their structural implications.**
     J. J. G. M. van Boeckel.   PhD dissertation, Universiteit van Amsterdam, 1968. 287p. maps. bibliog.

This thesis presents the results of a regional survey of gravity in northern Suriname and furthermore, studies the interpretational aspects of the aeromagnetic surveys of the same area performed by the Aero Service Corporation (Philadelphia). An integral part of the latter project is the study of the magnetic properties of Suriname rock samples. The first chapter gives a review of the geology in Suriname.

20   **A pedo-geomorphological classification and map of the Holocene sediments in the coastal plain of the three Guianas.**
     R. Brinkman, L. J. Pons.   Wageningen, The Netherlands: Soil Survey Institute, 1968. 40p. maps. bibliog.

Provides a classification of the sediments in the coastal plain of the Guianas on the basis of age, facies, geomorphology, and pedological characteristics. The main geomorphological elements are: beach ridges; marine tidal clay flats and marshes; natural levees of the rivers and estuaries; and peat swamps. A separate pedo-geomorphological sediment map of the area (scale 1:1,000,000) is included.

21   **The Guiana coast.**
     J. H. G. R. Diephuis.   *Tijdschrift van het Koninklijk Nederlandsch Aardrijkskundig Genootschap*, vol. 83 (1966), p. 145-52. maps. bibliog.

Extensive coastal measurements, a study of the properties of the sediments concerned, and a review of the literature enabled the author to present a quantitative picture of some of the coastal phenomena of the Guianas. He discusses the origin of the sediment, the properties of the silt, and the most important external factors that influence the coastal processes.

22   **Reconnaissance soil survey in northern Surinam.**
     J. J. van der Eijk.   PhD dissertation, Landbouw Hogeschool Wageningen, The Netherlands, 1957. 99p. maps. bibliog.

This is a publication of reconnaissance soil surveys in northern Suriname made by this soil scientist from the Central Bureau for Aerial Survey, Paramaribo, during the years 1949-54, in which aerial photographs were used to form the basis of the study. The team interpreting the photographs consisted of a forester, a geologist, and a soil scientist who made nineteen trips to conduct fieldwork, which was later supplemented by laboratory research. In this thesis, the author explains the working methods and elaborates on the landscapes and soil associations of northern Suriname. The volume includes twelve aerial photographs of various Surinamese landscapes.

23 **On the structure and origin of the sandy ridges in the coastal zone of Suriname.**
D. C. Geijskens. *Tijdschrift van het Koninklijk Nederlandsch Aardrijkskundig Genootschap*, vol. 69 (1952), p. 225-37. map.

Presents a report on an investigation of a group of sandy ridges carried out in 1939-40, in which drill holes were made to study the soil profile in the coastal zone. The results are supplemented with data obtained in later years. A general map and the profiles presented summarize a large part of the findings.

24 **Outline of the geology and petrology of Surinam (Dutch Guiana).**
Robert IJzerman. Utrecht, The Netherlands: Kemink en Zoon, 1931. 519p. maps. bibliog.

In 1926, a topographer, a botanist, a zoologist, and a geographer made an expedition to the Wilhelmina Mountains. The geological data gathered there are collected in this dissertation (Rijksuniversiteit Utrecht, the Netherlands, 1931). The petrographical descriptions are quite detailed and a short outline provides a summary of the state of the geology pertaining to Suriname at that time. This outline is, of course, incomplete as the author did not have the necessary quantitative data nor could he have had insight into the geological relation of the formations because vast regions of the country had only been superficially explored at that time, if at all. This thesis includes forty-eight plates.

25 **Heavy mineral investigation of samples of Surinam.**
H. Kiel. *Geologie en Mijnbouw*, vol. 17 (April 1955), p. 93-103. maps. bibliog.

The author investigated a large number of mineralogical samples with the purpose of classifying the heavy mineral content and to ascertain the distributive provinces of the clastic material of the rocks examined. He presents four mineral associations: tourmaline-metamorphic group-association; tourmaline-association; A-association; and B-association. Staurolite in considerable quantities characterizes the latter two associations.

26 **New facts on the geology of the 'young' unconsolidated sediments of Northern Surinam.**
D. G. Montagne. *Geologie en Mijnbouw*, vol. 43, no. 12 (Dec. 1964), p. 499-515. maps. bibliog.

Gives a short synopsis of the most important data on the stratigraphy of the 'young', unconsolidated sediments in central northern Suriname, as collected in and around bauxite mines there. The author also adds some information on heavy minerals, clay mineralogy, and grain size distribution. Montagne presents a stratigraphical table and finally focuses attention on the possible regional importance of some of the data presented.

27 **On geogenesis and pedogenesis in the Old Coastal Plain of Surinam (South America).**
Arthur Willem Lourens Veen. PhD dissertation, Universiteit van Amsterdam, 1970. 176p. maps. bibliog.

A presentation of the results of an investigation into the geogenesis and the pedogenesis in the Old Coastal Plain. The thesis serves a double purpose: first it contributes to the factual knowledge of the soils and deposits of Suriname and their mineralogy; and constructs a model for the Old Coastal Plain of the relation between stratigraphy and geogenesis on the one hand and the landscape and pedogenesis on the other hand. Details concerning the technique of mapping, profile description, and sample analysis are given in the appendix.

28 **Quantitative analysis of the available alumina content by (D. T. A.) in bauxite from 'Onverdacht', Surinam.**
A. H. van der Veen. *Geologie en Mijnbouw*, vol. 47, no. 6 (1968), p. 469-78.

In the evaluation of bauxite deposits, it is of great importance to know the available alumina content. Differential thermal analysis (DTA) is chosen as the principal method of analysis. The author describes in detail bomb digestion and subsequent filtration and titration procedures. The apparatus and the procedures used are also discussed.

29 **The geology of the Wilhelmina Mountains in Suriname, with special reference to the occurrence of precambrian ash-flow tuffs.**
J. Verhofstad.   PhD dissertation, Universiteit van Amsterdam, 1970. 97p. maps. bibliog.

An investigation of the jungle-covered Wilhelmina Mountains, which form a mountain range running east-west in central Suriname. These mountains are 'composed of granitoid and metamorphosed acid to intermediate volcanic rocks, as well as of doleritic intrusives'. The author has subjected eight samples from the area to radiometric determination.

30 **Shallow-water waves and fluid-mud dynamics, coast of Surinam, South America.**
John Thomas Wells.   PhD dissertation, Louisiana State University and Agricultural and Mechanical College, Baton Rouge, 1977. 98p. map. bibliog. (Available from University Microfilms International, Ann Arbor, Michigan, order no. 78-7566).

An examination of the process-form interactions between waves, fluid mud, and suspended sediment in the near shore region of the Atlantic coast between the Amazon and the Orinoco. The author describes the waves moving over a mobile, fluid-mud bottom and assesses the role of waves in suspending and transporting fluid mud. He conducted field experiments in four different hydrologic settings along the central coast of Suriname.

Maps

31 **Schakels met het verleden. 39 land- en zeekaarten van Suriname in facsimile. Geschiedenis van de kartografie van Suriname 1500-1971.**
(Links with the past. 39 maps and charts of Suriname in facsimile. History of the cartography of Suriname.)
Edited by C. Koeman.   Amsterdam: Theatrum Orbis Terrarum, 1973. 177p. maps.

These thirty-nine maps and charts are opulently presented in a wooden case. The earliest one dates from 1599, the most recent, a chart of the coast of Suriname, was made in 1971. The accompanying book, with texts in English, Spanish and Dutch, sketches the history of cartography in Suriname. In the case of Suriname the maps made in the late 19th and early 20th centuries are particularly important. The first topographical map covering the whole country was made as recently as 1966. This book contains forty-eight illustrations.

32 **Historie, techniek en maatschappelijke achtergronden der karteringswerkzaamheden in Suriname sinds 1667./History, techniques and social backgrounds of the mapping activities in Suriname since 1667. With summaries in English and Spanish.**
Justus Ben Christiaan Wekker.   PhD dissertation, Rijksuniversiteit Utrecht, The Netherlands, 1983. 144p. maps. bibliog.

This dissertation provides an insight into mapmaking and is based on maps, protocols, and reports and accounts concerning the map material. The book begins with a synopsis of colonial mapmaking and the following chapters discuss the period since the 19th century. Until the middle of that century interest was confined to the coastal belt of Suriname but expanded to the hinterland when gold was discovered in 1861. Around the turn of the century seven scientific expeditions collected topographical, geological, ethnographical, botanical, and zoological data. Nevertheless, vast stretches of land remained *terra incognita* until 1947, when photogrammetry was applied in mapping the country. The thesis includes summaries in English and Spanish. The appendices contain eighteen maps; a glossary; an index of personal names and one of subjects; as well as a list of maps cited in the text.

33 **Suriname in kaartencollecties.** (Suriname in map collections.)
Justus Ben Christiaan Wekker.   *Oso*, vol. 7, no. 2 (Dec. 1988), p. 175-88. bibliog.

A listing of map collections in and outside Suriname. The compiler discusses five categories of maps: maps printed prior to 1948; antique manuscript maps; aerial maps; printed thematic maps published after 1948; and working maps.

9

Travellers' Accounts

34 **An essay on the natural history of Guiana, in South America. etc.**
Edward Bancroft.   London: T. Becket & P. A. De Hondt, 1769. 402p.
This volume contains four letters with observations on the Dutch territory in Guiana.
The first letter provides a general geographic account of Guiana. In the second letter,
the author discusses the flora and fauna. In the third one, he focuses on the
Amerindians and their lifestyle. The final letter describes the Berbice, Essequibo, and
Demerara Rivers and the Dutch settlements thereon, as well as a slave insurrection,
government policy, and the discipline of the slaves.

35 **Dutch Guiana.**
W. G. Palgrave.   London: Macmillan, 1876. 264p. map.
This account is the result of a two-week stay in Suriname by the author, who was the
guest of the British consul and the governor of Suriname. Palgrave is very positive
about the colony, which he calls a 'Creole paradise' and focuses much of his attention
in this work on the coastal region and the capital of Paramaribo; the waterways; the
Maroons; and the Creole population at the Munnickendam plantation.

36 **Nachricht von Suriname und seinen Einwohnern, sonderlich den
Arawacken, Warauen und Karaiben, von den nüzlichsten Gewächsen und
Thieren des Landes, den Geschäften der dortigen Missionarien der
Brüderunität und der Sprache der Arawacken.** (Report about Suriname
and its inhabitants, especially the Arawaks, Waraos and Caribs, its
useful vegetation and animals of the country, the activities of the
missionaries of the Unity and the language of the Arawaks.)
Christlieb Quandt.   Amsterdam: S. Emmering, 1968. 316p. maps.
In 1768, Christlieb Quandt left for Suriname, where he was to become a missionary
among the Arawaks at Saron. From 1774 until 1780 he worked at the Hope mission on
the Corantijn River. From his diary and notes Quandt compiled a book of twenty-two
letters (first published in 1807) on his life in Suriname. The first ten of these provide a

chronological account of his work among the Amerindians. The other twelve consist of treatises on the flora and fauna of Suriname, as well as ethnographical and philological notes on the Amerindians.

37 A narrative of a voyage to Suriname; of a residence there during 1805, 1806, and 1807; and of the author's return to Europe by the way of North America.
Albert von Sack.   London: G. & W. Nicol, 1810. 282p. map.

This volume contains seventeen letters translated from the German of which fourteen discuss the author's residence in Suriname. In his first letter, the author explains the reasons for his voyage to Suriname. In letters two and three, he describes the journey and in letter four his arrival in Suriname. In letters four and five, the author sketches Paramaribo and its environment and letter six recounts a tour in the Commewijne district. In letter seven, Sack describes the New Year's celebrations in Paramaribo, while in number eight he gives a brief history of the country. In letter nine, the author makes another journey and recounts visits to plantations, a Maroon village, Amerindian villages, and Jodensavanne. In letter ten, he focuses in more detail on the plantations and slavery. Letter eleven describes the inhabitants of Paramaribo. Letters twelve, thirteen, and fourteen are devoted to the climate of the country. Letter fifteen is on the abolition of the slave trade. The flora and fauna are discussed in his final letter on Suriname. The seventeenth letter discusses the departure from Suriname. The appendices treat the vegetation and animal life in more detail.

38 A journey in Dutch Guiana.
Ivan T. Sanderson.   *Geographical Journal* (London), vol. 93, no. 6 (June 1939), p. 468-90.

An account of a one-year sojourn in Suriname. The first four months were spent in Paramaribo, while later scientific expeditions to the interior were made. Place names in Suriname are listed in an appendix.

Flora and Fauna

Flora

39 **Enumeration of the herbarium specimens of a Suriname wood collection made by Prof. G. Stahel.**
G. H. J. Amshoff.   Utrecht, The Netherlands:
Natuurwetenschappelijke Studiekring voor Suriname en Curaçao, 1948.
46p. (Uitgave, 2).

This is a review of the work of Professor G. Stahel of Paramaribo, who made an extensive collection of wood samples in several sets. To facilitate the identification, herbarium specimens were also collected under the same numbers as the wood samples. The herbarium material was often sterile; therefore, it had to be matched rather than determined.

40 **Notes on the Acanthaceae of Surinam.**
C. E. B. Bremekamp.   *Recueil des Travaux Botaniques Néerlandais*, vol 35 (1938), p. 130-76.

In the first section of this essay, the author discusses the subfamiles and 'tribes' of the *Acanthaceae* and presents a key by which the majority of the species in Suriname can be found. In the second part, Bremekamp comments on these Surinamese species.

41 **Orchid hunting in Suriname.**
Jan W. Broekuizen.   *Suralco Magazine*, vol. 1 (1973), p. 6-13.

A popular description of orchid hunting trips in the Surinamese jungle. Orchids are usually hidden among masses of vegetation and the author lists orchids found in savannas, forests, and gardens. The article includes drawings and six colour photographs.

42   **An ecological and phytogeographic study of northern Surinam savannas.**
      Johannes van Donselaar.   Amsterdam: North-Holland Publishing,
      1965. 163p. maps. bibliog.

A dissertation (Rijksuniversiteit Utrecht, the Netherlands, 1963) dealing with the flora
of the savannas in northern Suriname, based on fieldwork conducted in 1958 and 1959.
The author examined three savannas in detail: the Lobin savanna near Zanderij, the
Coesewijne savanna near Bigipoika, and the Gros savanna near Gros, all of which may
be regarded as fairly representative of the greater part of northern Suriname savannas.
Fieldwork and secondary literature enabled Van Donselaar to draw a general picture
of the savanna flora and vegetation occurring in these areas. The investigation is
mainly concerned with the description and classification of vegetation types on a
floristic basis, focusing on the distribution of the pertinent species and the vegetation
types, and on their relation to environmental factors.

43   **Structure, root systems and periodicity of savanna plants and vegetations
      in northern Surinam.**
      Wikje Aleida Elisabeth van Donselaar-Ten Bokkel Huinink.
      Amsterdam: North-Holland Publishing, 1966. 162p. bibliog. (Wentia,
      Royal Botanical Society of the Netherlands, 17).

A study examining the relationships between a number of vegetational units of
savannas and their environment, through a quantitative description of aspects other
than floristic composition, and through the establishment of environmental correlations.
The author investigated root systems; structure; periodicity; and characteristics of the
leaves, both of the species and of the different vegetation types.

44   **The mosses of Suriname.**
      Peter Arnold Florschütz.   Leiden, The Netherlands: E. J. Brill, 1964.
      271p. bibliog.

A dissertation (Rijksuniversiteit Utrecht, the Netherlands, 1964) treating all of the
varieties of mosses collected in Suriname which also briefly lists the species found in
Guyana and French Guiana. The first chapter includes a guide to the literature on
mosses of Latin America.

45   **Medicijn-planten in Suriname (den dresi wiwiri fu Sranan).** (Medicinal
      plants in Suriname.)
      Henrich Heyde.   Paramaribo: (no publisher), 1987. 112p. bibliog.

An introduction to and a listing of medicinal plants (with names in Latin and native
languages) traditionally used in Suriname. This booklet contains the description of
approximately eighty plants and more than fifty photographs. An index lists diseases
and refers to plants used to cure them.

46   **Vegetation and soil of a white-sand savanna in Suriname.**
      Petrus Cornelis Heyligers.   Amsterdam: Noord-Hollandse
      Uitgeversmaatschappij, 1963. 148p. maps. bibliog.

A dissertation (Rijksuniversiteit Utrecht, the Netherlands, 1961) describing the
vegetation and discussing the prevailing ecological factors of a savanna region near
Jodensavanne. The established units used for this description are called 'major
vegetation types', with 'variants', 'subvariants', and 'facies' as sub-units. The author

13

describes in detail three major vegetation types of scrub and five of herb vegetation, and he also pays attention to the surrounding woods and forests.

47 **The Pteriodophytes of Suriname: an enumeration with keys of the ferns and fern-allies.**

Karl Ulrich Kramer. Utrecht, The Netherlands: Natuurwetenschappelijke Studiekring voor Suriname en de Nederlandse Antillen, 1978, 198p. bibliog. (Uitgave, 93).

A publication of data on the Pteridophytes of Suriname, accumulated during the author's twenty-five year study of this group of plants. Kramer opts for the form of enumeration, using keys and noting some synonyms. In order to remedy the absence of descriptions and illustrations to some extent, much literature is cited, particularly references to critical publications, and to books and articles containing descriptions or figures or both.

48 **Additions to Pulle's Flora of Surinam.**

Joseph Lanjouw. *Extrait du Recueil des Travaux Botaniques Néerlandais*, vol. 32 (April 1935), p. 215-61. map. (Mededeelingen van het Botanisch Museum en Herbarium van de Rijksuniversiteit te Utrecht, 19).

During a trip to Suriname in 1933, the author collected herbs and shrubs in forests, coastal swamps, and savannas. In this enumeration with critical remarks the author only deals with the families of plants already published in the *Flora of Surinam* (1932-35). The descriptions of specimens belonging to other families have subsequently been published in later issues of the *Flora of Surinam* (q.v.).

49 **The Euphorbiaceae of Surinam.**

Joseph Lanjouw. Amsterdam: J. H. de Bussy, 1931. 195p. map. bibliog.

This book is divided into two parts: in section one the author critically discusses the different species, providing information about their uses and applications by the natives, and makes some geobotanical observations; the second part contains the taxonomical segment, with the description of the genera, the determination keys, and the description of the species with literature and localities. The investigations were carried out at the Botanical Museum in Utrecht, the Netherlands. In a later study called 'New or noteworthy Euphorbiaceae from Suriname' in *Recueil des Travaux Botaniques Néerlandais*, vol. 36 (1939) Lanjouw describes then new or rare *Euphorbiaceae* which were collected during the period 1935-38 on the Great Savanna near the sources of the Sipaliwini River, which forms part of the boundary between Brazil and Suriname.

50 **Studies of the vegetation of the Suriname savannahs and swamps.**

Joseph Lanjouw. *Nederlandsch Kruidkundig Archief*, vol. 46 (1936), p. 823-51. map. bibliog. (Mededeelingen van het Botanisch Museum en Herbarium van de Rijksuniversiteit te Utrecht, 33).

In the first section of this paper, the author describes some of the savannas in the northern part of Suriname. In the second part, he gives a brief account of the swamps.

Even though swamps and savannas have regularly been confused, the dominant plant species and the general aspect of the swamps are quite different from those of the savannas.

51 **Notes on the geology and geography of Tafelberg, Suriname.**
Bassett Maguire. *Geographical Review*, vol. 35, no. 4 (Oct. 1945), p. 563-79. maps.

A report of the New York Botanical Garden expedition of 1944 which set out to study and collect the vegetation of Tafelberg or Table Mountain. The researchers found that the flora of Tafelberg had a strong affinity with that of other and higher plateaus in Guyana and Venezuela and also with that of the coastal savannas. The article is illustrated with thirteen photographs. A more elaborate report has appeared in ten volumes of the journal *Memoirs of the New York Botanical Garden* published between 1953 and 1978.

52 **Suriname timbers I: general introduction, guttiferae, vochysiaceae, anacardiaceae, icacinaceae.**
Alberta M. W. Mennega. The Hague: Martinus Nijhoff, 1948. 59p. bibliog. (Uitgave van de Stichting Natuurwetenschappelijke Studiekring voor Suriname en Curaçao, 3).

An investigation into the anatomy of Suriname timber, principally based on the Stahel collection, which was the largest collection ever made in Suriname at the time and representative of the forests there. The Stahel collection of timber consists of 379 samples belonging to 54 families. The hand-lens method was used to provide descriptions and determination keys.

53 **The ferns of Surinam. Supplement to Flora of Surinam (Dutch Guyana).**
O. Posthumus. Amsterdam: Koninklijke Vereeniging Koloniaal Instituut, 1928. 196p. (Mededeeling no. XXX, Afd. Handelsmuseum, 11).

Even though this volume deals mainly with the ferns of Suriname, those in French and in British Guiana are mentioned as well. The work contains an alphabetical index and is arranged in accordance with the *Index Filicum* of C. Christensen.

54 **An enumeration of the vascular plants known from Surinam, together with their distribution and synonymy.**
August Adriaan Pulle. Leiden, The Netherlands: E. J. Brill, 1906. 555p. map. bibliog.

This dissertation (Rijksuniversiteit Utrecht, the Netherlands, 1906) starts with a history of the investigation of the flora of Suriname. The systematic part provides a general plant geography and the author indicates the position occupied by Surinamese flora with respect to the whole of the Americas.

55 **Flora of Surinam (Netherlands Guyana).**
Edited by August Adriaan Pulle. Amsterdam: Koninklijke
Vereeniging Koloniaal Instituut, 1932-51. 4 vols. map. bibliog.
(Mededeeling no. XXX, Afd. Handelsmuseum, 11).

The *Flora* consists of four volumes, each divided into several issues. Volume I deals
with the Pteridophyta, the Gymnosperms, the Gnetales, the Monocotyledonae, and
the Dicotyledonae-Monochlamydeae. Volumes II and III treat the Dicotyledonae-
Choripetalae and Volume IV is devoted to the Dicotyledonae-Sympetalae.

56 **The vegetation of four mounds in the coastal plains of western
Suriname/De vegetatie van 4 terpen in de Westsurinaamse kustvlakte.**
Marga C. M. Werkhoven, Aad H. Versteeg. *Mededelingen der
Surinaamse Musea*, no. 32 (Dec. 1980), p. 9-36. bibliog.

This study attempts to compare the present-day vegetation of this area with a
reconstruction of vegetation from the period between 300 and 1000 AD made on the
basis of pollen studies. Such investigations may prove useful for archaeologists,
botanists, pedologists, and ecologists as the effects of human activities in the distant
past on the vegetation and soil can be examined. This article is written in English and
in Dutch.

57 **The indiginous palms of Surinam.**
J. G. Wessels Boer. Leiden, The Netherlands: E. J. Brill, 1965. 172p.
bibliog.

A dissertation (Rijksuniversiteit Utrecht, 1965) which explores a number of various
localities throughout Suriname in order to collect a large sample of the palm species
native to this country. The author argues that clear-cut species and genera can be
distinguished in palms and discusses seventeen species in detail. The work contains
seventeen plates and ten figures.

58 **Fa joe kan tak' mi no moi. Inleiding in de flora en vegetatie van
Suriname.** (How can you say that I am not beautiful. Introduction to the
flora and vegetation of Suriname.)
J. G. Wessels Boer, W. H. A. Hekking, J. P. Schulz. Paramaribo:
Stinasu, 1976. 2 vols. (Natuurgids Serie B, 4).

A popular guide to the flora of Suriname describing 232 plants and flowers. Most of the
plants described here can be found in the coastal regions and the more accessible parts
of the interior. Two introductory chapters provide general information on botany. The
second part includes a glossary and an alphabetical index with names in Latin, Dutch,
and Sranan.

Fauna

59 **Notes on a collection of Surinam birds.**
    Outram Bangs, Thomas E. Penard. *Bulletin of the Museum of
    Comparative Zoölogy at Harvard College*, vol. 62, no. 2 (April 1918),
    p. 25-93.

An annotated list of 301 species of birds which were collected near Paramaribo or along the Marowijne and Saramacca Rivers between 1912 and 1914. This listing may be considered fairly representative of the lowland avifauna of Suriname, even though many species are missing from the list.

60 **Mosquitos of Surinam. A study on neotropical mosquitos.**
    C. Bonne, J. Bonne-Wepster. Amsterdam: Koninklijke Vereeniging
    van het Koloniaal Instituut, 1925. 558p. (Mededeeling no. XXI,
    Afdeeling Tropische Hygiene, 13).

This publication gives descriptions of 133 species of mosquitos, of which forty-six were then new to science. Specimens were collected from near the coast as well as from the interior. The authors approach the subject from a medical point of view; knowledge of the local mosquito fauna is necessary to combat human diseases. The appendix includes eighty-four figures.

61 **Ecology and management of deer in Suriname, South America.**
    William Vickers Branan. PhD dissertation, University of Georgia,
    Athens, Georgia, 1984. 153p. bibliog. (Available from University
    Microfilms International, Ann Arbor, Michigan, order no. 85–04585).

This thesis investigates the basic biology of the three deer species occurring in Suriname. White-tailed deer (*Odocoileus virginianus*) inhabit the Atlantic coastal marshes and grassland savannas bordering Brazil. Red brocket (*Mazama americana*) and brown brocket (*M. gouazoubira*) deer live in the rain forests. The author's research concentrates on antler cycles, fawning seasons, food habits, heterozygosity, morphology, and genetic variability.

62 **Birds of Suriname.**
    F. Haverschmidt   Edinburgh, Scotland: Oliver & Boyd, 1968. 45p.
    map. bibliog.

A fully illustrated handbook, containing information on the identification, occurrence, habitat, habits, nesting, food, and range of about 600 species in Suriname. The author gives additional information on the topography and climate of the country, and the state of future ornithological research in Suriname. The volume includes an annotated bibliography.

63 **Surinaamse vissen.** (Surinamese fish.)
    Henrich Heyde. Paramaribo: (no publisher), 1986. 154p.

In the first pages of this guide, the author sketches the history of commercial and recreational fishing in 20th-century Suriname, focusing mainly on the former. He then discusses the characteristics of fish found in Surinamese waters. In a glossary he lists the scientific and native (Sranan and Saramakan) names of the fish described. This volume contains approximately sixty drawings and forty-eight colour photographs.

64   **Surinam turtle notes 1-3.**
      Russell L. Hill.   Paramaribo: Foundation for Nature Preservation in
      Suriname (Stinasu), 1971. 16p. bibliog. (Mededeling, 2).
The author looks at three aspects of turtles in Suriname: the polymorphism of costal and vertebral laminae in the sea turtle *Lepidochelys olivacea*; the results of an investigaton into the damage done by the crab *Ocypode quadrata* to the green turtle *Chelonia mydas*; and the effect of the deliberate breakage of eggs in sea turtle nests on the hatchling emergence percentage.

65   **Notes on the herpetofauna of Surinam IV: the lizards and amphisbaenians**
      of Surinam.
      Marinus Steven Hoogmoed.   The Hague: W. Junk, 1973. 419p. maps.
Forty lizards and three amphisbaenians native to Suriname are presently known. In this publication eight species are reported for the first time, and two new subspecies are described. The occurrence of four species which reproduce parthenogenetically is noted: three of which do so exclusively and one which does so partially. The author presents extensive descriptions and ecological data of each species. The zoogeography of the lizards and amphisbaenians in the Guianas is discussed extensively. The author draws conclusions regarding the presence of a rainforest refuge on the Tumac Humac and Boundary Mountains during the last interpluvial period from the distribution of lizards which inhabit the savanna. In special chapters the author describes collectors and expeditions.

66   **The bats of Surinam.**
      Antonius Marie Husson.   Leiden, The Netherlands: E. J. Brill, 1962.
      282p. bibliog.
An account of the state of knowledge concerning the taxonomy of the bats inhabiting Suriname which is intended as a basis for future investigation. The author reviews Surinamese bats on the basis of the material and literature then available. The coastal region north of the anterior mountain range and the area east of the Saramacca and Suriname Rivers in particular have been relatively well explored as far as the chiropeterological fauna is concerned. However, there is little data on the occurrence of bats in the interior.

67   **Turtles on the beach.**
      J. J. Janssen.   *Suralco Magazine*, vol. 1 (Dec. 1969), p. 28-35. bibliog.
A popular scientific description of the wildlife along the Atlantic coast, and the turtles in particular. The author also discusses projects to protect the turtles from extinction.

68 **The cichlids of Surinam. Teleostei: Labrodei.**
Sven O. Kullander, Han Nijssen. Leiden, The Netherlands: E. J. Brill,
1989. 256p. maps. bibliog.

In this faunal survey six new species of South American *Cichlidae* (tropical freshwater fish) are described, resulting in a Surinamese cichlid fauna of twelve native genera and twenty-six species, based on thousands of specimens. This book comprises a key to the cichlids of Suriname with diagnoses of the genera, based mainly upon osteological studies. The species are extensively described and illustrated in 135 figures. Their distribution is plotted on maps.

69 **Metamorphosis insectorum Surinamensium of de verandering der Surinaamse insecten. Metamorphosis of the insects of Surinam.**
Maria Sibylla Merian. Zutphen, The Netherlands: De Walburg Pers,
1982. 2nd ed. 138p.

The first edition of *Metamorphosis* was published in Amsterdam in 1705 in Latin and in Dutch. During the 18th century some reprints were made and in 1976 a costly full size replica was prepared in Leipzig. This edition is unabridged, yet reduced in size and is published in Dutch and in English. The author was born in Frankfurt am Main, currently FRG, in 1647 and died in 1717 in the Netherlands, having travelled in Suriname between 1699 to 1701. The book contains sixty copper plates with pictures of about ninety observations of insects and a few other animals in all states of development on the plants on which they feed. There are several errors in the texts and the drawings but it should be borne in mind, that C. Linnaeus, who brought order into the taxonomy of plants, animals, and their nomenclature, was born two years after the book's original publication.

70 **The monkeys of Suriname/De Surinaamse apen.**
Russell A. Mittermeier, Marc G. M. van Roosmalen. *Suralco Magazine*, vol. 10, no. 3 (1978), p. 13-21. map.

A popular scientific article on the two families, seven genera, and eight species of monkeys occurring in Suriname. Seven of these species belong to the family *Cebidae*. The eighth, the saguwinchi, belongs to the family *Callitrichidae*. The article contains a list of vernacular names of Surinamese monkeys and eight colour illustrations.

71 **Surinaamse slangen in kleur.** (Surinamese snakes in colour.)
Joep Moonen, Wim Eriks, Kees van Deursen. Paramaribo: C.
Kersten, 1979. 119p. bibliog.

A popular scientific guide decribing the snakes of Suriname which provides the scientific name in Latin as well as the Dutch, Surinamese, and English names, and contains a short summary in English. The book is illustrated with approximately seventy colour photographs.

72 **Birdcatching in Surinam.**
Thomas E. Penard, Arthur P. Penard. *West-Indische Gids*, vol. 7
(1925/26), p. 545-66.

An article on bird-catching in the 1920s which lists a number of birds with their Latin, English, and Sranan Tongo names. The authors review several ways in which birds are caught, including the use of fall-traps, trap-cages, birdlime, snares and nest-robbing.

The trapping and keeping of *Euphonias* (canaries), finches, macaws, parrots, and parakeets is described in more detail.

73 **The marine Mollusca of Suriname (Dutch Guiana) Holocene and present. Part 1. General introduction.**
C. O. van Regteren Altena. Leiden, The Netherlands: E. J. Brill, 1969. 49p. map. bibliog. (Zoologische Verhandelingen Uitgegeven door het Rijksmuseum van Natuurlijke Historie te Leiden, 101).

A general introduction to the marine *Mollusca* of Suriname in which the author provides an overview of the history of the study of this fauna, discusses the coastal waters as an environment for *Mollusca* and deals with the occurrence of Holocene marine *Mollusca* and their economic importance. In the seventh chapter, the author lists the collections and collectors of the material studied. In the final section of the book, he compares the results of his research with data from Guyana and French Guiana.

Prehistory and Archaeology

74 **Hertenrits: an arauquinod complex in north west Suriname.**
Aad Boomert. *Journal of the Walter Roth Museum of Archaeology and Anthropology*, vol. 3, no. 2 (1980), p. 68-104. maps.
From 1956 onwards, artificially raised habitation mounds dating from 600 to 900 AD have been discovered in the western coastal region of Suriname. These mounds, the largest of which is Hertenrits, are situated in the middle of vast complexes of equally artificially raised agricultural plots, often grouped in small clusters. The mounds are connected with the raised-field clusters by seasonally inundated pathways running radially from them. This paper describes the sites and raised-field complexes and offers a detailed analysis of the pottery, bone, stone, and shell artifacts found at the Hertenrits site.

75 **The prehistoric stone axes of the Guianas: a typological classification.**
Aad Boomert. *Journal of the Walter Roth Museum of Archaeology and Anthropology*, vol. 2, no. 2 (1979), p. 99-124. maps. bibliog.
This paper presents a typology incorporating all the axe forms then known from the Guianas. Since the majority of stone axes from the Guianas is known only from individual finds, the approach is synchronic rather than diachronic. Nevertheless, the author describes some of the important lines of cultural diffusion. Most of the material discussed is from Suriname. Boomert has examined, drawn, and photographed more than 400 of the then known total of 600 or 700 axes. The article includes fifty drawings and eleven photographs.

76 **The Sipaliwini archeological complex of Surinam: a summary.**
Aad Boomert. *Nieuwe West-Indische Gids/New West Indian Guide*, vol. 54, no. 2 (1980), p. 94-107. map. bibliog.
A brief description of industrial activities in the Sipaliwini area between 8000 and 5000 BC, the distribution, cultural affiliations, and dating thereof. Since 1962, chipped stone implements and projectile points, dating from the Lithic times, have been found on various spots in the Sipaliwini savanna of southern Suriname. In 1980, twenty-nine

21

surface sites were known in total, all presumably belonging to the same cultural assemblage: the Sipaliwini complex. Related Lithic workshops, camp sites, and individual finds have been discovered in Guyana and in Venezuelan Guiana.

77 **Manufacture and trade of stone artifacts in prehistoric Surinam.**
Aad Boomert, S. B. Kroonenberg. In: *Ex Horreo: IPPL 1951-1976.*
Edited by B. L. van Beek, R. W. Brandt, W. Groenman-Van
Waateringe. Amsterdam: Universiteit van Amsterdam, 1977, p. 9-46.
maps. bibliog. (Albert Egges van Giffen Instituut voor Prae- en
Protohistorie Cingvla, IV).

The authors discuss the occurrence of a distinctive pre-Columbian ceramic style together with partially finished axes, adzes and chisels, and waste flaxes of metabasalt at sites in the Brownsberg-Afobaka area. They argue that between 1200 and 1500 AD there existed a regular trade of metabasalt tools from the Brownsberg-Afobaka area, in the vicinity of the grinding grooves, to the coastal region, which lacked the raw materials for axe manufacture. Furthermore, they discuss the Guianese trade in stone artifacts during post-Columbian times as well as the most recent stone axes of Suriname, made by 20th-century Akuriyo Amerindians

78 **The petroglyphs in the Guianas and adjacent areas of Brazil and Venezuela: an inventory. With a comprehensive bibliography of South American and Antillean petroglyphs.**
Cornelis Nicolaas Dubelaar. Los Angeles: Institute of
Archaeology, University of California, 1986. 326p. maps. bibliog.
(Monumenta Archaeologica, 12).

Perhaps the most important survey of petroglyphs of any region in South and Central America, this volume includes the rock art of four areas: Suriname, Guyana, French Guiana, and the adjacent areas of Brazil and Venezuela. All of the petroglyphs are extensively illustrated, both in line drawings and photographs. The documentation on Suriname is the result of the author's own investigations there, while the material from the other areas represents a distillation of existing literature. The material is arranged according to geographic area, and detailed maps and geographic coordinates are provided for most sites. An historically sequenced bibliography for each of the areas is supplied at the beginning of each chapter. A general comprehensive bibliography of South American and Antillean petroglyphs containing approximately 1,300 entries concludes the volume.

79 **South American and Caribbean petroglyphs.**
Cornelis Nicolaas Dubelaar. Leiden, The Netherlands: Koninklijk
Instituut voor Taal-, Land- en Volkenkunde, 1986. 249p. bibliog.
(Koninklijk Instituut voor Taal-, Land- en Volkenkunde Caribbean
Series, 3).

An elaborate study of rock inscriptions in South America and the Caribbean. The author discusses the origins of petroglyphs; the history of petroglyph investigation; the techniques and rock species used to make the inscriptions; the nature of the sites; and the orientation, dating, and interpretation of petroglyphs. Two-thirds of the book, however, concern the description and the isolation of pilot motifs. This approach enables Dubelaar to classify the rock inscriptions according to their geographical distribution. Many figures and appendices are added to illustrate this method. Suriname is one of several South American and Caribbean countries examined in this study.

80 **History of archeological investigations in Surinam.**
D. C. Geijskens. *Berichten van de Rijksdienst voor het Oudheidkundig Bodemonderzoek*, no. 10/11 (1960-61), p. 70-77. bibliog.
An overview of archaeological research carried out in Suriname during the period 1860-1960. The study of stone axes or celts formed the initial nucleus of research. Next came studies of objects sent to museums and in private collections in Europe. Scientific expeditions into the interior in the first decades of the 20th century provided much information about whetgrooves (or grinding grooves) and petroglyphs. Aerial photographs opened up new prospects for archaeological research. This article is also published as *Mededeling Surinaams Museum*, no. 4, (no date).

81 **De Kwatta Indianen: vroege bewoners van Suriname.** (The Kwatta Indians: early inhabitants of Suriname.)
M.R. Khudabux, Tj. D. Bruintjes. *Natuur en Techniek*, vol. 56, no. 2 (1988), p. 110-19.
In the 1950s human remains dating from 800 to 1000 AD were found near Paramaribo. These discoveries led to more excavations in this area. At present, more than fifty skeletons have been found, making it the largest collection of pre-Columbian skeletons in the northern part of South America. The authors discuss what can be learned from such a collection and conclude that there is still too little data to conduct a paleodemographic study. However, the bones reveal the occurrence of several diseases, as well as some demographic data such as age and gender.

82 **Archaeological investigations at Kwamalasamoetoe, South Suriname/Archeologisch onderzoek te Kwamalasamoetoe (Zuid-Suriname).**
Aad H. Versteeg. *Mededelingen Stichting Surinaamse Musea*, no. 30 (June 1980), p. 22-46. map. bibliog.
A report in English and Dutch on four archaeological sites in southern Suriname. These are situated on an elevated riverbank, and all contain evidence of repeated use. The fieldwork took place in 1980, when a large quantity of Taruma pottery and a small amount of Koriabo pottery were discovered at the Trio village of Kwamalasamoetoe. The comparatively large number of stone artifacts also found there can be connected only with Koriabo pottery and is an indication of a Koriabo inhabitation phase at the site. At the other three sites both decorated and undecorated Taruma pottery was found. The article includes twenty-six photographs.

83 **Archeological investigations in Suriname by C. J. Hering.**
Aad H. Versteeg. In: *Latijns Amerika-studies in Leiden 1982: opstellen op het gebied van de archeologie, geschiedenis, sociolinguistiek, letterkunde en culturele antropologie.* Edited by Raymond Th. J. Buve, Jan Lechner. Leiden, The Netherlands: Werkgroep Latijns Amerika, 1983, p. 7-18. map. bibliog.

Christiaan Johannes Hering (1829-96) was the first person to draw attention to the pre-Columbian inhabitants of Suriname. He concentrated on collecting and studying stone artifacts and petroglyphs. The fact that modern archaeological studies concentrate on ceramic artifacts may be the reason for the limited attention his work received after his death; nobody has continued the research started by Hering.

84 **A distinctive kind of pottery in western Suriname.**
Aad H. Versteeg. *Mededelingen Stichting Surinaamse Musea* no. 23/24 (June 1978), p. 16-26. maps. bibliog.

An article on pottery with a hitherto unknown kind of decoration. In 1977 a large quantity of this pottery was found in western Suriname during excavations, although only a small percentage of this find was decorated. Appliqué decorations in geometrical patterns are typical for the majority of the decorated sherds. The temper of the pottery is for the greatest part unusual. The article includes four plates.

85 **A fortified pre-Columbian village in East Suriname?/Een versterkt pre-Columbiaans dorp in Oost-Suriname?**
Aad H. Versteeg. *Mededelingen Stichting Surinaamse Musea*, no. 33 (May 1981), p. 38-48.

A report on archaeological investigations at Pondo Creek in the district of Commewijne. The striking feature of the site is an encircling trench, in which a number of potsherds were found and brought to the Surinaams Museum. The author concludes that the trench was dug by Amerindians during pre-Columbian times. No further indications were found regarding the purpose of the trench. This publication is written in English and Dutch.

86 **Prehistoric cultural ecology of the Coastal Plain of western Suriname.**
Aad H. Versteeg. In: *Proceedings of the Eighth International Congress for the Study of pre-Columbian cultures of the Lesser Antilles.* Edited by Suzanne M. Lewenstein. Tempe, Arizona: Arizona State University, 1980, p. 88-97, map. bibliog. (Anthropological Research Papers, 22).

A reconstruction of the ecology in the Hertenrits area in prehistoric times. The prehistoric population there lived in the border zone between fresh water and sea water influence. Although some sherds have been ascribed to the pre-1250 BP period, the author has found no convincing evidence of human habitation at an earlier date than 1250 BP. Versteeg also presents data obtained from two other excavations carried out in 1977 and 1978.

87   **The prehistory of the Young Coastal Plain of west Suriname.**
Aad H. Versteeg.   *Berichten van de Rijksdienst voor het Oudheidkundig Bodemonderzoek*, no. 35 (1985), p. 653-750. maps. bibliog.

Excavation sites in west Suriname demonstrate an influence from, contact with, and immigration from the Orinoco Basin over a very long period. The present study concentrates on two mounds near the Hertenrits: Buckleburg-I and Wageningen-I, and includes all the sites known in the coastal plain of west Suriname up to the mid-1980s. The research indicates that there existed a selective adaptation strategy to various environments.

History

General

88 **A short history of the Netherlands Antilles and Surinam.**
Cornelis Ch. Goslinga.   The Hague; Boston, Massachusetts; London:
Martinus Nijhoff, 1979. 198p. bibliog.

An introduction to three centuries of history, in which the general reader will find six short chapters of useful information dealing exclusively with Suriname, encompassing the period from Amerindian prehistory to independence in 1975, although coverage of the period since 1960 leaves much to be desired. Four chapters deal with both the Netherlands Antilles and Suriname. Here the emphasis is on differences in Dutch colonization; 20th-century political and economic development; and society and culture during the last two centuries.

89 **De foltering van Eldorado. Een ecologische geschiedenis van de vijf
Guyana's.** (The torture of Eldorado. An ecological history of the five
Guianas.)
Albert Helman.   The Hague: Nijgh en Van Ditmar, 1983. 494p. map.
bibliog.

A well-written history of the five Guianas, based on an impressive number of secondary sources. The author emphasizes the ecological unity of French Guiana, Suriname, Guyana, Brazil and Venezuela. He draws political conclusions from the ecological data by suggesting that the national boundaries are arbitrary. Some critics have argued that because of the mixture of fact and fiction, the book loses some of its scholarly merit. It includes a fine chronological table.

90   **Van Priary tot en met De Kom. De geschiedenis van het verzet in
     Suriname, 1630-1940.** (From Priary to De Kom. The history of resistance
     in Suriname, 1630-1940.)
     Sandew Hira.   Rotterdam, The Netherlands: Futile, 1983. 360p.
     bibliog.
An economist's Marxist interpretation of the history of resistance in Suriname from
slavery to the social unrest of the 1930s. The first chapter contains a sharp critique of
Van Lier's theoretical concept of a plural society as described in *Frontier society: a
social analysis of the history of Surinam* (q.v.) and *The development and nature of
society in the West Indies* (q.v.). In the following chapters Hira chronologically
discusses the resistance movements of the Amerindians, slaves, indentured labourers,
peasants, and finally the labourers and the unemployed during the depression of the
1930s.

91   **The Dutch peasants in Surinam.**
     C. de Jong.   *Plural Societies*, vol. 5, no. 3 (1974), p. 19-42. map.
An overview of the history of the colonization of Suriname by Dutch farmers from the
17th century to the Second World War. The author emphasizes the colonization
project of 1845, when 320 emigrants left for Suriname, and which failed utterly because
of mistakes made by the authorities in the Netherlands and in Suriname. A lack of local
knowledge resulted in the wrong choice of settlement and of products. Some of the
settlers moved to Paramaribo and prospered, while others suffered extreme poverty.

92   **Nosotros, esclavos de Surinam.** (We, slaves of Suriname.)
     Anton de Kom.   Havana: Casa de las Americas, 1981. 131p.
First published in 1934, this book is a classic written by the Creole anti-imperialist
activist Anton de Kom, who from 1920 lived in the Netherlands almost continuously.
In 1932 he returned to Suriname, causing an uproar and as a result he was deported.
He describes this episode, but more importantly he writes the first history of Suriname
from a Surinamese perspective. Using 18th and 19th-century sources he turns the then
existing colonial ideology upside-down. He emphasizes the relationship between
slavery and racism and tries to overcome the ethnic divisions which plague Suriname.
In 1935, a German translation of this work appeared in the USSR and there are several
editions in Dutch.

93   **Frontier society: a social analysis of the history of Surinam.**
     Rudolf A. J. van Lier, translated from the Dutch by Maria J. L. van
     Yperen.   The Hague: Martinus Nijhoff, 1971. 441p. bibliog.
     (Koninklijk Instituut voor Taal-, Land- en Volkenkunde Translation
     Series, 14).
The first edition of this standard work was published in 1949 as *Samenleving in een
grensgebied* (The Hague: Martinus Nijhoff). This up-dated version is a translation of
the second edition published in 1971. In this study the author presents a structural and
historical analysis of the development of Suriname from a colony of exploitation based
on slavery into an independent republic with an ethnically mixed population. As point
of departure Van Lier choses the concept of pluralism. The first half of the book is
devoted to the period of slavery. Each chapter deals with a separate population group:
the whites, the Jews, the free-coloureds, and the slaves. In the second half, Van Lier
chronologically discusses the socio-historical developments from the emancipation of

the slaves to 1971. He pays relatively little attention to post-war Suriname. Since no comparable studies have appeared since 1949, Van Lier's work still ranks as the only profound social analysis of three centuries of Surinamese history.

94 **Overview of the importation of Chinese contract-laborers into Suriname/Overzicht van de invoer van Chinese contract-arbeiders.**
Willem L. Man A Hing. *Mededelingen Stichting Surinaams Museum*, no. 36 (1982), p. 36-51. bibliog.
An overview of the indentured immigration of Chinese labourers. The first group of eighteen workers residing in Java, then the Dutch East Indies, arrived in 1853. During the subsequent period from 1858 to 1874, about 2,500 additional Chinese indentureds were imported from Macau, Hong Kong, and Java. The author concludes his article with a poem called *A Surinamese song for 1867* by an anonymous writer. The essay is written in Dutch and English.

95 **Le Surinam; des origines à l'independence.** (Suriname; from its origins to independence.)
Jean-Louis Poulalion. Paris: Académie des Sciences d'Outre-mer, 1986. 93p.
A general history, probably only of interest to the French-reading public, since there exist virtually no other studies in that language. The emphasis is on slavery, although the entire period from pre-Columbian times until independence is covered. The author has used only secondary sources for this synthesis.

96 **Dutch Guiana: a problem in boundaries.**
Engel Sluiter. *Hispanic American Historical Review*, vol. 13, no. 1 (Feb. 1933), p. 2-22. bibliog.
Presents an historical overview of boundary disputes which still concern Suriname. A series of upheavals caused territory in the Guianas to change hands at various times during the period 1665-1814. With the discovery of gold in the second half of the 19th century the question of the boundaries became important again. International arbitration in 1891 and again in 1896-97 resulted in treaties to solve the problems. A final settlement, however, has not been reached yet.

97 **Suriname: geschiedenis in hoofdlijnen.** (Suriname: outline of its history.)
Stan Verschuuren. Utrecht, The Netherlands: Hes, 1987. 133p. map. bibliog.
A general introduction to the history of Suriname. More than half of the volume is devoted to the post-Emancipation period. The author argues that the current problems of the country, including economic dependency and underdevelopment, can be traced back to its colonial past.

98 **Vestigingen aan en ontvolking van de Boven-Commewijne.** (Settlements
along and depopulation of the upper Commewijne River.)
Justus Ben Christiaan Wekker. *Oso*, vol. 8, no. 1 (May 1989),
p. 38-54. map. bibliog.

A sketch of the economic and the social history of the settlements and plantations
along the upper Commewijne River (from Fort Sommelsdijck to the Tempati creek)
from the 17th to the 20th century.

Pre-Emancipation (-1863)

99 **Schweizer Tropenkaufleute und Plantagenbesitzer in Niederländisch-West
Indien im 18. und zu Beginn des 19. Jahrhunderts.** (Swiss merchants and
plantation owners in the Dutch West Indies in the 18th and early 19th
centuries.)
Walter Bodmer. *Acta Tropica*, vol. 3, no. 4 (1946), p. 289-321. maps.

Since 1699 commercial bankers from Geneva had owned plantations in Suriname,
which they probably acquired through financial dealings in Amsterdam. A number of
Swiss traders in this city took part in the commercial traffic with the Caribbean. The
author focuses on the Faesch brothers who became the owners of several plantations in
Suriname, one of which was Hooyland which remained in the Faesch family for nearly
a century. The essay includes summaries in English and French.

100 **Plantation slavery in Surinam in the last decade before emancipation:
the case of Catharina Sophia.**
Ernst van den Boogaart, Pieter C. Emmer. In: *Comparative
perspectives on slavery in New World plantation societies.* Edited by
Vera Rubin, Arthur Tuden. New York: New York Academy of
Sciences, 1977, p. 205-25.

An examination of slavery at the Catharina Sophia plantation. The authors suggest
that improvement in the condition of slaves did not significantly reduce the natural
decrease of the population. The continuation of the slave system, however, did not
improve the economic position of Suriname. In both Cuba and Brazil planters seemed
able to take greater advantage of their slave labour than their counterparts in
Suriname. The essay includes nine tables on economy and demography.

101 **The Arawak Indians of Trinidad and coastal Guiana, ca 1500-1650.**
Arie Boomert. *The Journal of Caribbean History* , vol. 19, no. 2
(Nov. 1984), p. 123-88. maps.

The author aims to trace the 16th and early 17th-century history of the Arawaks or
Lokono ('the People') as they call themselves at present. In those days the Arawaks
inhabited parts of Trinidad, the lower Orinoco valley of Venezuela, and the coastal
plain of Guyana, Suriname, and French Guiana. Boomert discusses Arawak socio-
political organization; their traditional trade network; Arawak warfare and slave-
raiding practices; as well as the end of the Spanish-Arawak alliance.

102   **Opstand in Tempati, 1757-1760.** (Revolt in Tempati, 1757-1760.)
      Harry van den Bouwhuijsen, Ron de Bruin, Georg Horeweg.
      Utrecht, The Netherlands: Instituut voor Culturele Antropologie,
      Rijksuniversiteit Utrecht, 1988. 127p. map. bibliog. (Bronnen voor de
      Studie van Afro-Surinaamse Samenlevingen, 12).

Based on more than 1,000 documents the authors present a reconstruction of the
Tempati rebellion, which started when the slaves from La Paix timber plantation
refused to move to a sugar plantation. Soon the mutiny spread to all plantations along
the Tempati creek and after approximately six months the rebels moved southward to
join a group of Maroons. In 1760, the colonial authorities concluded a peace with these
Ndjukas. In return for their freedom the latter promised to stop their raids on the
plantations.

103   **The manumission of slaves in Suriname, 1760-1828.**
      Rosemary Brana-Shute.   PhD dissertation, University of Florida,
      Gainesville, 1985. 426p. maps. bibliog. (Available from University
      Microfilms International, Ann Arbor, Michigan, order no. 86-15444).

A study of the social processes which resulted in manumission during a period ranging
from the prosperity of the plantations to their decline, in which the author looks at
manumission from a social rather than a legal point of view. Based on an analysis of
943 petitions from owners, profiles are constructed of more than 1,300 slaves, their
owners, and other free persons instrumental in their manumission. The author argues
that manumission should be considered as a kin and gender-related phenomenon and
indicates that females constituted about two-thirds of those freed and that kinship was
frequently mentioned in petitions. This closely resembles patterns elsewhere in the
Caribbean. An article entitled 'Approaching freedom: the manumission of slaves in
Suriname, 1760-1828' in *Slavery and Abolition*, vol. 10, no. 3 (Dec. 1989), p. 40-63, is
based on this dissertation.

104   **Governor Johannes Heinsius: the role of Van Aerssen's predecessor in
      the Surinam Indian war, 1678-1680.**
      Raymond Th. J. Buve.   In: *Current anthropology in the Netherlands.*
      Edited by Peter Kloos, Henri J. M. Claessen. Rotterdam, The
      Netherlands: Anthropological Branch of the Netherlands Sociological
      and Anthropological Society, 1975, p. 39-47.

An article stressing the historical role of Johannes Heinsius and his administration in
the critical years of 1679 and 1680. On his arrival Heinsius found the colony in
great confusion; the authorities were already onboard ship, fleeing the dissident
Amerindians. In a few weeks Heinsius managed to secure the main strategic points and
keep the Amerindians at bay. However, lack of military support from the Netherlands
frustrated attempts to pacify the whole of Suriname.

105 **Patterns of marriage and remarriage among the sephardi Jews of Surinam, 1788-1818.**
R. Cohen. In: *The Jewish nation in Surinam.* Edited by R. Cohen. Amsterdam: S. Emmering, 1982, p. 88-100. bibliog.

An historical account of the marriage customs and demographic origins of the Jewish population in Suriname. The generation studied here lived in the late 18th and early 19th centuries and was overwhelmingly Suriname-born, forming a stable urban group. They were able to maintain a relatively normal marriage and remarriage pattern. The author demonstrates how different the Jewish community was from the rest of the white population.

106 **Soldier in paradise: the life of Captain John Stedman, 1744-1797.**
Louise Collis. New York: Harcourt, Brace & World, 1966. 231p. maps. bibliog.

A biography of John Stedman, author of the classic *Narrative of a five years' expedition* (q.v.), who in 1772 volunteered to join the Dutch military expedition against the Maroons in Suriname. The illustrations in this biography are taken from the *Narrative*.

107 **The migration from Surinam to Jamaica.**
Frank Cundall. *Timehri*, no. 6, third series, (Sept. 1919), p. 145-72. map.

An account of the fate of the 17th-century British settlers after they were forced to leave Suriname after the conclusion of the Treaty of Breda in 1667 which made Suriname a Dutch possession. Some of the settlers retired to Barbados and Antigua; the bulk of them, however, went to Jamaica. The article includes a list of British subjects and their slaves transported from Suriname to Jamaica.

108 **Abolition of the abolished: the illegal Dutch slave trade and the mixed courts.**
Pieter C. Emmer. In: *The abolition of the Atlantic slave trade: origins and effects in Europe, Africa, and the Americas.* Edited by David Eltis, James Walvin, Svend E. Green-Pedersen, with an introduction by Stanley L. Engerman. Madison, Wisconsin: University of Wisconsin Press, 1981, p. 177-92. map. bibliog.

The author shows that the abolition of the Dutch slave trade was effective as far as the triangular trade between the Netherlands, Africa, and the Caribbean was concerned. Yet, slave imports into Suriname continued after the Dutch slave trade had been abolished. The essay is divided into four sections. The first deals with the legal abolition of the Dutch slave trade at home, as well as the lack of reaction to this legislation in the Netherlands. The second and third sections focus on the Mixed Courts of Justice in Freetown, Sierra Leone, and Paramaribo. Finally, Emmer reviews the factors that were of importance in stopping the illegal trade.

109 **De binnenlandse oorlog in Suriname 1613-1793.** (The internal war in
Suriname 1613-1793.)
Hugo A. M. Essed. Paramaribo: Anton de Kom Universiteit, 1984.
128p. maps.

This is a compilation of several articles based on secondary literature, which examines
the struggle of the Maroons and the Amerindians against the Europeans in Suriname.
The four main topics discussed are slavery and legitimized violence; the development
of large Maroon communities; the colonial army; and the military organization of the
Maroons.

110 **Director Generals of the Netherlands West India Company: an accurate
list for the eighteenth century.**
H. M. Feinberg. *Bijdragen tot de Taal-, Land- en Volkenkunde*, vol.
130, no.1/2 (1974), p. 306-12.

All hitherto existing lists of the Director Generals of the West India Company (WIC)
contain errors. Feinberg's listing from 1702 to 1804 is based on the *Dagregisters* of the
Castle of St. George d'Elmina kept by the WIC and (after 1792) by the Dutch
government, with some dates confirmed by other archival sources. The author attempts
to cite the precise day of inauguration, and interim Director Generals are included
where appropriate. A complete list covering the 17th century is not included as most of
the records of the first WIC had been destroyed.

111 **The Dutch in the Caribbean and in the Guianas, 1680-1791.**
Cornelis Ch. Goslinga. Dover, New Hampshire; Assen, The
Netherlands: Van Gorcum, 1985. 712p. maps. bibliog.

A sequel to *The Dutch in the Caribbean and on the Wild Coast*, (q.v.) covering the rise
and fall of the second West India Company. During this period, Dutch colonial and
agricultural societies developed in the Windward and Leeward Antilles, Suriname,
Berbice, Essequebo, and Demerara. Social history receives attention in chapters
treating Surinamese colonial society, which include a description of Paramaribo, and
the Dutch Black and Red Codes. The portrayal of plantation life deals mainly with the
planters. Two chapters are devoted to the Surinamese Maroons and the Berbice slave
rebellion of 1763.

112 **The Dutch in the Caribbean and on the Wild Coast 1580-1680.**
Cornelis Ch. Goslinga. Gainesville, Florida: University of Florida
Press; Assen, The Netherlands: Van Gorcum, 1971. 647p. maps.
bibliog.

This volume represents a pioneer effort to chronicle the activities of the Dutch fleet in
the Caribbean during the 17th century. The author describes the formation, growth,
and demise of the Dutch West India Company, whose principal purpose was the
privateering of Spanish holdings and the colonization of the 'Wild Coast'. The profits
from smuggling, piracy, and kidnapping proved to be significant. After the peace with
Spain, concluded in 1648, privateering gradually gave way to colonization and the slave
trade. A sequel covering the period from 1680 to 1791 is called *The Dutch in the
Caribbean and in the Guianas, 1680-1791* (q.v.).

113   **International trade and the abolition of slavery in Suriname.**
Ruben S. Gowricharn.   *Caraibisch Forum*, vol. 2, no. 2/3 (1982),
p. 70-100. bibliog.
A (neo-)Marxist analysis of the economic forces that caused the abolition of slavery in
Suriname in 1863. The author argues that the late emancipation of the Surinamese
slaves had at least one important economic consequence; at a time when competition
from 'new' plantation colonies was increasing, its own economy continued to decline.
In the adjacent British territories technological innovations were introduced thirty
years earlier than in Suriname, resulting in higher output and lower costs.

114   **The Boni Maroon war 1765-1793, Surinam and French Guyana.**
Silvia Wilhelmina de Groot.   *Boletín de Estudios Latinoamericanos y
del Caribe*, no. 18 (June 1975), p. 30-48. maps.
A short overview of the history of the Aluku (or Boni) Maroons during the final
decades of the 18th century. The Alukus, who still live in the border area between
Suriname and French Guiana; started to attack planations in 1765 and continued to
wage an intermittent war against the colonial authorities until 1793, when their chiefs
Boni and Cormantin Codjo were killed by Ndjukas.

115   **A comparison between the history of Maroon communities in Surinam
and Jamaica.**
Silvia Wilhelmina de Groot.   In: *Out of the house of bondage:
runaways, resistance and marronage in Africa and the New World.*
Edited by Gad Heuman. London: Frank Cass, 1986, p. 173-84.
A comparison and an explanation of the similarities and differences in the
development of Surinamese and Jamaican Maroon communities. The author focuses
on their origins; their relationship with the colonial authorities; the peace treaties; and
the extent of their geographical, social, and economic isolation. De Groot concludes
that the contact between the Maroons and the colonial authorities was more intense in
Jamaica than in Suriname, and that conflicts were due to shortage of land in Jamaica
and shortage of labour in Suriname. The appendix contains comparative statistics. This
article is also published in *Oso*, vol. 3, no 1 (May 1984).

116   **An example of oral history: the tale of Boni's death and of Boni's head.**
Silvia Wilhelmina de Groot.   In: *Lateinamerika-Studien*. Edited by
Jürgen Schneider. Munich: Wilhelm Fint Verlag, 1982, p. 181-216.
map. bibliog. (Band 11).
The author concentrates upon the reinterpretation of one case study in oral history, to
shed additional light upon and provide new insights into the history of the Maroons
and the Alukus in particular. The tale concerns the period between 1780 and 1812 and
reports the death of Boni, the Paramount Chief, and Cormantin Codjo, an important
Aluku captain. The few facts dealing with the episode as reported in the 19th-century
literature often vary and contradict one another. This article is also published in Dutch
in *De Gids*, no. 1 (1980) and in French in *L'histoire et ses méthodes. Actes du Colleque
Franco-Néerlandais de novembre 1980 à Amsterdam* (Lille, France: Presse Universitaire
1981).

117   **From isolation towards integration. The Surinam Maroons and their colonial rulers: official documents relating to the Djukas (1845-1863).**
Silvia Wilhelmina de Groot.   The Hague: Martinus Nijhoff, 1977.
111p. bibliog. (Verhandelingen van het Koninklijk Instituut voor Taal-, Land- en Volkenkunde, 80).

This survey is the revised version in English of a publication in this same series called *Van isolatie naar integratie* (The Hague: Martinus Nijhoff, 1963). Based on archival sources, this study analyses the contacts between the Maroons and the colonial government as reflected in the correspondence between the government and the 'postholders' who were military officials entrusted with the task to maintain relations between the government and the Maroons after the conclusion of the peace treaties in 1760, 1762, and 1767. Until 1845 the authorities were eager to keep the Maroons isolated; later the government attempted to induce them to participate in the colonial labour market.

118   **Het Korps Zwarte Jagers in Suriname: collaboratie en opstand I en II.**
(The Black Chasseurs Corps in Suriname: collaboration and rebellion I and II.)
Silvia Wilhelmina de Groot.   *Oso*, vol. 7, no. 2 (Dec. 1988), p. 147-60; vol. 8, no. 1 (May 1989), p. 7-20. bibliog.

An account of the history of the Black Chasseurs, who were founded by the Dutch colonists in order to fight the Maroons in the early 19th century. Three hundred slaves were bought by the government and became free men when the Corps was founded. They functioned satisfactorily until their short but fierce rebellion against the authorities which caused much consternation in Suriname. The author analyses this rebellion which broke out in 1805, when the British occupied the Dutch colony (1804-16), and places it in a wider colonial, as well as international perspective.

119   **The Maroons of Surinam: agents of their own emancipation.**
Silvia Wilhelmina de Groot.   In: *Abolition and its aftermath: the historical context 1790-1916.* Edited by David Richardson. London; Totowa, New Jersey: Frank Cass, 1985, p. 55-79. map.

An article relating how the Maroons initially fought to protect their freedom and autonomy. However, their growing numbers, and their desire to settle down to a more sedentary lifestyle, encouraged the Maroons to seek peace with the whites after 1730. Various treaties were ratified to protect the integrity of Maroon culture. The article also includes a brief description of the main features of Maroon society.

120   **Notes on the history of the Jews in Surinam.**
P. A. Hilfman.   *Publications on the American Jewish Historical Society*, no. 18 (1909), p. 179-207.

Presents an outline of the history of the synagogue and cemetery of Jodensavanne. The author also lists the rabbis of the Dutch-Portuguese Jewish Congregation in Suriname from 1642 to 1750 as well as the marriages solemnized by the different rabbis of the Congregation during the same period.

121 **Oral history and archival data combined: the removal of the Saramakan Granman Kofi Bosuman as an epistemological problem.**
Joris Hoeree, Wilhelmus S. M. Hoogbergen. *Communication and Cognition*, vol. 17, no. 2/3 (1984), p. 245-89. bibliog.
An investigation into the problems of the relationship between archival and oral data, in which the authors employ an ethnographical illustration, taken from the history of Suriname: the removal of the Saramakan Granman or Paramount Chief, Kofi Bosuman in 1835. In this example two versions are juxtaposed: an archival version and an oral one. The authors construct a synthesis in which they note the differences between the two versions while pointing out their uniqueness.

122 **Surinam and Curaçao.**
Harry Hoetink. In: *Neither slave nor free: the freedman of African descent in the slave societies of the New World.* Edited with an introduction by David W. Cohen, Jack P. Greene. Baltimore, Maryland; London: Johns Hopkins University Press, 1974, p. 59-83.
Although Suriname and Curaçao were both subjected to Dutch authority and to similar metropolitan cultural influences, the conditions of the free blacks and coloureds in these colonies were different. Hoetink attributes this divergence to economic and demographic factors. Because of its climate and geography, Curaçao never became a plantation colony. Consequently, only a limited number of slaves lived on the island. A benign paternalistic slave system produced, through frequent manumissions, a large number of free coloureds for whom there was hardly any place in the economic and political structure, because their relatively large number threatened the position of the whites. In contrast, in the typical Caribbean plantation society of Suriname the great majority of the population was enslaved. This more cruel system, with fewer manumissions, however, could lead to the improvement of the social and economic position of the free coloureds, because the whites accepted their relatively small numbers more readily.

123 **De Boni-oorlogen, 1757-1860: marronage en guerilla in Oost-Suriname. The Boni wars, 1757-1860: Maroons and guerilla warfare in eastern Suriname (with a summary in English).**
Wilhelmus S. M. Hoogbergen. PhD thesis, Rijksuniversiteit Utrecht, The Netherlands, 1985. 528p. maps. bibliog. (Bronnen voor de Studie van Afro-Amerikaanse Samenlevingen, 11).
An exhaustive study of the Boni wars (1757-1860) which are placed in the context of Suriname's colonial society in the second half of the 18th century. Following guerrilla warfare against the planters and the colonial troops, the Aluku Maroons crossed the Marowijne River into French Guiana in 1776. After a period of relative calm, the Alukus resumed war against the Dutch in 1789. The author published documents on the residence of the Alukus in French Guiana and the second Boni war (which ended in 1793) in *De Boni's in Frans Guyana en de tweede Boni-oorlog, 1776-1793* (Utrecht, the Netherlands: Centrum voor Caraibische Studies, Rijksuniversiteit Utrecht, 1984.) The appendix includes a chronology as well as a listing of Surinamese plantations and their geographical location.

124 **The economic contribution of Dutch Sephardi Jewry to Holland's golden age, 1595-1713.**
Jonathan I. Israel. *Tijdschrift voor Geschiedenis*, vol. 96, no. 4 (1983), p. 505-35.
The author argues that the widespread conviction that the Dutch Sephardi contribution to Holland's prosperity was marginal is incorrect. A wide variety of evidence indicates that this group were of central importance in prolonging Holland's commercial growth. The Sephardim dominated a large part of Dutch trade with the West Indies and the Sephardi colony in Suriname continued to flourish down to the 1770s. By the mid-18th century Dutch Sephardi overseas commerce, which had once been a trading network based on Portuguese cities, evolved into a system based essentially on Curaçao, Suriname, and St. Eustatius.

125 **The conduct of the Dutch relating to their breaches of treaties with England. Particularly their breach of the Articles of Capitulation, for the surrender of Surinam, in 1667; and their oppressions committed upon the English subjects in that colony. With a full account of the case of J. Clifford, late merchant and planter of Surinam, etc.**
Ch. Jenkinson. London: W. Bristow, 1760. 206p.
An attack by an English author on the Dutch regarding their conduct concerning the Articles of Capitulation and the Treaty of 1667 as well as the Dutch treatment of English subjects living in Suriname. The volume includes a full account of the case of Jeronimy Clifford, an English planter and merchant, who addressed the governments in both the Dutch Republic and England about the injustices the Dutch had inflicted upon him.

126 **Seidenraupe, Dschungelblüte: die Lebensgeschichte der Maria Sibylla Merian.** (Silkworms, jungle blossoms: the biography of Maria Sibylla Merian.)
Charlotte Kerner. Weinheim, FRG; Basel, Switzerland: Beltz, 1988. 112p. bibliog.
A biography of Maria Sibylla Merian who, at fifty-two years of age, sailed to Suriname in 1699 to study butterflies and plants. Some of her observations have been published in *Metamorphosis insectorum Surinamensium* (q.v.), a book which made her famous, but not rich. Maria Merian died in Amsterdam in 1717. The biography contains books by Maria Merian as well as books, articles, and novels about her.

127 **Guerrilla warfare: a Bush Negro view.**
Johannes King, translated by Richard Price, Sally Price. In: *Maroon societies: rebel slave communities in the Americas.* Edited by Richard Price. Garden City, New York: Anchor Press/Double Day, 1973, p. 298-304.
A rather free translation by Richard Price and Sally Price of parts of *Skrekiboekoe* (Book of horrors), written in Sranan by Johannes King in 1885. An edited version of the original text, together with a Dutch translation and extensive notes, may be found in the anthology *Suriname: spiegel der vaderlandse kooplieden*, edited by Ursy M. Lichtveld, Jan Voorhoeve (The Hague: Martinus Nijhoff, 1980). The selection

presented by the Prices recounts the living conditions of a Maroon community at war; the conclusion of a peace treaty with the colonial government; and the subsequent celebrations within the community.

128 **Schets van de historische ontwikkeling van de manumissie in Suriname 1733-1863.** (Sketch of the historical development of manumission in Suriname 1733-1863.)
Paul Koulen. *Mededelingen Stichting Surinaams Museum*, no. 12 (Dec. 1973), p. 8-36. bibliog.

An essay dealing with the policy towards the manumission of slaves before the general abolition in 1863. The author's most important sources are the consecutive laws on manumission which were issued during the period 1733-1863. The author also speculates on the motives behind the manumission policy and their social and economic background. The degree to which the law was observed is hard to assess, but Koulen argues that there existed a wide discrepancy between the laws and the actual practices. The article includes a summary in English.

129 **Afwijking en tolerantie bij slavenhandel en negerslavernij, 1600-1863.** (Deviance and tolerance concerning slave trade and negro slavery.)
Maarten Kuitenbrouwer. In: *Een schijn van verdraagzaamheid. Afwijking en tolerantie in Nederland van de zestiende eeuw tot heden.* Edited by Marijke Gijswit-Hofstra. Hilversum, The Netherlands: Verloren, 1989, p. 211-35.

A study of the Dutch participation in the slave trade as well as of the official policy and public opinion in the Netherlands concerning this topic. The author also compares the Dutch slave trade with that of other countries, Britain in particular, and to other forms of trade and labour.

130 **Bijdragen tot de kennis van de kolonie Suriname dat gedeelte van Guiana hetwelk bij Tractaat ten jare 1815 aan het Koningrijk Holland is verbleven tijdvak 1816 tot 1822.** (Contributions to the knowledge of the colony of Suriname that part of Guiana which with the Treaty of the year 1815 is left to the Kingdom Holland period 1816 to 1822.)
Adriaan François Lammens, edited by G. A. de Bruijne. Amsterdam: Vrije Universiteit Amsterdam, Geografisch en Planologisch Instituut, Vakgroep Sociale Geografie van Ontwikkelinglanden; Leiden, The Netherlands: Caribbean Department, Royal Institute of Linguistics and Anthropology, 1982. 198p. maps.

The Surinaams Museum in Paramaribo and the General State Archives in The Hague house the eighteen volumes containing the writings of A. F. Lammens. Part of one of these volumes is reprinted in this book. Lammens (1767-1847) was a high official in Suriname and he sketches here the geography and social conditions of that country and of Paramaibo in particular. It is one of few 19th-century descriptions of the town and is thus exceedingly important.

131 **Demographic performance of two slave populations of the Dutch speaking Caribbean.**
Humphrey E. Lamur. *Boletín de Estudios Latinoamericanos y del Caribe*, no. 30 (June 1981), p. 87-102. bibliog.
Most Caribbean plantation colonies such as Suriname showed a substantial natural decrease in the slave population. One of the few exceptions to this pattern was the demographic performance of the slaves in Curaçao. The fertility rate in Suriname was twice as low as in Curaçao. The author suggests that this differential was caused by differences in the average birth interval between the two populations. This, in turn, was related to differences both in the nature of slavery and the labour conditions on the estates, and probably to nutrition as well.

132 **Fertility differentials on three slave plantations in Suriname.**
Humphrey E. Lamur. *Slavery and Abolition*, vol. 8, no. 3 (1987), p. 313-35.
An analysis of the differences in fertility and child-spacing intervals at three Surinamese plantations: Andressa (timber), Catharina Sophia (sugar), and Mijn Vermaak (coffee/cacao). The author examines demographic and socio-economic aspects related to fertility differentials. He concludes that the slaves' fertility level was dependent on the crop and the resulting labour conditions at the estates.

133 **De kaping van een Surinaamse schoener door de slaaf Philip, 1853.** (The hijacking of a Surinamese schooner by the slave Philip, 1853.)
Humphrey E. Lamur. *Oso*, vol. 2, no. 1 (May 1983), p. 35-65. map.
An account of the escape of a slave by hijacking a ship. The author focuses on the historical and anthropological aspects of this case and analyses the relation between the master and the slave, and traces the origin of a class of 'privileged slaves'. Lamur discusses the events of 1853, the role of the slave, Philip, and the reasons for his flight. The archival documents used to study this case are presented in six appendices.

134 **Het onstaan van het eigendomsrecht bij slaven in Suriname.** (The origin of the right of ownership of slaves in Suriname.)
Humphrey E. Lamur. *Oso*, vol. 8, no. 1 (May 1989), p. 29-37. bibliog.
According to the dependency theory concerning the development of the Caribbean in the 18th and 19th centuries pre-capitalist modes of production continued to exist during slavery. Adherents of this theory explain this by pointing to the planters' interests, which were not threatened by pre-capitalist modes of production. Lamur argues however that it was not only the planters' interests which determined the survival of this mode of production, but also those of the slaves.

135 **The production of sugar and the reproduction of slaves at Vossenburg, Suriname, 1705-1863.**
Humphrey E. Lamur. Amsterdam: Centre for Caribbean Studies, 1987. 164p. maps. bibliog. (Caribbean Culture Studies, 1).
In this case study of the Vossenburg and Wayampibo plantations, Lamur examines the evolution of joint ownership; the demographic development of the slave population;

and the profitability of sugar cultivation in Suriname during the period 1700-1863. The author concludes that in spite of the scarcity of slave labour, the cultivation of sugar at these two plantations had been profitable. In a separate section a number of tables and figures illustrate that the general reproduction rate of the slave population was negative, or zero at best.

136 **Outalissi; a tale of Dutch Guiana.**
Christopher Edward Lefroy. London: J. Hatchard & Son, 1826. 324p.
The author of this first-hand but partly fictional account about the condition of the slaves in Suriname was a judge in the Mixed Court in the colony. The book is dedicated to the abolitionist William Wilberforce and is intended to expose some of the features in the unreformed system of slavery in Suriname.

137 **The Jewish community in Surinam: a historical survey.**
Rudolf A. J. van Lier. In: *The Jewish nation in Surinam.* Edited by R. Cohen. Amsterdam: S. Emmering, 1982, p. 19-27. bibliog.
A survey of the history of the Jews in Suriname, who first arrived in 1652. The Jewish village of Jodensavanne was the centre of Jewish life in the colony and contained a large synagogue which was inaugurated in 1685. The Jews formed a separate group which in 1665 was granted a number of important privileges, such as free worship. After 1750, anti-Semitism began to develop, mainly caused by political tensions and the relationship between Jews and non-Jews gradually worsened. However, the position of the Jews improved again in the 19th century.

138 **Jan Willem Kals 1700-1781: leraar der hervormden; advocaat van Indiaan en Neger.** (Jan Willem Kals 1700-1781: teacher of the protestants; counsel of Amerindians and blacks.)
J. M. van der Linde. Kampen, The Netherlands: Kok, 1987. 202p. bibliog.
A biography of Jan Willem Kals, who was a preacher in Suriname during the 18th century whose concern for the welfare of the Amerindians and the slaves brought him into conflict with the authorities. Kals was expelled within two years, but continued to preach and write about the plight of these 'heathens'. This book contains summaries in English and German. Seven appendices include archival material.

139 **Organisatie, sterkte en samenstelling van de Militie, 1724-1795.**
(Organization, strength and composition of the Militia, 1724-1795.)
M. J. Lohnstein. *Oso*, vol. 7, no. 1 (May 1988), p. 47-62. bibliog.
The purpose of this article is twofold. First, the author checks primary and secondary sources to establish a truthful account of the history and functioning of the Militia in the 18th century. Second, the author analyses the place and function of the Militia in a plantation colony. This analysis forms the background for a discussion of the changing organizational structure of the Militia.

140 **De zaak van Semire de antropofage: Geregtshof te Suriname, 21 juni 1837.** (The case of Semire the anthropophagus: Court of Justice in Suriname, 21 June 1837.)
William L. Man A Hing. *Oso*, vol. 8, no. 1 (May 1989), p. 55-64. bibliog.

A case study of cannibalism involving a female slave who killed and ate a child. The article includes the court records.

141 **Betwist bestuur. Een eeuw strijd om de macht in Suriname 1651-1753.** (Contested rule: a century of struggle for dominance in Suriname 1651-1753.)
Gerard Willem van der Meiden. Amsterdam: De Bataafsche Leeuw, 1986. 167p. bibliog.

An analysis of the functioning of the administration in Suriname during the period 1651-1753. These years were particularly conflict-ridden, as five governors had to be recalled from the colony. The author establishes relationships between individual crises and the structural problems that allowed them to proliferate. He pays little attention, however, to the relationships between the different population groups. This dissertation (Rijksuniversiteit Leiden, the Netherlands, 1987) includes a brief summary in English.

142 **Governor Mauricius and the political rights of the Surinam Jews.**
Gerard Willem van der Meiden. In: *The Jewish nation in Surinam.* Edited by R. Cohen. Amsterdam: S. Emmering, 1982, p. 48-55. bibliog.

A short article on the political tensions during the middle of the 18th century, in which the Jews played a major role. The author analyses the conflict from the political point of view, paying particular attention to the role of Governor Mauricius, who objected to any infringement on the rights of the Jews.

143 **The Dutch and British policy of Indian subsidy: a system of annual and triennial presents.**
Mary Noel Menezes. *Caribbean Studies*, vol. 13, no. 3 (Oct. 1973), p. 64-88.

A description of the relations between the Dutch and the British colonists and the Amerindians in the Guianas. The Dutch exerted themselves to foster good relations with the native tribes. After all, the Amerindians were familiar with the terrain and they were instrumental in the containment of African slaves as well as in setting up and maintaining trade relations. According to the author, the Amerindians accepted the jurisdiction of the Dutch, and after the colonies were ceded to the British, the Amerindians recognized the British as heirs to the Dutch. The natives claimed the same privileges they had enjoyed under Dutch rule.

144 **Roosenburg en Mon Bijou. Twee Surinaamse plantages, 1720-1870.**
(Roosenburg and Mon Bijou. Two Surinamese plantations, 1720-1870.)
Gert Jan Oostindie. Dordrecht, The Netherlands: Foris, 1989. 548p.
map. bibliog. (Koninklijk Instituut voor Taal-, Land- en Volkenkunde
Caribbean Series, 11).

A study of a sugar plantation (Roosenburg) and a coffee estate (Mon Bijou), in which
the author focuses on the economic and agricultural development of the plantations as
well as on labour relations. He also looks at the world the slaves made and places his
findings in a Caribbean context. He deals with the relations between plantation
management and the owners and creditors who lived in the Netherlands. The volume
contains six appendices. This study was originally a dissertation (Rijksuniversiteit
Utrecht, the Netherlands, 1989) which included a six-page summary in English.

145 **An early Jewish colony in western Guiana, 1658-1666; and its relation to
the Jews in Surinam, Cayenne and Tobago.**
Samuel Oppenheim. *Publications of the American Jewish Historical
Society*, no. 16 (1907), p. 95-186.

An account of the history of the Jews in Brazil, Cayenne, and Suriname. The author
sketches the surrounding conditions up to the beginning of the first settlement and
refers to a sister colony in Tobago to which some of the colonists departed.

146 **First-time: the historical vision of an Afro-American people.**
Richard Price. Baltimore, Maryland; London: Johns Hopkins
University Press, 1983. 189p. maps. bibliog.

This volume contains the oral history of the Saramaka Maroons relating to the period
from 1685 to 1762, as conveyed to Price by historians from various Saramaka clans.
Running simultaneously with the texts representing Saramaka collective knowledge,
the author provides commentaries, explanations, and comparisons with other written
sources. Price's extensive knowledge of Saramaka history earned him a formal
appointment as an official tribe chronicler. 'First-time' is the era of the 'Old-time'
people, the formative years of the Saramaka way of life: the years in which the
Saramakas escaped to freedom, built their early settlements in the rain forest, raided
plantations, and conducted a guerrilla war against the white colonists. This book
publishes the oral history of village movements, interclan rivalries, and the process of
building towards a peace treaty with the colonists, which was finally achieved in 1762.
This classic study includes an extensive methodological introduction.

147 **Kwasímukámba's gambit.**
Richard Price. *Bijdragen tot de Taal-, Land- en Volkenkunde*, vol.
135, no. 1 (1979), p. 151-69. map. bibliog.

This paper considers and compares the two separate historical traditions about
Kwasi, a Saramaka Chief who was also a healer and a diviner and who was the
colony's principal intermediary in dealing with runaway slaves .The Saramaka Maroons
call him Kwasímukámba, and they have preserved a detailed image of this man for
over 200 years. In written sources Kwasímukámba is known as Quacy or Kwasi,
and was, according to John Stedman, one of the most extraordinary black men in
Suriname.

148 **Representations of slavery: John Gabriel Stedman's 'Minnesota' manuscripts.**
Richard Price.   Minneapolis, Minnesota: Associates of the James Ford Bell Library, University of Minnesota, 1989. 35p. (The James Ford Bell Lectures, 26).
A lecture introducing J. G. Stedman's 'Minnesota' manuscripts. Price assesses their significance and recounts the history of editing the 1988 version of Stedman's *Narrative of a five years expedition against the revolted negroes of Surinam* (q.v.) which led him and Sally Price to Suriname, Germany, the Netherlands, and England. The lecture draws upon the introduction of the aforementioned edition of the *Narrative*.

149 **To slay the hydra: Dutch colonial perspectives in the Saramaka wars.**
Richard Price.   Ann Arbor, Michigan: Karoma, 1983. 247p. maps. bibliog.
The title of this book, intended as a companion volume to *First-time: the historical vision of an Afro-American people* (q.v.), was taken from a poem by Governor Mauricius who felt that since military expeditions had proven to be worthless, diplomacy and cunning behaviour would be the only ways to destroy the Maroon 'hydra'. On the basis of diaries and reports, mainly by military men and peace negotiators such as Louis Nepveu, this book offers the view of the white protagonists on the years between the abortive Peace Treaty of 1749 and the making of the Saramaka Peace in 1762. It encompasses Saramaka raids on plantations, massive colonial expeditions against these rebel slaves, the schemes of spies and counter-spies, the influence of the Ndjuka Peace Treaty of 1760, the political negotiations leading to the Saramaka Peace Treaty, and the celebrations following the final outcome.

150 **John Gabriel Stedman's 'Journal of a voyage to the West Indies in ye year 1772. In a poetical epistle to a friend'.**
Richard Price, Sally Price.   *Nieuwe West-Indische Gids/New West Indian Guide*, vol. 59, no. 3/4 (1985), p. 185-96. bibliog.
In preparing the critical edition of J. G. Stedman's *Narrative of a five years expedition against the revolted negroes of Surinam* (q.v.) the authors discovered a previously unknown poem recounting Stedman's outward voyage to Suriname in 1772-73. Since it was not intended to be published with the *Narrative. . .*, the authors have therefore published it here, with a few introductory comments and notes.

151 **Analysis of the annals relating to early Jewish settlement in Surinam.**
L. L. E. Rens.   In: *The Jewish nation in Surinam*. Edited by R. Cohen. Amsterdam: S. Emmering, 1982, p. 28-46. map. bibliog.
This article originally appeared in *Vox Guyana*, no. 1 (1954). It focuses on the legend regarding the supposed departure of many hundreds of Jews in the decade following on the Treaty of Breda in 1667. It is said that these migrants left for Jamaica and other English Caribbean possessions. The author concludes that these statements are entirely unfounded and even seem very improbable.

152   **Additional notes on the history of the Jews in Surinam.**
      J. S. Roos.   *Publications of the American Jewish Historical Society*, no.
      13 (1905), p. 127-36.
A short article containing notes on the history of Jewish settlement in Suriname. The
author investigated the old Colonial Archives, the records of the Portuguese Jewish
Congregation, and the records of the Dutch Jewish Congregation.

153   **Jewish jurators in Surinam.**
      J. A. Schiltkamp.   In: *The Jewish nation in Surinam*. Edited by R.
      Cohen. Amsterdam: S. Emmering, 1982, p. 57-63. bibliog.
A description of the unique institute of the Jewish jurator, or notary, and its origins.
The first member of the Jewish nation to be appointed jurator, and thus the first Jewish
notary in the Western hemisphere, was Samuel Nassy in 1684. The author examines
the role of the Nassy family in the development of this office in Suriname.

154   **Emancipation in British Guyana and its influence on Dutch policy**
      regarding Surinam.
      J. P. Siwpersad.   In: *Abolition and its aftermath: the historical context*
      1790-1916. Edited by David Richardson. London; Towota, New Jersey:
      Frank Cass, 1985, p. 168-80.
The author demonstrates how the abolition of slavery in the British colonies initiated a
process of gradual acceptance of the emancipation principle in Dutch government
circles. The assessment of the results of emancipation in other colonies shaped the
Dutch authorities' approach to abolition. Developments in British Guiana were
followed particularly closely. The author argues that reports about the unsatisfactory
behaviour of former slaves and the decline of large-scale agriculture following abolition
in British Guiana, served as an obstacle to slave emancipation in Suriname. This article
is a summary of several chapters of the author's dissertation *De Nederlandse regering*
en de afschaffing van de Surinaamse slavernij (The Dutch government and the
abolition of slavery in Suriname) (Groningen, The Netherlands: Bouma's
Boekhuis, 1979).

155   **Narrative of a five years expedition against the revolted negroes of**
      Surinam. Transcribed for the first time from the original 1790
      manuscript. Edited, and with an introduction and notes, by Richard
      Price and Sally Price.
      John Gabriel Stedman.   Baltimore, Maryland; London: Johns
      Hopkins University Press, 1988. 708p. maps. bibliog.
A beautifully produced volume of John Stedman's *Narrative*, which unlike all previous
publications is based on Stedman's personal copy of the 1790 manuscript rather than
on the heavily edited first published edition of 1796. The text is presented intact and
discusses several themes: the military campaigns against the Maroons and Stedman's
relations with other soldiers and his superiors; a description of Surinamese flora and
fauna; a detailed analysis of plantation life, and finally, Stedman's romance with the
slave Joanna. The commentary by the Prices appears separately in the introduction,
the notes, and two appendices. The first appendix contains identifications of flora and
fauna, the second one lists the sources for literary citations.

156 **The Surinam rat race: labour and technology on sugar plantations, 1750-1900.**
Alex van Stipriaan. *Nieuwe West-Indische Gids/New West-Indian Guide*, vol. 63, no. 1/2 (1989), p. 95-119.

Preceding a dissertation on this subject, the author discusses the history of labour and technology on sugar plantations in Suriname. He discusses technological innovations in the factory and in the field, as well as the development of productivity and profitability. Van Stipriaan concludes that the introduction of more advanced technology did not have to wait for the abolition of slavery.

157 **The Guyana-Suriname boundary dispute: an historical appraisal, c. 1683-1816.**
Alvin O. Thompson. *Boletín de Estudios Latinoamericanos y del Caribe*, no. 39 (Dec. 1985), p. 63-84. maps.

This article looks at the origins of the boundary dispute between Suriname and Guyana. By the mid-18th century the Dutch possessed several colonies on the South American mainland: Essequibo, Demerara, Berbice, and Suriname. Since these territories were contiguous to each other the authorities had never exactly demarcated the boundaries. This became a problem when the first three colonies became British territories. Before the 19th century two attempts were made to establish the boundaries between Berbice and Suriname. Both of these attempts failed, however, and a definitive settlement has still not been reached.

158 **Dutch capital in the West Indies during the eighteenth century: the financing and expansion of plantations before 1750.**
J. P. van de Voort. In: *The Low Countries history yearbook. Acta Historiae Neerlandicae, no. 14*. The Hague: Martinus Nijhoff, 1981, p. 85-105.

Plantations in the West Indies were highly capital intensive, and most planters were dependent on credit to raise capital. Van de Voort describes the commission system that characterized English and Dutch trade with the plantations in the West Indies. With the significant expansion of agricultural production in Suriname during the first half of the 18th century, the demand for credit increased concomitantly. The bullish market in plantation loans ended with the bank crisis of Amsterdam in 1772. The author argues that the primary cause of the fiasco of West Indian financial dealing lay in the lack of insight regarding plantation agriculture among Dutch capitalists.

159 **Die Rolle der niederländischen Publizistik bei der Meinungsbildung hinsichtlich der Aufhebung der Sklaverei in den westindischen Kolonien.**
(The role of Dutch publicists in the formation of public opinion regarding the abolition of slavery in the West Indian colonies.)
Eugenius Theodorus Waaldijk. PhD dissertation, Westfälischen Wilhelms-Universität zu Münster, FRG, 1959. 229p. bibliog.

A discussion of the role Dutch publicists played in the formation of public opinion regarding slavery during the period 1833-63. Many commentators lamented the situation of the slaves and called for the abolition of the system. On the other hand, slave owners and many merchants wanted to maintain the existing source of labour.

Both groups tried to influence people without a set opinion, government officials in particular.

160 **Geschiedenis van Suriname.** (History of Suriname.)
J. Wolbers. Amsterdam: S. Emmering, 1970. 849p.

A classic history of Suriname from 1492 to 1858, originally published in 1861 and based on documents deposited at the General State Archives in The Hague. The author did research in England in order to describe the period of the English occupation of Suriname (1804-16). The book was intended to increase knowledge about the colony and its slave population in particular. Prior to its publication, some good histories of Suriname existed but only covered the period up to 1770. Other essays mainly discussed the agricultural aspects of the colony. The author divides the history of Suriname into five periods. The first describes the discovery of America to the conquest of Suriname by the province of Zeeland (1666). The second one treats the time from Abraham Crijnssen who conquered Suriname (1666) to C. van Aerssen Sommelsdijck (1683). The third period studies the history until the English occupation, while the fourth discusses the English occupation, which lasted from 1804 to 1816. The final section recounts the time from 1816 to 1858. Despite a number of factual errors, the book is still eminently useful and contains a chronology of the major events in the history of Suriname.

Post-Emancipation (1863-)

161 **Chinese contract migrants in Surinam between 1853 and 1870.**
J. Ankum-Houwink. *Boletín de Estudios Latinoamericanos y del Caribe*, no. 17 (Dec. 1974), p. 42-68. bibliog.

In the period 1853-70 more than 2,500 Chinese were imported to work on the plantations in Suriname. The author discusses various aspects of this Chinese indentured migration, such as the labour shortage; public opinion about the Chinese at the time; and the so-called 'coolie-trade' and its regulations.

162 **War, cooperation, and conflict: the European possessions in the Caribbean, 1939-1945.**
Fitzroy André Baptiste. New York: Greenwood Press, 1988. 351p. maps. bibliog. (Contributions in Comparative Colonial Studies, 23).

This study on the Second World War centres on the Caribbean. It examines the place of the Caribbean possessions of Britain, France, and the Netherlands within the complex strategy and diplomacy of the opposing coalitions during the war. The author notes the strategic importance of bauxite to the Allied war effort which made Suriname a pawn in the war. One chapter is devoted to the German occupation of the Netherlands and the repercussions of this in the Caribbean, another discusses the entry of US Forces into Suriname.

163 **Aantekeningen over de geschiedenis van de Kwinti en het dagboek van Kraag (1894-1896).** (Notes on the history of the Kwinti and the diary of Kraag [1894-1896].)

Chris de Beet, Miriam Sterman. Utrecht, The Netherlands: Centrum voor Caraïbische Studies, Instituut voor Culturele Antropologie, Rijksuniversiteit Utrecht, 1980. 76p. maps. bibliog. (Bronnen voor de Studie van Bosneger Samenlevingen, 6).

The diary of the evangelist Christiaan Kraag sheds light on a relatively little known episode in the history of the Kwinti Maroons. Kraag was a missionary in the village of Copenkrissi on the Coppename River from 1893 to 1903. In the introduction, the authors focus on the escape from the plantations, the first contacts with other Maroon groups, and the first missionary efforts to convert the Kwinti to Christianity. The diary is printed in Sranan and Dutch.

164 **Jungle gold. Van de goudvelden in Suriname.**

Will DeGrouchy, William L. Magee, introduced and annotated by Frans C. Bubberman. Zutphen, The Netherlands: De Walburg Pers, 1985. 160p. maps.

A version in Dutch and English of *Jungle gold, Dad Pedrick's story* (Indianapolis, Indiana: Bobbs-Merrill, 1930) introduced and annotated by Frans Bubberman. Howard A. Pedrick arrived in Paramaribo in 1899. He trained as an engineer, and was employed by the rich businessman R. H. Foerderer from Philadelphia to manage the technical side of a gold-mining venture, the Marowijne Company. His lively letters bear witness to a born storyteller and give an impression of the advent of modern industrialism in the jungle, complete with the heroic tales of its pioneering executives. *Jungle gold* was put to paper by others, and therefore the names are sometimes transmuted, while texts are exaggerated at times. Yet, according to Bubberman, *Jungle gold* has a solid foundation in fact.

165 **The meek Hindu: the recruitment of Indian labourers for service overseas, 1870-1916.**

Pieter C. Emmer. In: *Colonialism and migration; indentured labour before and after slavery.* Edited by Pieter C. Emmer. Dordrecht, The Netherlands: Martinus Nijhoff, 1986, p. 187-208.

An examination of the recruitment of Indian indentured labourers. Emmer argues that fraud, deception, and kidnapping were not widely used. On the contrary, there were many laws and regulations to prevent irregular recruiting practices. Emmer prefers to compare indentured migration to 'free' emigration out of Europe during the 19th century, rather than liken it to the slave trade. This study is based on archival records in England and in the Netherlands.

166 **Contractimmigranten voor Suriname/Contract immigrants for Suriname.**

Jos Fontaine. *Suralco Magazine*, vol. 16, no. 2 (1984), p. 1-10.

A brief popular article describing the immigration of Portuguese from Madeira, Chinese, British Indians, and Javanese, who were recruited to work on the plantations in Suriname. The author also pays attention to the activities of the Suriname Immigration Company, which never really became successful.

167 **Djuka society and social change; history of an attempt to develop a Bush Negro community in Surinam 1917-1926.**
Silvia Wilhelmina de Groot. Assen, The Netherlands: Van Gorcum, 1969. 259p. maps. bibliog.
During the years 1917-26, the Surinamese government tried to persuade the Ndjukas to establish contact with Western civilization by offering them education, agricultural instruction, and medical aid. The government aimed to integrate them into the colonial scheme and thus enlarge the number of potential labour recruits. W. F. van Lier assumed the task of 'postholder' of the Tapanahoni river, along which most Ndjukas live, to execute these plans. Notwithstanding Van Lier's thorough ethnographic knowledge of the Ndjukas, the development plan met with insuperable opposition. Apart from unforeseen events, several factors contributed to this failure; for instance the historically conditioned distrust of the Ndjukas towards Western civilization, as well as the autonomy and the rigid stratification of Ndjuka society.

168 **Kleine boeren in de schaduw van de plantage. De politieke ekonomie van de na-slavernij periode in Suriname.** (Smallholders in the shadow of the plantation. The political economy of the post-slavery period in Suriname.)
Waldo Heilbron. Amsterdam: Stolk, 1982. 302p. bibliog.
A neo-Marxist thesis concerning the early developments in small-scale agriculture following the abolition of slavery and the period of State supervision during 1873-1923. The book is divided into three parts: the first describes the changing social basis of the smallholders; the second discusses the changing economy and the market; and the final part deals with the transformation of the State during this time. The volume includes a summary in English.

169 **Control and resistance: indentured labor in Suriname.**
Rosemarijn Hoefte. *Nieuwe West-Indische Gids/New West Indian Guide*, vol. 61, no. 1/2 (1987), p. 1-22. bibliog.
An examination of the degree and quality of control exerted over indentured labourers at the largest plantation, Mariënburg, in particular, during the period 1880-1940. During indentureship the planters and the State exercised control over contractants. The author analyses the functioning of the judicial system in Suriname and discusses the ways in which indentured workers opposed domination. Hoefte looks at passive resistance, such as non-cooperation and illegal absences, as well as forms of active resistance such as mass uprisings.

170 **Plantation labor after the abolition of slavery: the case of plantation Mariënburg (Suriname), 1880-1940.**
Rosemarijn Hoefte. PhD dissertation, University of Florida, Gainesville, 1987. 501p. bibliog.
After the abolition of slavery in 1863, planters generally complained about a lack of workers. The immigration of contract labourers seemed to be the means to provide Suriname with a new supply of workers. Between 1873 and 1917 more than 34,000 British Indians migrated to Suriname. In addition, almost 33,000 Javanese arrived between 1890 and the beginning of the Second World War. This dissertation examines the necessity and quality of indentured labour in Suriname, and its largest plantation, Mariënburg, in particular. The introductory chapters contain an analysis of Suriname's

inclusion into the global economic system. These sections are followed by an account of indentured immigration and the social, economic, cultural, and demographic impact that this migration had on both the receiving colony and on the Asian contractants.

171 **A. de Kom: zijn strijd en ideeën.** (A. de Kom: his struggle and ideas.) Edited by Instituut Anton de Kom-Abraham Behr. Amsterdam: Sranan Buku, 1989. 130p.

Publication of papers presented at a conference held in the Anton de Kom year (1988) which celebrated the ninetieth anniversary of his birth. Some of the contributions focus on De Kom's life as an anti-colonialist activist, while others emphasize his ideas, which continue to be an inspiration for the Left.

172 **Life at Marispaston.**
Johannes King, edited by H. F. Ziel, preface by Jan Voorhoeve. The Hague: Martinus Nijhoff, 1973. 142p. map. (Verhandelingen van het Koninklijk Instituut voor Taal-, Land- en Volkenkunde, 64).

The Matawai Maroon, Johannes King wrote the manuscript on which this volume is based between 1891 and 1894. King had had a vision which instructed him to be baptized by the Moravian Brethren and to become an apostle to his people. He writes about his visions, his youth, and the history of his family. He also recounts his voyages, preaching the gospel among other Maroon populations, and gives descriptions of life in Maroon communities. This monograph contains an edited account of the difficulties between King and his brother, Chief Noah Adrai, together with some letters, a diary fragment, and a travel account of 1865. The introduction provides biographical and bibliographical notes as well as references to King's style. A summary in English preceeds the Sranan text.

173 **De roemloze ondergang van het stoomschip 'Goslar'.** (The inglorious end of the steamer 'Goslar'.)
Evert van Laar, William L. Man A Hing. *Tijdschrift voor Zeegeschiedenis*, no. 1, vol. 8 (1989), p. 67-78.

Relates the story of the German steamer *Goslar*. In September 1939 the *Goslar* entered Surinamese waters, and in May 1940 (several days after Germany had occupied the Netherlands) the crew deliberately sunk the ship in the Suriname River near Paramaribo. The wreck has never been removed and the keel, which sticks out of the water, now forms an iron 'island' in the river.

174 **Anton de Kom, luchador anticolonialista de Suriname.** (Anton de Kom, anti-colonialist fighter from Suriname.)
Armando Lampe. *El Caribe Contemporáneo*, no. 13 (Dec.1986), p. 99-106.

A discussion of the life of Surinamese activist Anton de Kom. In the first section the author describes the situation in Suriname during De Kom's lifetime. Lampe treats various aspects of De Kom's thinking on nationalism, racism, and the class struggle and underlines the importance of his writings for Suriname and the Caribbean as a whole. The paper includes summaries in French and English.

175 **The American takeover; industrial emergence and Alcoa's expansion in
     Guyana and Suriname 1914-1921.**
     Carlo Lamur. Dordrecht, The Netherlands: Foris, 1985. 209p.
     bibliog. (Koninklijk Instituut voor Taal-, Land- en Volkenkunde
     Caribbean Series, 1).

This work deals with the expansion of the American bauxite company Alcoa
(Aluminum Company of America) into Guyana and Suriname. The author describes in
great detail the colonial policies, which led on the one hand to the nationalization of
the bauxite sector in Guyana, and on the other hand to the denationalization of the
Surinamese bauxite ores by Alcoa. According to Lamur, the latter was to a great
extent due to the ignorance, indifference, and sometimes even illegal actions by the
then governors of Suriname. A historiographical introduction to Surinamese bauxite,
and a chapter on the emergence of the bauxite and aluminum industry in general
precede the presentation of data, which was derived mainly from archival sources.

176 **De Algemene Rekenkamer als 'bijzondere kraamkamer': de wording
     van de Rekenkamer van Suriname.** (The general auditor's office as
     'special delivery room': the birth of the auditor's office of Suriname.)
     Lou A. M. Lichtveld.   In: *Van Camere vander Rekeninghen tot
     Algemene Rekenkamer: zes eeuwen Rekenkamer. Gedenkboek bij het
     175-jarig bestaan van de Algemene Rekenkamer.* Edited by P. J.
     Margry, E. C. van Heukelekom, A. J. R. M. Linders. The Hague:
     Staatsdrukkerij en Uitgeverij, 1989, p. 351-75.

Former president of the Auditor's Office of Suriname, Lou Lichtveld, sketches the
history of this institution, emphasizing the early years, when he was closely involved
with its activities. In fact, he writes his memoirs concerning the creation of this office.
He is, however, critical of the developments since the 1960s.

177 **West-Indië in het parlement 1897-1917: bijdrage tot Nederland's
     koloniaal-politieke geschiedenis.** (West India in parliament 1897-1917:
     contribution to Dutch colonial political history.)
     J. M. Plante Fébure.   The Hague: Martinus Nijhoff, 1918. 196p.

A guide to Dutch Caribbean policy during the years 1897-1917 as discussed in the
Dutch parliament in The Hague. More than half of the text is devoted to Suriname.
The contents are arranged alphabetically by subject. The section on Suriname covers
101 topics.

178 **De bacovencultuur met gouvernementssteun in de jaren 1905-1910.** (The
     cultivation of bananas with government subsidies in the years 1905-
     1910.)
     Adriaan van Putten.   *Oso*, vol. 7, no. 1 (May 1988), p. 31-46. bibliog.

A description of the closely interwoven relationship between the government and the
business community during the years in which A. W. F. Idenburg was the Governor of
Suriname (1905-08). Idenburg promoted tropical agriculture and the cultivation of
bananas in particular. His plans did not bring Suriname the prosperity that was hoped
for.

179 **Suriname 1933-1944: koloniale politiek en beleid onder Gouverneur Kielstra.** (Suriname 1933-1944: colonial politics and policy under Governor Kielstra.)
Hans Ramsoedh. Delft, The Netherlands: Eburon, 1990. 255p. bibliog.

A study of the administration of Governor J. C. Kielstra (1933-44). His administration marked a distinct watershed in the history of Suriname for Kielstra broke with the policy of assimilation, which intended to promote the Dutch language and culture in Suriname. The author looks at the reasons for this new course, its consequences, and the reactions to it. This monograph, originally a dissertation (Rijksuniversiteit Utrecht, the Netherlands, 1990) includes a summary in English.

180 **Opkomende arbeidersbeweging in Suriname. Doedel, Liesdek, De Sanders, De Kom en de werklozenonrust 1931-1933.** (Emerging labour movement in Suriname. Doedel, Liesdek, De Sanders, De Kom and the unemployment unrest 1931-1933.)
Ben Scholtens. Nijmegen, The Netherlands: Masusa, 1986. 222p. bibliog.

A detailed description of social unrest during the 1930s, based on primary sources and interviews. The author describes the well-known Anton de Kom (1898-1945) as well as the lesser-known leaders, Louis Doedel (1905-80), Heinrich Liesdek (1903-67), and Theo de Sanders (1893-1976) and places the labour movement and its leaders in a historiographical context. Scholtens' thesis that during this time the labour movement entered a new and modern phase is not, however, entirely convincing. The book contains more than fifty photographs and illustrations. In *Louis Doedel: Surinaams vakbondsleider van het eerste uur. Een bronnenpublikatie* (Paramaribo: Anton de Kom Universiteit van Suriname, 1987) Scholtens compiled, annotated, and introduced twenty-three texts authored by Doedel. During the period 1931-37 Doedel was active as a writer of pamphlets, manifestos, journalistic articles, and as the publisher of several newspapers.

181 **Suriname and the Second World War/ Suriname en de Tweede Wereldoorlog.**
Ben Scholtens. *Suralco Magazine*, vol. 18, no. 1 (1986), p. 16-25.

This is an article in English and Dutch, first published in the Surinamese newspaper *De Ware Tijd* (7 May 1985), describing the military involvement of Suriname in the Second World War. The author also focuses attention on Surinamese men fighting overseas and on the war morale in Suriname.

182   **De Tapanahoni Djuka rond de eeuwwisseling: het dagboek van Spalburg (1896-1900). Ingeleid door H. U. E. Thoden van Velzen, Chris de Beet.** (The Tapanahoni Djuka around the turn of the century: the diary of Spalburg (1896-1900). Introduced by H. U. E. Thoden van Velzen, Chris de Beet.)
J. G. Spalburg.   Utrecht, The Netherlands: Centrum voor Caraïbische Studies, Instituut voor Culturele Antropologie, Rijksuniversiteit Utrecht, 1979. 129p. maps. bibliog. (Bronnen voor de Studie van Bosneger Samenlevingen, 5).
The major part of this volume is devoted to the diary of the teacher and evangelist Johan Spalburg, who from 1896 to 1900 worked in the Ndjuka village of Diitabiki. The diary provides an insight into Ndjuka society around the turn of the century and the important social, economic, and religious changes, which characterized this period. The first part of the introduction by De Beet places the missionary activities of Spalburg in an historical context, while Thoden van Velzen gives a brief history of the Ndjukas in the 19th century.

183   **Female religious responses to male prosperity in turn-of-the-century Bush Negro societies.**
H. U. E. Thoden van Velzen, Wilhelmina van Wetering. *Nieuwe West-Indische Gids/New West Indian Guide*, vol. 56, no. 1/2 (1982), p. 43-68. map. bibliog.
An analysis of the drastic changes in gender relations which occurred among the Maroons at the end of the 19th century. Many men migrated to the coastal areas to participate in the expanding national economy. Consequently, they failed to perform their share in the traditional subsistence economy and women were left to fend for themselves in these disadvantageous conditions. This article explores the various female responses to this new situation.

184   **A Klondike in the tropics: an article on legendary El Dorado, now Surinam.**
John W. Vandercook.   *World's Work*, (March 1926), p. 510-22. map.
An article singing the praises of US energy and imagination in the attempts to acquire wealth in Suriname. The author states that gold ore deposits compared favourably with California, and discusses gold mining in Suriname. He also focuses on other enterprises such as the cultivation of Sea Island cotton, the mining of bauxite, and the exploitation of tropical hardwood. Notwithstanding its errors, this article is a fine example of the optimism regarding Suriname's economic future during the early decades of the 20th century. This essay is illustrated with thirteen photographs.

185   **A brief outline of the Suriname gold industry. Geology, technique, hygiene. Description of the gold placer and the prospects of the Guiana gold placer.**
J. H. Verloop.   Amsterdam: J. H. de Bussy, 1911. 107p. maps. bibliog.
The first gold ore discoveries in Suriname were made in 1865 but despite appreciable financial investments, the gold industry never flourished. The author discusses some of

the factors causing this disappointing development. He feels that the poor state of hygiene was the major problem. Many foreign experts left the colony with health problems after only a short stay, some even died there. The appendix contains a large geographical and geological map of the concessions of the Guyana gold placer, the De Jong placer, and the Bibaz placer as well as technical drawings.

186   **Money magic in a modernizing Maroon society.**
       Diane Vernon.   Tokyo: Institute for the Study of Languages and
       Cultures of Asia and Africa. 50p. bibliog. (AA-Ken Caribbean Study
       Series, 2).
In the 19th century many Ndjuka men embarked on a series of economic ventures, such as trading timber, producing gold and balata, and transporting people from the coast to the interior. The author looks at two beliefs which developed concurrently with the financial ventures: the *Bankuu* cult, which incarnates danger inherent in the pursuit of wealth and *Papa obia*, which offers a positive, traditional magic to seduce coastal people into lavishing riches on emigrants from the interior.

187   **Koloniale politiek en transformatieprocessen in een plantage-economie,**
       Suriname 1873-1940. (Colonial policy and transformation processes in a
       plantation colony, Suriname 1873-1940.)
       Glenn Willemsen.   PhD dissertation, Erasmus Universiteit
       Rotterdam, The Netherlands, 1980. 356p. bibliog.
This thesis forms part of a larger research project concerning the political and economic development of Suriname since the abolition of slavery in 1863. The general hypothesis is that the type of relation between the metropole and the colony resulted in the simultaneous cumulative processes of underdevelopment in Suriname and of economic growth in the Netherlands. This book discusses the most important policy plans made between 1873 and 1940 to revive the Surinamese economy. The author argues that the Netherlands never attempted to systematically develop the economy of Suriname.

188   **Through revolution or the remarkable Killinger trial in the Dutch colony**
       of Surinam.
       Rudolph L. Worst.   Paramaribo: J. H. Oliveira, 1911. 80p.
An account of a rather curious episode in the history of Suriname known as the 'Killinger-affair'. In 1910, the Hungarian-born Franciscus Killinger, Inspector of Police in Paramaribo, conspired to overthrow the government and to proclaim a republic. In this pamphlet the author, a supporter of Killinger, relates the trial against Killinger and his six co-conspirators. It reveals the varied backgrounds of the defendants, their plans, and their betrayal by a former policeman and a priest. The seven were condemned to death; their sentences were later commuted to a relatively short term of imprisonment.

Population

General

189 **Les habitants de Suriname à Amsterdam.** (The inhabitants of Suriname in Amsterdam.)
Roland Bonaparte.   Paris: A. Quantin, 1884. 227p. maps.
The first part of this curious book contains a geographic description of Suriname and an outline of Amerindian society. This is followed by a meticulous physical description, plus photographs, of fifteen Amerindians who were part of the colonial exhibition in Amsterdam in 1883. Their head-dresses, ornaments, and several utensils are also pictured. The second section deals with Maroons and describes two Saramakans and two Ndjukas exhibited in Amsterdam. The final part focuses on Creoles and profiles eight of them who were at the exhibition.

190 **The development and nature of society in the West Indies.**
Rudolf A. J. van Lier.   Amsterdam: Koninklijke Vereeniging Indisch Instituut, 1950. 19p. bibliog. (Mededeling no. XCII, Afdeling Culturele en Physische Antropologie, 37).
A translation of Rudolf van Lier's inaugural lecture as professor extraordinary of cultural sociology of Suriname and the Netherlands Antilles at the Rijksuniversiteit Leiden, the Netherlands. He characterizes the segmentary societies of the English, French, and Dutch-speaking Caribbean from the early 17th century to 1950. As defined by Van Lier, segments are population groups founded on cultural traditions and racial origins. Since he considers Suriname to be one of the best examples of a segmentary society, this country serves as the case study in the lecture.

191 **Suriname, land of seven peoples: social mobility in a plural society: an ethnohistoriographical study.**
F. E. M. Mitrasing.   Paramaribo: Mitrasing, 1979. 176p. maps. bibliog.

According to the author, seven ethnic groups make up the population of Suriname: Amerindians, Europeans, Creoles (including Maroons), Jews, Chinese, British Indians, and Javanese. The very small group of Lebanese or Syrians is only mentioned in the epilogue. The cultural background of each population group is briefly discussed. Mitrasing pays attention to horizontal or geographical (spatial) mobility, and vertical or intellectual mobility. He also examines immigration, emigration, and internal migration. The final part of this introductory book deals with interethnic relations, again with migration, and political life in Suriname.

Demography

192 **Life table for Suriname 1964-1970.**
A. C. Boldewijn, Humphrey E. Lamur, R. A. Lamur.   *Nieuwe West-Indische Gids/New West Indian Guide*, vol. 52, no. 1/2 (Nov. 1977), p. 51-57.

A short contribution on the decline of mortality and the fluctuating trends in life expectancy in Suriname between 1964 and 1970. The article contains comparative demographic data with respect to Guyana and Trinidad.

193 **De europeesche landbouwkolonisatie in Suriname-The Dutch rural settlers in Surinam 1845-1950.**
Joh. Gemmink.   Zuidwolde, The Netherlands: The author, 1980. 296p. (Socio-Demographische Studien, V).

The author discusses Dutch colonization in Suriname, emphasizing two aspects: political leadership and demographic development. The book consists of four parts: a text in Dutch; sixty-seven demographic tables; a listing of all 1,521 Dutch descendants living in Suriname in 1950; and a twenty-page summary in English.

194 **The demographic evolution of Surinam 1920-1970: a socio-demographic analysis.**
Humphrey E. Lamur.   The Hague: Martinus Nijhoff, 1973. 207p. map. bibliog. (Verhandelingen van het Koninklijk Instituut voor Taal-, Land- en Volkenkunde, 65).

Within the context of a general study of the demographic evolution of Suriname, specific attention is paid to interethnic differentiation. Variations in the relative distribution of fertility, mortality, and migration manifest the demographic differentiation of the main population groups. The fertility rate of the British Indians is rather high in comparison to that of the Javanese and the Creoles. As for the mortality rate, the Javanese have a higher rate than the British Indians and the Creoles. Concerning migration, the proportional figures demonstrate the highest migration rates for the Creoles, followed respectively by the British Indians and the Javanese.

195 **Fertility decline in Surinam, 1964-1970.**
Humphrey E. Lamur. *Boletín de Estudios Latinoamericanos y del Caribe*, no. 16 (June 1974), p. 28-49. bibliog.
A comparison of the three major ethnic groups with regard to the decline in fertility during the 1960s. The author attempts to determine the degree to which the fertility of women of varying age-brackets between fifteen and forty-four years contributed to this decline. Lamur examines fertility and age structure in order to find a correlation.

196 **Recent fertility trends in Suriname.**
Humphrey E. Lamur. *Journal of Biosocial Science*, no. 18 (1986), p. 57-62.
Between 1962 and 1974 fertility rapidly declined in Suriname, and since that time this trend has stabilized. The author thinks this a surprising, yet not an unusual, development. Similar trends have occurred in other Caribbean countries. According to Lamur the 1962-74 fertility decline may be explained as a consequence of socio-economic developments. Furthermore, the activities of the Suriname Family Planning Association, founded in 1968, has led to a decreasing birth rate.

197 **Urban survival strategies and infant mortality in Paramaribo, Surinam.**
Humphrey E. Lamur. *Genus*, vol. 42, no. 1/2 (1986), p. 103-12. bibliog.
An examination of the link between infant mortality and living conditions in Paramaribo. In the first part of this article, the author deals with the evolution of infant mortality in Suriname. He goes on to discuss survival strategies and infant mortality in an urban neighbourhood. The main results point to an increase in infant mortality during the past years, which is mainly due to a shortening of the duration of breastfeeding the babies. This change in feeding practices results from a shift in the survival strategies of the mothers which is associated with conflicting interests concerning land use in the inner city of Paramaribo. The article includes summaries in French and Italian.

Amerindians

198 **Report of a contact with stone-age Indians in southern Surinam.**
M. W. H. de Boer. *Nieuwe West-Indische Gids/New West Indian Guide* , vol. 47, no. 3 (1970), p. 249-59.
While doing pedological-geological research in eastern and southern Suriname, the author encountered some Akuriyos, stone-age Amerindians, tracked down for the first time in the 1930s. He discovers that physically they are not like the Trios or the Wayanas, their Amerindian neighbours. De Boer characterizes them as nomads, who do not use canoes and whose most valuable tools are the axe, bow, and arrow. Hunting is the task of the Akuriyo men, while the women traditionally prepare the game brought back by their husbands. At the time there existed at least two Akuriyo groups which had not been contacted.

199 **Cariben (Paragoto's?) aan de Perica.** (Caribs [Paragotos?] along the
Perica.)
G. Bos. *Bijdragen tot de Taal-, Land- en Volkenkunde*, vol. 145, no. 1
(1989), p. 8-29. maps. bibliog.

The author argues that Caribs, and in all likelihood Paragotos, inhabited the coastal
lowland between the Coppename and Amana Rivers between the 17th and early 19th
centuries. The article is based on archival sources and antique maps.

200 **Comparative studies of the social structure of Guiana Indians and the
problem of acculturation.**
Audrey J. Colson Butt. In: *The ongoing evolution of Latin American
populations*. Edited by Francisco M. Salzano. Springfield, Illinois:
Thomas, 1971, p. 61-126.

The first part of this discussion provides a selection of the features, similarities, and
differences which have characterized Amerindian tribes in French Guiana, Guyana,
and Suriname in historical times. In the second part, the author discusses the levels of
contact between tribesmen and communities of foreign settlers. She differentiates types
of isolation, semi-isolation, and full and regular contact, each connected with different
degrees of acculturation. In the final part, the author focuses attention on the main
problems of the Amerindians in the contemporary world.

201 **Political and economic mobilisation and the Arawak-Carib relation in
Surinam.**
Ferdinand Emile Ricardo Derveld. *Nieuwe West-Indische Gids/New
West Indian Guide*, vol. 51, no. 4 (Dec. 1976), p. 127-46. bibliog.

A case study dealing with the Arawak and Carib Amerindian communities of
Bernarddorp, a village about fifteen miles from Paramaribo. The author distinguishes
two categories of villagers. He uses the concept 'cosmopolitan' for those who take part
in the national economy and are involved in national politics. 'Local' is the term used
for those whose frame of reference is mainly determined by the village. Derveld finds
that the 'cosmopolitan' Arawaks and Caribs are willing to cooperate to achieve
common goals, and that the contrast between the two tribes in this category has
weakened. The differences between 'local' Caribs and Arawaks, however, continue to
exist.

202 **Some data on the physical anthropology of Oajana Indians.**
A. B. Droogleever Fortuyn. Amsterdam: Koninklijke Vereeniging
Indisch Instituut, 1946. 24p. bibliog. (Mededeeling no. LXIX,
Afdeeling Volkenkunde, 22).

A study of the physical characteristics of fifteen male and twelve female Wayanas who
belong to the Carib Indians. In fifteen pages of text and as many tables, the author
presents data on their (relative) body weight; stature; (relative) height; head length;
head breadth; cephalic index; hand lengths; hair; and blood groups.

203 **Documentary information about the Surinam Wama or Akurio Indians.**
   D. C. Geijskens. *Nieuwe West-Indische Gids/New West Indian Guide*,
   vol. 47 (1969/70), p. 260-85. bibliog.
A review of the known facts about the Akuriyo Indians. The first contacts were made
in 1937, and in 1938 a none too successful expedition to study these Amerindians was
organized. Contact was re-established in 1968 by I. Schoen and M. de Boer among
others. The article contains four photographs.

204 **Philosophy, initiation and myths of the Indians of Guiana and adjacent
   countries.**
   C. H. de Goeje. In: *Internationales Archiv für Ethnographie, volume
   XLIV*. Edited by A. W. Nieuwenhuis, W. H. Rassers, B. J. O.
   Schriek, W. D. van Wijngaarden. Leiden, The Netherlands: E. J. Brill,
   1943, p. 1-136. bibliog.
This treatise is the result of many years of study by the author, as well as by other
researchers such as the Penard brothers and W. Abbenhuis, who also studied the
Arawaks. The author discusses three inter-related subjects: the philosophy of the
Amerindians, and their gods and spirits; the mediceman (shaman) and his initiation;
and the myths and fairy tales.

205 **Alemi songs of the Turaekare of southern Surinam.**
   Fabiola Jara. *Latin American Indian Literatures Journal*, vol. 2, no. 2
   (Fall 1989), p. 4-14.
Alemi is a complex set of beliefs and practices related to hunting and to the
relationships between men and animal societies. An *alemi* specialist's assistance is
requested whenever people feel that a person has been captured or kidnapped by
animal societies, that is when a person has fallen ill.

206 **Monos y roedores. Rito, cosmología y nociones zoológicas de los
   turaekare de Surinam.** (Monkeys and rodents. Ritual, cosmology and
   zoological notions of the Turaekare of Suriname.)
   Fabiola Jara. *América Indígena*, vol. 48, no. 1 (1988), p. 9-26. bibliog.
An exploration of the representational systems used by the Turaekare and the
Akuriyo. The sociological and symbolic relationships between these two groups are
close. The author examines the significance of the existing differences between the two
Amerindian groups.

207 **Astronomy of the coastal Caribs of Surinam.**
   Fabiola Jara, Edmundo J. L. N. R. Magaña-Torres. *L'Homme,
   Revue Française d'Anthropologie*, vol. 23, no. 1 (1983), p. 111-33.
   bibliog.
The Carib sky, as conceived in this paper, includes the fifty-three Carib stars and
constellations recorded between the 16th century and 1980. Basing this article on
fieldwork in three Carib villages in Suriname, the authors discuss the aspects of life the
Caribs consider when establishing star-constellations, and the relevance of the Carib
social structure to an understanding of their astronomy. Finally, the authors briefly
analyse the myths concerning the origins of the constellations in order to determine

their underlying meaning. Their findings question the validity of the theory stating that the functions of astronomy are mainly connected to economic activities.

208   **The Akuriyo of Surinam: a case of emergence from isolation.**
Peter Kloos.   Copenhagen: International Work Group of Indigenous Affairs, 1977. 31p. maps. bibliog.

The Akuriyo of Suriname are an Amerindian Carib-speaking community. Until 1968 they led a completely nomadic life in southeastern Suriname. In that year they were (re)discovered by the West Indies Mission, who established contact and brought the majority, voluntarily, to Amerindian Trio villages. This case study describes how between 1968 and 1973 circumstances forced the Akuriyo to lose their own identity and acquire a new, Trio identity.

209   **The Akuriyo way of death.**
Peter Kloos.   In: *Carib-speaking Indians: culture, society and language.* Edited by Ellen B. Basso. Tucson, Arizona: University of Arizona Press, 1977, p. 114-22. map. bibliog. (Anthropological Papers of the University of Arizona, 28).

The author argues that the unusual degree of isolation from the outside world is responsible for the relatively low rate of infant mortality among the Akuriyo. A major factor of mortality among children between one and twelve years of age is the irregular and unvaried supply of food. As a result of the high child mortality, those who survive childhood are a highly selected group, able to withstand the harshness of adult life. The Akuriyo age early and during old age·(between thirty and forty) the majority of men meet death during their search for food. Women live longer, but are left behind if they lack the strength to follow the group. The Akuriyo have developed an attitude of resignation in the face of approaching death and are not inclined to assist anyone who is no longer able to help himself.

210   **The Maroni River Caribs of Surinam.**
Peter Kloos.   Assen, The Netherlands: Van Gorcum, 1971. 304p. maps. bibliog.

An ethnohistory and social analysis of a Carib village, exemplified by Christiaankondre and Langamankondre, located along the Marowijne (or Maroni) River. The author looks at the basic structure of Carib society and the way the village is integrated. The development of social structure, both in a sociological and in a historical sense, including the integration of the Carib village in Suriname are considered. Kloos demonstrates that this Carib society, despite centuries of contact, change, and near extinction, has maintained intact fundamental structural principles or features. The Maroni River Caribs share these characteristics with all known Carib societies.

211   **Contribuciones al estudio de la mitología y astronomía de los indios de las Guayanas.** (Contributions to the study of the mythology and astronomy of the Indians of the Guyanas.)
Edmundo J. L. N. R. Magaña-Tórres.   Dordrecht, The Netherlands: Foris, 1987. 306p. bibliog. (CEDLA Latin America Studies, 35).

This so-called preliminary work is based on fieldwork conducted among Amerindian peoples in Suriname and French Guiana. The author studied the mythology and astronomy among the Wayana, the Apalai, the Trio, and the Carib Indians. The work includes theoretical introductions, some 300 narratives, as well as the identification of 136 constellations. Moreover, Magaña briefly discusses the ethnography of the various groups. This volume contains illustrations made by native informants, glossaries, and detailed bibliographies. The appendices include zoological, ornithological, and icthyological vocabularies.

212 **El cuerpo y la cocina en la mitología Wayana, Tarëno y Kaliña.** (The body and cooking in the Wayana, Trio and Kalihna mythology.)
Edmundo J. L. N. R. Magaña-Tórres. *América Indígena*, vol. 68, no. 3 (July-Sept. 1988), p. 571-604. bibliog.
Employing the Claude Lévi-Strauss hypothesis on the relationship between the body and cooking, the author studies some of the personages found in the Wayana, Trio, and Carib mythology of Suriname, Brazil, and French Guiana. These Amerindian peoples use cookery as a means of body control as well as a means of general sociological classification of the structure of social systems and of matrimony.

213 **The old-head woman and the penis man.**
Edmundo J. L. N. R. Magaña-Tórres. *Latin American Indian Literatures Journal*, vol. 5, no. 2 (fall 1989), p. 15-30.
The author deals with two bizarre and intriguing myths in Wayana mythology in his study of the Amerindian lifestyle. In the first one the women of a village abandoned their men because the latter had killed their penis lover. The second myth relates the adventures of the rolling skull: a head went up to the sky to become a star and with its rising it announces the dry season.

214 **Orion y la mujer Pléyades: simbolismo astronómico de los indios kaliña de Surinam.** (Orion and the woman of the Pleiades: astronomical symbolism of the Kalihna Indians in Suriname.)
Edmundo J. L. N. R. Magaña-Tórres. Dordrecht, The Netherlands: Foris, 1988. 373p. bibliog. (CEDLA Latin America Studies, 44).
An analysis of the formal structure of Carib astronomy. To elucidate the main concepts in operation in the native astronomy, the author focuses on myths, which are vehicles used to transmit astronomical knowledge from generation to generation. He concludes that Guianese astronomy is consistently inconsistent. Furthermore, Magaña demonstrates the relationship between astronomy and cosmology with other aspects of society. The book contains summaries in Dutch and in English.

215 **Marriage among the Trio: a principle of social organisation.**
Peter G. Rivière. Oxford: Clarendon Press, 1969. 353p. maps. bibliog.
A detailed analysis of the values underlying the marriage system of the Trio Indians, who prefer to marry within their own small communities. The author shows how the same principle of organization can be seen operating in other Trio social institutions. Part one provides a background to Trio history and culture. Part two describes the criteria of social classification and Trio marriage. In the final section two different levels of approach are used: conventionally expected attitudes and behaviour, as well as actual behaviour between different relationship categories.

216 **A report on the Trio Indians of Surinam.**
Peter G. Rivière. *Nieuwe West-Indische Gids/New West Indian Guide*, vol. 55, no. 1/2 (1981), p. 1-38. bibliog.

This article is an abbreviated version of a report prepared for the government of Suriname in 1979. It updates an earlier report, published under the title 'A policy for the Trio Indians' in the *Nieuwe West-Indische Gids/New West Indian Guide*, vol. 45, no. 2/3 (1966). Since the Trio Indians of Suriname developed contacts with the Maroons, official institutions such as the Surinamese government and the Government Mining Department, with the West Indies Mission, as well as casual visitors and tourists, life in Trio society has changed considerably. Rivière even speaks of a 'social revolution'. In this report, he recommends a government policy of gradual assimilation between Trio society and the coastal society of Suriname, but that this process should in no way be enforced or hastened. He gives concrete suggestions concerning health, diet, economy, authority, and visitors of the Trios. The author is struck by how little many of the problems facing the Trio Indians have changed, despite the fact that numerous changes did take place in their lifestyles. The first part of this paper provides a general description of the Trio Indians. The second section contains a summary of the recommendations sent to the Surinamese government.

217 **An inquiry into the animism and folk-lore of the Guiana Indians.**
Walter E. Roth. New York, London: Johnson Reprint, 1970. 453p. bibliog.

This volume was originally published in 1915 as one of two papers accompanying the Thirtieth Annual Report of the US Bureau of American Ethnology to the Secretary of the Smithsonian Institution, 1908-09. The author was a stipendiary magistrate, medical officer, and protector of Indians in the district of Pomeroon (British Guiana) during the first decades of the 20th century. He made an ethnographical survey of the native tribes of British Guiana, Venezuela, Suriname, and French Guiana. The legends, myths, and fables which Roth collected have been drawn mainly from Arawak, Carib, and Warrao sources. The book comprises twenty-one chapters, some 120 myths and tales, as well as plates, figures, and a glossary.

218 **Guianas: indigenous period.**
Irving Rouse. Mexico: Instituto Panamericana de Geografia e Historia, 1953. 100p. bibliog (Program of the History of America, I, 7).

An overview of Amerindian history and culture in the Guianas. The booklet is divided into fifty-six topics and eight chapters. In commenting on each topic, the author explains the points which may be obscure, brings out differences in interpretation, and, wherever possible, discusses the historical significance of the topic. A brief bibliography concludes each topic. Following some general considerations, the chapters are ordered according to historical period from the pre-ceramic age (pre-900 AD) to the late historic age (1800 to the present).

219 **Report of the emergency trip made by the West Indies Mission to the Akoerio Indians, June 1971.**
Ivan L. Schoen.   Washington, DC: Smithsonian Institution, Center for Short-lived Phenomena; Paramaribo: West Indies Mission, 1971. 9p.

A report of the prelude to the integration of the Akuriyo tribe into Trio villages in Suriname. The author describes the Akuriyo people and their situation in order to demonstrate that intervention by the West Indies Mission was really necessary.

220 **American Indians from Suriname: a physical-anthropological study.**
J. Tacoma.   PhD dissertation, Rijksuniversiteit Utrecht, The Netherlands, 1963. 180p. bibliog.

An investigation of skeletal remains of Surinamese Indians, dating from over 1000 years ago. A comparison of the features of this collection with anthropometric and osteometric data of recent Surinamese Indians proves that only the cranial index shows significant differences. These can partly be ascribed to the influence of the artificial deformation of the head. Part one of the thesis includes a review of the pertinent literature, while part two provides descriptions, measurements, and plates of the skull.

Creoles

221 **On the corner: male social life in a Paramaribo Creole neighbourhood.**
Gary Brana-Shute.   Assen, The Netherlands: Van Gorcum, 1979. 124p. maps. bibliog. (Studies of Developing Countries, 22).

Based on fieldwork conducted in 1972 to 1974, this is a detailed case study of the social behaviour and social networks of lower-class black males living near the centre of Paramaribo. The 'corner' is a spatial reference to the neighbourhood shop (the *winkel*) where men drink together and share their experiences. This study is a revised edition of the author's doctoral dissertation, *Streetcorner winkels and dispersed households: male adaptation to marginality in a lower-class Creole neighborhood in Paramaribo* (University of Florida, Gainesville, 1974, available from University Microfilms International, Ann Arbor, Michigan, order no. 75-19315).

222 **Some aspects of youthful identity management in a Paramaribo Creole neighbourhood.**
Gary Brana-Shute.   *Nieuwe West-Indische Gids/New West Indian Guide*, vol. 53, no. 1/2 (Sept. 1978), p. 1-20.

An exploration of some key aspects of identity management and status maintenance among a group of lower-income Surinamese youths in Paramaribo neighbourhoods. The author concentrates on boys and young men acting out public dramas that will award them certain reputations. Individual style and flair are notable characteristics of this behaviour.

223 **Death in the family; ritual therapy in a Creole community.**
Rosemary Brana-Shute, Gary Brana-Shute. *Bijdragen tot de Taal-,
Land- en Volkenkunde*, vol. 135, no. 1 (1979), p. 59-83.
An ethnographic description of the ceremonies and symbols employed by Creoles from
Paramaribo to deal with death. The authors discuss the specific rituals, prayers and
incantations, the time when and the place where the sacred activities take place, and
the people who participate in them. The data are presented in the form of a case study
seen 'through the eyes of the ritual participants themselves'.

224 **The family system of the Paramaribo Creoles.**
Willem F. L. Buschkens. The Hague: Martinus Nijhoff, 1974. 324p.
bibliog. (Verhandelingen van het Koninklijk Instituut voor Taal-,
Land- en Volkenkunde, 71).
This book is the English edition of the author's dissertation (Rijksuniversiteit Leiden,
the Netherlands, 1973) on the family lives of the lower-class Creole population of
Paramaribo. Based on fieldwork conducted in 1964-65, the author discusses topics such
as: household structure; economic aspects of the household; alternative unions
between men and women; illegitimacy of birth; and social relations within the family.
The introduction provides a discussion of social research on the Caribbean family. An
historical background for the understanding of contemporary Afro-Caribbean family
life in Suriname is given in four chapters covering the initial period of settlement of the
plantation colony up to the 1960s.

225 **The historical context of Nengre kinship and residence: ethnohistory of
the family organization of lower status Creoles in Paramaribo.**
Benjamin Edward Pierce. In: *Old roots in new lands: historical and
anthropological perspectives on black experiences in the Americas*.
Edited by Ann M. Pescatello. Westport, Connecticut: Greenwood
Press, 1977, p. 107-31. bibliog.
A study of the family system of lower status Creoles, or the Nengre, of Paramaribo.
The author maintains that Nengre kinship is similar to that of other Afro-American
proletariats. He distinguishes three factors that have influenced the Nengre family
organization: remains of surving African culture; European, that is Dutch, cultural
influence; and, finally, uniquely Surinamese historical, ecological, and demographic
factors. According to Pierce, no single aspect provides an adequate explanation of the
urban Nengre. Pierce also published a dissertation on this topic called *Kinship and
residence among the urban Nengre of Surinam* (Tulane University, New Orleans,
Louisiana, 1971. Available from University Microfilms International, Ann Arbor,
Michigan, order no. 71-27303).

226 **Status competition and personal networks: informal social organisation
among the Nengre of Paramaribo.**
Benjamin Edward Pierce. *Man*, vol. 8, no. 4 (Dec. 1973), p. 580-91.
A description and analysis of the system of informal social relationships among non-
kinsmen in lower status Creole society in Paramaribo, which is based on data gathered
during participant observation. The author demonstrates that the strategies utilized by
these Creoles in managing their interpersonal relationships and the relative sizes of
their personal networks depend to a large extent on their positions in the system of
personal stratification and on their status aspirations.

Maroons

227 **Male absenteeism and nutrition: factors affecting fertility in Matawai Bush Negro society.**
Chris de Beet, Miriam Sterman. *Nieuwe West-Indische Gids/New West Indian Guide* , vol. 52, no. 3/4 (June 1978), p. 131-63.
The Matawai Maroons value children highly and generally prefer to raise large families. Their fertility level, however, is notably low compared to similar societies. On the basis of extensive fieldwork, the authors draw the conclusion that male absenteeism and nutrition are the key factors explaining this discrepancy.

228 **People in between: the Matawai Maroons of Suriname.**
Chris de Beet, Miriam Sterman. PhD dissertation, Rijksuniversiteit Utrecht, 1981. 530p. maps. bibliog.
A study of a Matawai village society is combined with the presentation of quantitative data on aspects of the social organization and demography of this ethnic group. The authors emphasize the significance of regional differences among this relatively small Maroon group and give particular attention to marriage and divorce; matrilineal kinship; household; and the system of foster-parentship. Matrilineality plays a dominant role in Matawai society. Finally, the authors present data on the growth of the population and migration among the Matawais.

229 **I sought my brother: an Afro-American reunion.**
S. Allen Counter, David L. Evans. Cambridge, Massachusetts; London: MIT Press, 1981. 276p.
The fascinating story of a meeting between Counter, a neurobiologist, Evans, an electrical engineer, and Maroons in the Suriname rain forest. It relates the dangerous journey over river waters filled with rapids, rocks, and piranha that took the two men to a Maroon village. The text and hundreds of illustrations document their participation in village life and ceremonies, including hunting and fishing; medical practices; dance and other rituals; childbirth; and the building of a house and a canoe. The film *I sought my brother* based on the book, appeared on television throughout the world.

230 **The Bush Negro tribes of Surinam, South America: a synthesis.**
Dirk Hendrik van der Elst. PhD dissertation, Northwestern University, Evanston, Illinois, 1970. 377p. bibliog. (Available from University Microfilms International, Ann Arbor, Michigan, order no. 71-30974).
An introductory synthesis aimed at an English-language audience. In the first part, the author discusses the history of Suriname and the tribalization of the Maroons, although the historiographical overview is now rather dated. In part two, Van der Elst focuses on the organization of the households and subtribes, as well as on tribal relations. In the third section, the ideology of the Maroons is examined. The final chapters describe the changes which have taken place during the 20th century.

231 **The Coppename Kwinti: notes on an Afro-American tribe in Surinam.**
Dirk Hendrik van der Elst. *Nieuwe West-Indische Gids/New West Indian Guide*, vol. 50, no. 1/3 (1974-75), p. 7-17; 107-22; 200-11.

An article in three parts on the Kwinti Maroons, detailing their history and development; organization and ideology; as well as cultural change and viability. The author expresses the fear that Kwinti society might disappear and suggests several measures which may help the Kwinti way of life to survive: Granmanship for their Chief; the right to exclude strangers from their villages; and regulation of the trade in fish and game.

232 **A preliminary investigation of social conditions in Suriname's 'transmigration villages'.**
Adiante Franszoon. *Mededelingen Stichting Surinaams Museum*, nos 19/20 (1976), p. 11-23. maps.

A report on 'transmigration villages' developed to house several thousand Maroons after the construction of the hydroelectric project in Brokopondo in the 1960s. The fieldwork for this report was conducted in 1975 and covered all of the fourteen villages relocated above the artificial lake, but only some of the villages below the lake. The author concludes his report with a set of recommendations: modernization of machinery; provision of adequate transportation; provision of roofing materials for the new villages; the protection of traditional tribal territories; and the creation of employment for the Maroons. The editor of the *Mededelingen Stichting Surinaams Museum* not only thinks the author's investigative techniques to be rudimentary, but that the same holds true for his efforts to expose the facts.

233 **An ethnographic study of social control and dispute settlement among the Aluku Maroons of French Guiana and Surinam South America.**
Shelby Matthew Givens. PhD dissertation, University of California, Berkeley, 1984. 368p. maps. bibliog. (Available from University Microfilms International, Ann Arbor, Michigan, order no. 84-26971).

This study is the result of the first conventional anthropological fieldwork conducted among these Maroons. Following a brief socio-historical background of the Alukus, the author outlines the domains of their traditional law in their relationships with the administrative government of the nation state. Givens examines traditional and administrative sanctions with respect to their influence upon the traditional measures of social control and dispute settlement.

234 **Matawai lineage fission.**
Edward Crocker Green. *Bijdragen tot de Taal-, Land- en Volkenkunde*, vol. 133, no. 1 (1977), p. 136-54. maps. bibliog.

In this essay the author explains the process of lineage fission in Matawai society, in which new lineage groups are formed. He compares the native's ideal model of this process with the anthropologist's empirically-derived model of the same process. Finally, Green evaluates the usefulness of such contrasts between the ideal and the real generally.

235 **The Matawai Maroons: an acculturating Afro-American society.**
Edward Crocker Green. PhD dissertation, Catholic University of
America, Washington, DC, 1974. 331p. bibliog. (Available from
University Microfilms International, Ann Arbor, Michigan, order no.
75-00081).
On the basis of participant observations and interviews, the author presents
ethnographic data on the Matawai Maroons. The focus is on ethnohistory, kinship, and
religion. Since Matawai society is undergoing rapid transformation, a constant theme
throughout this study is change. Urban influences are responsible for many socio-
cultural developments and for the migration of Matawais to the coastal area.

236 **The Maroon chiefs visit Africa: diary of an historic trip.**
Silvia Wilhelmina de Groot. In: *Maroon societies: rebel slave societies
in the Americas.* Edited by Richard Price. Garden City, New York:
Anchor Press/Doubleday, 1973, p. 389-98.
The Paramount Chiefs or *Granmans* of the Maroons had several times expressed a
wish to journey to the land of their fathers. The government of Suriname offered them
a trip to West Africa, which was made in 1970. This article is an account of that
journey.

237 **Rebel destiny: among the Bush Negroes of Dutch Guiana.**
Merville J. Herskovits, Frances Herskovits. New York: McGraw-Hill,
1934. 366p.
A popular account of fieldwork conducted among the Saramakas during the 1920s. The
authors argue that the bush is like 17th-century Africa, thus implying that Maroon
civilization is static, although later researchers have strongly challenged this position.
The book also contains some exaggerations and minor errors. Yet, this pioneering
effort by English-language researchers is still considered a classic.

238 **Djuka: the Bush Negroes of Dutch Guiana. With an introduction by
Blair Niles and a foreword by Clark Wissler.**
Morton C. Kahn. New York: Viking Press, 1931. 233p. bibliog.
A narrative of personal observations of Maroon life made by Kahn, who visited
Suriname to study public health measures which is not intended as an ethnological or
anthropological account. The author uses the name 'Ndjuka' to designate all Maroons,
not only those belonging to the Ndjuka population. The volume contains more than
sixty photographs. The phonograms in Ndjuka appear in appendix A. The symbols
found in Maroon art are presented in appendix B.

239 **Notes on the Saramaccaner Bush Negroes of Dutch Guiana.**
Morton C. Kahn. *American Anthropologist, New Series,* vol. 31, no. 3
(July-Sept. 1929), p. 468-90.
An essay based on fieldwork conducted in 1927. The author outlines various aspects of
Saramakan life, such as government, nutrition, religion, ceremonies, health, language,
and culture. The article includes six plates.

240 **Continuity in change: Cottica Djuka society as a changing system.**
André J. F. Köbben. *Bijdragen tot de Taal-, Land- en Volkenkunde*, vol. 124, no. 1 (1968), p. 56-90. bibliog.

A description of the social structure and culture of the Ndjuka Maroons, who possess strong defence mechanisms opposing acculturation. The external factors of change such as governmental interference, missionary activities, and medical aid, are not sufficient, not even in combination, to break this resistance. Although this Maroon society does absorb new elements and exhibits change, continuity of the old Ndjuka ways is still dominant.

241 **Unity and disunity: Cottica Djuka as a kinship system.**
André J. F. Köbben. *Bijdragen tot de Taal-, Land- en Volkenkunde*, vol. 123, no. 1 (1967), p. 10-52.

The Ndjuka matrilineal kinship system distinguishes three categories: matrilineal descendants of the ancestress, descendants of the men of the matrilineage, and the affines. The author demonstrates how the kinship system is fundamental in that all legal, political, economic, and religious relations are expressed in terms of kinship. Reciprocal relationships characterize the Ndjuka village, yet in some respects individual interests come to the fore more than in Western society. This article is reprinted in *Maroon societies: rebel slave communities in the Americas*, edited by Richard Price (q.v.).

242 **Planned research into the criminological consequences of the mass migration of the Bush Negroes in Suriname.**
A. Leerschool-Liong A Jin. In: *Crime and punishment in the Caribbean*. Edited by Rosemary Brana-Shute, Gary Brana-Shute. Gainesville, Florida: Center for Latin American Studies, University of Florida, 1980, p. 114-23. maps.

This article provides background information on a research project on crime among migrant Maroon populations. The construction of the hydro-electric plant and the resulting man-made Lake Brokopondo forced thousands of Maroons to move. The project intends to ascertain whether and how this migration has changed social, legal, and criminological aspects in the lives of the Maroons.

243 **The Paramacca Maroons: a study in religious acculturation.**
John D. Lenoir. PhD dissertation, New School for Social Research, New York, 1973. 213p. bibliog. (Available from University Microfilms International, Ann Arbor, Michigan, order no. 74-19518).

An illustration of the dynamics of Maroon religious acculturation as part of the Paramakan transition from isolation to participation in the Surinamese state and larger society. The active competition between Roman Catholic and Moravian missionaries for adherents among the Paramakas provided the institutional setting for the articulation of internal controversies. The cultural conversion to Christianity caused problems concerning the succession to chieftaincy through opposing mission affiliations. The Paramakas were ultimately divided in a religious schism through contrary processes of syncretism.

244 **Aboikoni, granman in een woelige overgangsperiode.** (Aboikoni, granman during a turbulent transition period.)
André Mosis, Ben Scholtens. *SWI Forum*, vol. 5, no. 2 (Dec. 1988), p. 89-111.
In January 1989, Granman Aboikoni passed away in Asidonopo. He was 98 years old, and for almost forty years had been involved in local government. The authors provide both biographical information on this remarkable individual and insights to some important changes which took place during his administration. The most dramatic event, no doubt, was the forced transmigration of approximately 6,000 Maroons to enable the construction of Lake Brokopondo.

245 **Wirtschaft und materielle Kultur der Buschneger Surinames: ein Beitrag zur Erforschung afroamerikanischer Probleme.** (Economy and material culture of the Surinamese Bush Negroes: a contribution to the study of Afro-American problems.)
Peter Neumann.   Berlin, GDR: Akademie-Verlag, 1967. 181p. map. bibliog. (Abhandlungen und Berichte des Staatliches Museum für Völkerkunde Dresden, 26).
Following an introduction to the history and social organization of the Maroons, the author elaborates on their economic system. First, he discusses economic activities such as agriculture, fishing, hunting, husbandry, and industries. Second, Neumann examines trade between the Maroons and Amerindians on the one hand, and Maroons and Europeans on the other.

246 **Vluchtelingen, opstandelingen en andere Bosnegers van Oost-Suriname, 1986-1988.** (Refugees, rebels and other Maroons from east Suriname, 1986-1988.)
T. S. Polimé, H. U. E. Thoden van Velzen.   Utrecht, The Netherlands: Instituut voor Culturele Antropologie, Centrum voor Caraibische Studies, 1988. 127p. maps. (Bronnen voor de Studie van Afro-Surinaamse Samenlevingen, 13).
A collection of impressions by the authors, who reflect the experiences of the Maroon refugees and rebels. Some of the articles were published earlier in the Dutch daily *Het Parool*. Polimé concentrates on the refugees in French Guiana who have fled the guerrilla war, while Thoden van Velzen focuses on the Maroons who still live in eastern Suriname, some of whom are active in the 'Jungle Commando' led by Ronnie Brunswijk, which fights against the National Army. The sympathy of the authors is clearly with Brunswijk's men.

247 **Avenging spirits and the structure of Saramaka lineages.**
Richard Price.   *Bijdragen tot de Taal-, Land- en Volkenkunde/Antropologica 15*, vol. 129, no. 1 (1973), p. 86-107.
Following a brief introduction to the Saramaka Maroons, this paper is divided into five parts. The first introduces the concept of avenging spirits (*kúnu*). The second section describes *kúnu* as the central symbol of ideal lineage structure. In the third part, the author outlines the nature of real lineages and the causes of division. The fourth section comes to the heart of the problem in examining the role of avenging spirits in

the process of lineage fission. The final section deals briefly with certain divisive effects of the *kúnu* belief on a daily level, where it functions analogously to witchcraft or sorcery beliefs in many other societies.

248 **To everything a season: the development of Saramaka calendric reckoning.**
Richard Price.   *Oso*, vol. 3, no. 1 (May 1984), p. 63-71. bibliog.

An exploration of the development of the Saramaka calendar from the 18th century to the present. From an 18th-century beginning that was African, yet at the same time influenced by the experience of plantation slavery, the Saramaka calendar has evolved into a flexible instrument. It continues to serve local horticultural needs, yet is sufficiently compatible with the Western calendar to permit effective communication between Saramakas and coastal people. Price argues that the fact that the intercalation between the Saramaka lunar calendar and the Western solar calendar is done by ongoing negotiation among Saramakas rather than by a periodic mathematical 'correction' preserves the flexibility of the system. Moreover, it expresses the more general predominance of political rather then normative solutions to conflicts in Saramaka life.

249 **The Guiana Maroons: changing perspectives in 'Bush Negro' studies.**
Richard Price.   *Caribbean Studies*, vol. 11, no. 4 (Jan. 1972), p. 81-105. map. bibliog.

In this review article of Jean Hurault's *Africains de Guyane. La vie máterielle et l'art des Noirs Réfugiés de Guyana* (q.v.) Price looks at developments since 1960 and evaluates the extant knowledge of Maroon societies.

250 **Saramaka social structure: analysis of a Maroon society in Surinam.**
Richard Price.   Rio Piedras, Puerto Rico: Institute of Caribbean Studies, University of Puerto Rico, 1975. 177p. bibliog. (Caribbean Monograph Series, 12).

First presented as a doctoral dissertation at Harvard University, Cambridge, Massachusetts, in 1969, this study is aimed primarily at describing some central aspects of Saramaka social structure. The author outlines some basic Saramaka premises and assumptions about the world and how one operates within it, as well as the dominant role of divination in every aspect of Saramaka social life. In subsequent discussions of emigration, residence, marriage, child rearing, inheritance, land tenure, and lineage fission, he demonstrates how the Saramaka view of men and society marks each aspect of social life. In the article 'Saramaka emigration and marriage: a case study of social change' in *Southwestern Journal of Anthropology*, vol. 26, no. 2 (summer 1970), Price elaborates on Saramaka emigration and marriage. Since the late 19th century Saramaka men have worked for many years of their lives far from their tribal territory. The shortage of marriageable men at home has produced significant changes in traditional patterns of betrothal, polygyny, and conjugal residence, as well as in the role definitions of husband and wife. An analysis of how these, and other related, changes occurred is supported by comparative data from neighbouring Maroon groups. These data also suggest that differences in patterns of emigration may account for many of the hitherto unexplained differences in social structure among these groups.

251 **The great father and the danger: religious cults, material forces, and collective fantasies in the world of the Surinamese Maroons.**
H. U. E. Thoden van Velzen, Wilhelmina van Wetering. Dordrecht, The Netherlands: Foris, 1988. 451p. maps. bibliog. (Koninklijk Instituut voor Taal-, Land- en Volkenkunde Caribbean Series, 9).
Records an extensive study of the history of the cults of the Ndjuka Maroons who have managed to maintain their cultural and social autonomy, despite sweeping economic changes. These economic transformations form the background for a detailed examination of religious movements over time. The book explores the relation between cult, myth, and the everyday world and compares the interpretations of native and foreign intellectuals. The authors use an idiosyncratic mix of Karl Marx, Max Weber, and Sigmund Freud to establish a theoretical framework, containing infrastructural and superstructural explanations as well as a political and symbolic analysis.

252 **Bakuu: possessing spirits of witchcraft on the Tapanahony.**
Diane Vernon. *Nieuwe West-Indische Gids/New West Indian Guide*, no. 54, vol. 1 (1980), p. 1-38. maps. bibliog.
A report on one pantheon of possessing spirits known as *Bakuu*. While even the author's oldest informants denied ever having seen *Bakuu* mediums in the village of Tabiki before, the *Bakuu* phenomenon was experienced in the 1970s as visions in the night, as an interpretation of illness and death, as accusations of witchcraft, and as possession by spirits. The author recounts one example of *Bakuu* social drama and situates the *Bakuu* in relation to other pantheons of possessing spirits.

253 **Witchcraft among the Tapanahoni Djuka.**
Wilhelmina van Wetering. In: *Maroon societies: rebel slave communities in the Americas.* Edited by Richard Price. Garden City, New York: Anchor Press/Doubleday, 1973, p. 370-88. bibliog.
An article based on fieldwork carried out in 1961 and 1962. During this time eighty persons in the village of Diitabiki were denounced as witches after their death. Women formed the majority of these witches. The author presents seven case histories to shed light on the dynamics of witchcraft accusations, on how they grow and spread. A more extensive and theoretical version of this paper is published in *Structure, function and process: contributions of Dutch anthropologists*, edited by Peter Kloos, André J. F. Köbben (Assen, The Netherlands: Van Gorcum, 1972).

British Indians

254 **Pandits, power and profit: religious organization and the construction of identity among Surinamese Hindus.**
Cors van der Burg, Peter van der Veer, *Ethnic and Racial Studies*, vol. 9, no. 4 (Oct. 1986), p. 514-28. bibliog.
An inquiry into the relationship between religious and ethnic organization and leadership. The authors argue that the dynamics of religious politics have been fundamental to the construction of a Surinamese Hindu identity as well as to the

construction of a British Indian ethnic identity. Ethnicity derives its importance in Suriname from ethnic politics, whereas in the Netherlands it is important in the context of the organization of the welfare society.

255 **The evolution of the social, economic and political position of the East Indians in Surinam 1873-1980.**

Sandew Hira. *India in the Caribbean*. Edited by David Dabydeen, Brinsley Samaroo. London: Hansib, 1987, p. 189-209. bibliog.

An analysis of the social, economic, and political position of the British Indians in the context of inter-ethnic relations in Suriname. The author focuses on the factors which determine the position of an ethnic group and how inter-ethnic relations evolve. He argues that material rather than psychological factors have determined the social and economic position of the British Indian population. A similar article by the same author covering the period 1873-93 appeared in *Indians in the Caribbean*, edited by I. J. Bahadur Singh (New Delhi: Sterling, 1987).

256 **The caste system and the Hindustani group in Surinam.**

Johan Dirk Speckmann. In: *Caste in overseas Indian communities*. Edited by Barton M. Schwartz. San Francisco: Chandler, 1967, p. 201-12. bibliog.

The author studies the extent to which the Indian caste system still exists among British Indians in Suriname. He finds that the meaning of this internal stratification system has decreased, particularly since 1940 while status differentiation based on education, profession, economic position, and political influence has become increasingly more important. The author argues that the caste system did not survive migration, instead one national caste developed in Suriname to which all British Indians belong.

257 **Dutch colonial policy and East Indians in Surinam.**

Johan Dirk Speckmann. In: *Asie du Sud: traditions et changements/ actes du VIe colloque européen sur les études modernes concernant l'Asie du Sud; Sèvres, 8-13 juillet 1978/ organisé par Marc Gaboricau et Alice Thornes*. Paris: Centre National de la Recherche Scientifique, 1979, p. 605-9. (Colloques Internationaux du Centre National de la Recherche Scientifique, 582).

An article dealing with the impact of Dutch colonial policy on the integration of the British Indian community. The arrival and settlement of Asian immigrants intensified the pluralist character of Surinamese society. The colonial government followed a policy of assimilation directed towards the inclusion of all population groups into one Dutch cultural community. During the period 1933-40 a change in this colonial policy led to the issuing of new laws, which reflected a pragmatic adaptation to the persisting cultural and racial heterogeneity. After the Second World War the process of economic differentiation diminished ethnic solidarity. Political autonomy weakened the European influence and a cultural reorientation followed. Since independence the Surinamese government has strongly encouraged an assimilation policy to unify the community.

258　**The Indian group in the segmented society of Surinam.** -
Johan Dirk Speckmann.　*Caribbean Studies*, vol. 13, no. 1 (1963),
p. 3-17.
Speckmann describes the plural society of Suriname, basing his discussion on the
theories of J. S. Furnivall (see *Colonial policy and practice*, London: Cambridge
University Press, 1948), M. G. Smith (see *The plural society in the British West Indies*,
Berkeley; Los Angeles: University of California Press, 1965), R. A. J. van Lier (q.v.),
and H. Hoetink (see *De gespleten samenleving in het Caribisch gebied*, Assen, The
Netherlands: Van Gorcum, 1962). He then sketches the place of the British Indians
within this segmented society and the willingness of this population group to adjust to
the values and standards of Western civilization.

259　**Marriage and kinship among the Indians in Surinam.**
Johan Dirk Speckmann.　Assen, The Netherlands: Van Gorcum,
1965. 302p. 2 maps. bibliog.
A study of three essential institutions in the life of the British Indians: marriage,
kinship, and the family. The author pays attention to the system of selecting of a
partner; the wedding ritual; and the dissolution of a marriage. An analysis of the
household group, the relations between its members; and economic aspects are
covered. British Indian kinship relations and the related terminology are studied. In
addition, Speckmann gives information on the history of the British Indians and he
discusses social change in Suriname in general and in the British Indian community in
particular.

260　**A Hindu wedding in Suriname/ Een hindoestaans huwelijk in Suriname.**
Ger D. van Wengen, Anne Marie Woerlee.　*Mededelingen Stichting
Surinaams Museum*, no. 35 (Dec. 1981), p. 15-38. bibliog.
A description of a wedding between two young teachers from Sanatan Dharm (an
orthodox sect of Hinduism maintaining the caste system) families. The wedding took
place under the regulations prescribed by the Asiatic Marriages Statute which came
into effect in 1939. This article in English and in Dutch presents a chronological
account of the activities during the last three days before the wedding. In the
conclusion these rites are viewed in their religious, sociological, and historical contexts.

Javanese

261　**Politieke mobilisatie en integratie van de Javanen in Suriname:
Tamanredjo en de Surinaamse nationale politiek.** (Political mobilization
and integration of the Javanese in Suriname: Tamanredjo and
Suriname national politics.)
Ferdinand Emile Ricardo Derveld.　Groningen, The Netherlands:
Bouma's Boekhandel, 1982. 168p. maps. bibliog.
A fine study of the Javanese role in the political system of Suriname between the
Second World War and the *coup d'état* of 1980. The author places much emphasis on
such phenomena as patronage, social brokerage, and the spoils system. In this case
study of the village of Tamanredjo, he focuses on the structural and cultural

characteristics of the Javanese community: the kinship system, language, and religion. The original dissertation (Rijksuniversiteit Leiden, the Netherlands, 1981) contains a two-page summary in English.

262 **Kulturwandel der indonesischen Einwanderer in Surinam: kulturelle und gesellschaftliche Veränderungen einer javanischen Minderheit in Latein Amerika.** (Cultural transformation among the Indonesian immigrants in Suriname: cultural and social changes of a Javanese minority in Latin America.)
Gabriele Grodd. PhD dissertation, Albert-Ludwigs-Universität, Freiburg im Breisgau, FRG, 1971. 159p. bibliog.

A German dissertation discussing the cultural changes experienced by the Javanese population. These changes consist of the loss of the Javanese cultural heritage, in particular language and the social order. Surinamese values increasingly influence young Javanese, who in great numbers leave the agricultural sector in their search for upward mobility, while older people hang on to tradition and stay in Suriname even though they would rather return to Java.

263 **De betovering verbroken. De migratie van Javanen naar Suriname en het rapport-Van Vleuten (1909).** (The magic spell broken. The migration of Javanese to Suriname and the report-Van Vleuten [1909].)
Rosemarijn Hoefte. Dordrecht, The Netherlands: Foris, 1990. 131p. bibliog. (Koninklijk Instituut voor Taal-, Land- en Volkenkunde Caribbean Series, 12).

In the early years of the 20th century, the Surinamese planters requested an investigation into the conditions of the Javanese indentured labourers. The report by the Dutch East Indian government official, H. van Vleuten, was rather negative and had never been published. This is the first time that this unique contemporary source has been published in an abridged and edited version. The introduction describes the history and culture of the Javanese in Suriname and the background of Van Vleuten. Hoefte compares the findings of Van Vleuten to other contemporary reports on contract labour in Suriname and to labour conditions in Sumatra (Dutch East Indies), where the majority of Javanese indentureds toiled.

264 **De immigratie van Indonesiërs in Suriname.** (The immigration of Indonesians in Suriname.)
Joseph Ismael. Leiden, The Netherlands: Luctor et Emergo, 1949. 170p. bibliog.

A classic account of the migration and settlement of the Javanese population in Suriname, this dissertation discusses the slow demographic growth of the Javanese with respect to their low birth rate and high death rate. The last chapter treats the position of the Javanese in Surinamese society in which the author studies their relationship with the other population groups as well as their own social and economic progress.

265 **The Indonesian minority in Surinam.**
Justus M. van der Kroef. *American Sociological Review*, vol. 16, no. 5 (1951), p. 672-79.
A brief review of the history of the Javanese population in Suriname and an analysis of the economic and social status of this group in the years immediately following the Second World War. At the time of writing, the author did not foresee any changes in the inferior position of the Javanese unless the Indonesian government actively protected the rights of its 'nationals'.

266 **Repatriation movements among the Javanese in Suriname: a comparative analysis.**
Craig A. Lockard. *Caribbean Studies*, vol. 18, no. 1/2 (April-July 1978), p. 85-113.
The author compares two repatriation movements among Javanese peasants in Suriname: the first in the early 1930s and the second in the late 1940s and early 1950s. In both cases one dynamic leader was clearly dominant: Anton de Kom in 1933 and Ideng Sumita during the period 1946-54. Lockard analyses the organization, leadership, social origins, and ideology of these movements, as well as the social, political, and cultural context in which they were generated. He explores the role of millenarianism and compares the movements to other lower-class repatriation movements.

267 **The Javanese in Surinam: ethnicity in an ethnically plural society.**
Parsudi Suparlan. PhD dissertation, University of Illinois at Urbana-Champaign, 1976. 390p. maps. bibliog. (Available from University Microfilms International, Ann Arbor, Michigan, order no. 76-24184).
This thesis shows that ethnicity is an individual phenomenon that emerges in social interaction. Individual behaviour, including the expression of ethnicity, is a manifestation of an individual's interpretation of himself and others. The author demonstrates that ethnicity is expressed in various ways, focusing on inter-ethnic relationships and variations in the expression of ethnicity among the Javanese.

268 **The Javanese of Surinam: segment of a plural society.**
Anna Maria de Waal Malefijt, preface by Margaret Mead. Assen, The Netherlands: Van Gorcum, 1963. 206p. map. bibliog.
This study deals with the Javanese population, who came to Suriname as indentured labourers. After the expiry of their contract approximately two-thirds of the almost 33,000 immigrants settled in Suriname, mainly as smallholders. Following an examination of the reasons for and the circumstances of the Javanese migration, the author presents a topical discussion of the various aspects of Javanese culture in Suriname: household; family and kinship; marriage, religion; and social organization. De Waal Malefijt concludes that the most salient feature of Javanese culture in Suriname is its resistance to cultural change, accompanied by the overt expression of the ideal to retain the cultural practices as the migrants remember existing in Java. This volume is a revised edition of the author's dissertation, *The Javanese population of Surinam* (Columbia University, New York, 1960. Available from University Microfilms International, Ann Arbor, Michigan, order no. 60-05101).

269 **Respect patterns and change among the Javanese of Surinam.**
Anna Maria de Waal Malefijt. In: *Family and kinship in Middle America and the Caribbean: proceedings of the 14th seminar of the Committee on Family Research of the International Sociological Association, Curaçao, September 1975*. Edited by Arnaud F. Marks, René A. Römer. Curaçao: Institute of Higher Studies; Leiden, The Netherlands: Department of Caribbean Studies, Royal Institute of Linguistics and Anthropology, 1978, p. 87-98.

The most pervasive aspect of the Surinamese Javanese family organization is the built-in respect pattern for older members of the family. This traditional pattern is one of several factors prohibiting rapid cultural change. Since the late 1960s, however, drastic cultural changes have been observed. The author discusses these transformations and their effect on the nature and structure of the Javanese family.

270 **The cultural inheritance of the Javanese in Surinam.**
Ger D. van Wengen. Leiden: E. J. Brill, 1975. 55p. (Ministerie van Cultuur, Recreatie en Maatschappelijk Werk, Mededelingen van het Rijksmuseum voor Volkenkunde, Leiden, 19).

A discussion of the religion and certain traditional art forms currently or formerly practised in the Javanese communities in Suriname. Where the literature permits, a comparison is made with the situation in Java. Particularly with respect to the art forms, there exists in many cases complete agreement between the area of origin and the Javanese art forms in Suriname.

Lebanese

271 **The Lebanese in Suriname.**
G. A. de Bruijne. *Boletín de Estudios Latinoamericanos y del Caribe*, no. 26 (June 1979), p. 15-37.

Although numerically a small group, the Lebanese have become a characteristic 'trade minority' in Suriname, with control over an appreciable portion of the textile market. The author discusses the trek of the Lebanese migrants to Suriname, their development into a dominant textile-trade group, their position in urban society, and their contribution to the economic development of Suriname.

Overseas Populations

272 **Immigration and the formation of minority groups: the Dutch experience 1945-1975.**
Hans van Amersfoort, translated from the Dutch by Robert Lyng.
Cambridge, England: Cambridge University Press, 1982. 234p. bibliog.
An analysis of the social position of the main groups of immigrants in Dutch society in the post-war period, in which the author raises the question concerning the necessary conditions under which immigration leads to the formation of minority groups. In the first part of this volume, Van Amersfoort develops a theory of race relations. In the second section, he applies this theory to a descriptive analysis of four immigrant populations in the Netherlands: the Indonesian Dutch, the Moluccans, the Surinamese, and 'guest labourers' from the Mediterranean area. The chapter on the Surinamese amounts to approximately forty pages and discusses migration and assimilation of this ethnic group, and compares it with other ethnic populations. The book was originally published in Dutch as *Immigratie en minderheidsvorming: een analyse van de Nederlandse situatie 1945-1973* (Alphen aan den Rijn, the Netherlands: Samsom, 1974).

273 **Reluctant hosts: immigration into Dutch society 1970-1985.**
Hans van Amersfoort, Boudewijn Surie. *Ethnic and Racial Studies*, vol. 10, no. 2 (April 1987), p. 169-85. bibliog.
Between 1970 and 1980 thousands of immigrants from Suriname, Turkey, and Morocco entered the Netherlands. This development seemed to have taken the Dutch by surprise and the authors analyse the reactions and perceptions of Dutch society. They break down the abstraction 'Dutch society' into three realms of discourse: the social sciences; politics; and public opinion.

274 **The Dutch plural society: a comparative study in race relations.**
Christopher Bagley. London, New York, Toronto: Oxford University
Press, for the Institute of Race Relations, London, 1973. 293p. bibliog.

An analysis of race relations and the integration of immigrants in the Netherlands, with
detailed comparisons with the British situation. The author argues that the Netherlands
have attained a reasonable degree of success in absorbing a large number of
immigrants from the East and the West Indies. He suggests the implementation in the
United Kingdom of several measures applied in the Netherlands to improve British
race relations.

275 **The hustler culture of young unemployed Surinamers.**
Wim E. Biervliet. In: *Adaptation of migrants from the Caribbean in
the European and American metropolis.* Edited by Humphrey E.
Lamur, Johan Dirk Speckmann. Amsterdam: Department of
Anthropology and Non-Western Sociology of the University of
Amsterdam; Leiden, The Netherlands: Department of Caribbean
Studies, Royal Institute of Linguistics and Anthropology, 1975,
p. 191-201.

A paper focusing on young unemployed Surinamese in major cities in the
Netherlands. The author presents a picture of their life-style and socio-economic
conditions. He demonstrates the deficient participation of the Surinamese migrants in
the institutional framework of the host society.

276 **Surinamers in the Netherlands.**
Wim E. Biervliet. In: *Contemporary Caribbean: a sociological reader.*
vol. 1. Edited by Susan Craig. Maracas, Trinidad: College Press, 1981,
p. 75-99.

An overview of the migration of Surinamese to the Netherlands in the 1970s. The
author describes the problems immigrants encountered in the labour and housing
market, and in the field of education. He also discusses government policy towards the
integration of Surinamers in Dutch society, and touches upon the conflicts between
Dutch and Surinamese people competing for the same resources. Biervliet pays minor
attention to remigration, crime, and the hustler sub-culture.

277 **Culture, structure, and ethnic enterprise: the Surinamese of
Amsterdam.**
Jeremy Boissevain, Hanneke Grotenbreg. In: *Lost illusions:*
Caribbean minorities in Britain and the Netherlands. Edited by Malcolm
Cross, Han Entzinger. London: Routledge, 1988, p. 221-40. bibliog.

The authors explore why the style of entrepreneurship should differ between ethnic
groups, all of whom migrated from the same place during the same period. The focus is
on the Chinese, the British Indians, and the Creoles, all of whom emigrated from
Suriname. British Indians and Chinese are more active as entrepreneurs than are
Creoles. The first group is most strongly established in the retail trade, while the latter
two are concentrated in the café and restaurant sector. Factors explaining these
differences are experience, family structure, saving and work ethic, financial resources,
networks, and ambition. A similar article by the same authors called 'Entrepreneurs
and the law: self-employed Surinamese in Amsterdam' appears in *History and power in*

the study of law: new directions in legal anthropology, edited by June Starr and Jane Collier (Ithaca, New York: Cornell University Press, 1989).

278   **Caribbean migration to the Netherlands. From elite to working class.**
Frank Bovenkerk.   In: *The Caribbean exodus*. Edited by Barry B.
Levine. New York; Westport, Connecticut; London: Praeger, 1987,
p. 204-13. bibliog.

Emigration used to be a prerogative for the white and mulatto upper classes alone, but from the mid-1960s the lower social classes began to leave for the Netherlands as well. The development of the ethnic and socio-economic composition of the migratory flow reflects the emancipation of the various groups in Surinamese society. First there were the whites and mulattos, followed by the dark-skinned Creoles, and then came the British Indians. Meanwhile Surinamese society fell apart at the seams. After the government opted for independence in 1973 a sharp increase in emigration took place. The author analyses how such a disastrous reduction of the population was possible and compares Surinamese and Antillean emigration.

279   **The sociology of return migration: a bibliographic essay.**
Frank Bovenkerk.   The Hague: Martinus Nijhoff, 1974. 67p. bibliog.

In this essay the author discusses a number of issues: the definition of return migration; the 'laws' and types of return migration; the motives migrants have for returning; the readjustment problems they face; the influence of returnees on their home communities; and the research techniques used to study return migration. In a concluding chapter the author suggests directions for future research.

280   **Why returnees generally do not turn out to be 'agents of change': the case of Suriname.**
Frank Bovenkerk.   *Nieuwe West-Indische Gids/New West Indian Guide*, vol. 55, no. 3/4 (1981), p. 154-73. bibliog.

Through the story of the fictional Romeo Pengel, the author explains that return migrants usually make no more than a negligible contribution to the modernization of their native countries in the Third World. Bovenkerk concentrates on the dynamics of the process of return migration itself. He elaborates on the characteristic features of the migration from Suriname to the Netherlands and vice versa, as well as on the idea that returnees form a new minority. In the final section the influence of the *coup d'etat* of 1980 on migration patterns is discussed.

281   **The draining of Surinam.**
Edward Dew.   *Caribbean Review*, vol. 5, no. 4 (1973), p. 8-15.

An overview of Surinamese migration to the Netherlands and the (brain-)draining of Suriname before independence in 1975. Emigration is valued as a safety-valve for both socio-economic and political strains. However, in the 1970s Surinamese in the Netherlands increasingly encountered racial discrimination and political opposition to the free influx of migrants.

282 **The underdevelopment of ex-colonial immigrants in metropolitan society: a study of Surinamers in the Netherlands.**
Vernon Albert Domingo. PhD dissertation, Clark University, Worcester, Massachusetts, 1980. 309p. bibliog. (Available from University Microfilms International, Ann Arbor, Michigan, order no. 80-27961).

In this study of underdevelopment and migration, the author argues that ethnic inequality in the Netherlands is institutionalized. The author attributes the inferior position of Surinamese migrants in the Netherlands to the Dutch political system which inhibits the improvement of the position of migrants. Their general lack of the skills needed for upward mobility in a Western industrial society has served as a catalyst in a period of economic decline.

283 **Horse, coke en kansen: sociale risico's en kansen onder Surinaamse en Marokkaanse harddruggebruikers in Amsterdam. I. Surinaamse harddruggebruikers.** (Horse, coke and chances: social risks and chances among Surinamese and Maroccan hard drug users in Amsterdam. I. Surinamese hard drug users.)
Paul van Gelder, Jelle H. Sijtsma. Amsterdam: AWIC, Antropologisch Sociologisch Centrum en Instituut voor Sociale Geografie, Universiteit van Amsterdam, 1988. 164p. bibliog.

A two-part report on the use of hard drugs by Surinamese in Amsterdam. The first part provides a theoretical framework and a short history of the use of hard drugs in Amsterdam. Part two discusses the use of hard drugs among Surinamese in 1987 and 1988. Interviews with twenty-six men and five women as well as data from social workers and policy makers form the basis of this investigation.

284 **Bonoeman, rasta's en andere Surinamers. Onderzoek naar etnische groepen in Nederland.** (Bonuman, rastas and other Surinamese. Study of ethnic groups in the Netherlands.)
Edited by Paul van Gelder, Peter van der Veer, Wilhelmina van Wetering. Amsterdam: AWIC, 1984. 255p. bibliog. (Publicatie, 1).

A volume divided into four parts which consist respectively of three general articles on studying ethnic minorities, five essays on religion among Creoles and British Indians, a discussion of economic organization and a final section dealing with youth and education.

285 **Suriname is mijn moeder en iedere moeder koestert haar kind.
Onderzoek naar remigratiemotieven van potentiële Surinaamse
remigranten.** (Suriname is my mother and every mother loves her child.
An inquiry into reasons for remigration of potential Surinamese
repatriates.)
Edward Headley.   Amsterdam: Wetenschapswinkel van de
Universiteit van Amsterdam, 1988. 60p. bibliog. (Deelrapport I Project
Remigratie Surinamers).
This report is based on interviews with twenty-five Surinamese Creole migrants living
in the Netherlands. The author discusses the reasons why some of these migrants might
want to return to Suriname. The main two reasons mentioned are discrimination and
that life in Suriname is considered to be more relaxed and free. Most of the
respondents, however, only want to repatriate when the political and the economic
circumstances in Suriname have improved. The structure of this report is similar to
Radj Ramcharan's *Dromen kost geen geld* (q.v.).

286 **Onder Surinamers: een pastorale handreiking.** (Among Surinamese: a
pastoral helping hand.)
P. Jansen.   The Hague: Boekencentrum, 1988. 103p. bibliog.
This volume provides information on the religious background of Creole immigrants in
the Netherlands. The author focuses on the traditions and religion of the Moravian
Church. Topics discussed by Reverend Jansen include hymns, baptism, Communion,
and the early morning service.

287 **Over massa's en kaders. Een theoretische basis voor het Surinaams
organisatie-leven.** (Of masses and cadres. A theoretical basis for
Surinamese organizations.)
Carlo Joemrati.   *Sranan Akademia*, vol. 1, no. 1 (May 1988), p. 63-80.
A theoretical analysis of the BSL or Beweging Surinaams Links (Movement
of the Surinamese Left). Since its establishment in 1982 this organization has been a
small academically-oriented group. The author argues that the BSL should transform
itself into a mass organization to lobby for the interests of the Surinamese population
in the Netherlands.

288 **De eerste neger: herinneringen aan de komst van een nieuwe
bevolkingsgroep.** (The first negro: memories of the arrival of a new
population group.)
Rudie Kagie.   Houten, The Netherlands: Het Wereldvenster, 1989.
138p.
A journalistic account of the history of the first black, mainly Surinamese, immigrants
to the Netherlands during the first decades of the 20th century. The author bases his
study on interviews and secondary sources.

289 **Surinamese settlement in Amsterdam 1973-83.**
Leo de Klerk, Hans van Amersfoort. In: *Lost illusions: Caribbean minorities in Britain and the Netherlands.* Edited by Malcolm Cross, Han Entzinger. London: Routledge, 1988, p. 147-63. maps. bibliog.

An analysis of the development of the settlement patterns of the Surinamese in Amsterdam. The authors argue that in 1983 the Surinamese lived in better houses and were less segregated than in 1973. De Klerk and Van Amersfoort call this remarkable because that decade was characterized by high unemployment. They therefore conclude that an overwhelming and total pessimism is too one-sided and not based on facts.

290 **Surinaamse jongeren in Nederland.** (Surinamese youth in the Netherlands.)
Willem Koot. In: *Adolescenten in vele gedaanten: bijdragen over adolescentie en adolescenten zorg.* Edited by R. A. C. Hoksbergen, R. v. d. Meer, G. P. Schoon. Lisse, The Netherlands: Swets en Zeitlinger, 1987, p. 88-96. bibliog.

In 1986, an estimated 55,000 Surinamese between 15 and 24 years of age were resident in the Netherlands. The author discusses their role in the educational process and their position in the labour market, and focuses on their ethnic identity and cultural orientation. The author concludes that many problems confront these young Surinamese and he briefly outlines some of the possibilities in case they need assistance.

291 **Processes of ethnic identification among Surinamese children in the Netherlands.**
Willem Koot, Varina Tjon-A-Ten, Petrien Uniken Venema. In: *The Caribbean in Europe: aspects of the West Indian experience in Britain, France and the Netherlands.* Edited by Colin Brock. London: Frank Cass, 1986, p. 166-87. bibliog.

Even though many experts maintain that there exists a correlation between self-concept and ethnic identity on the one hand and school achievement on the other, these researchers do not think it necessary to introduce mother tongue education and cultural reinforcement to improve the achievement of Surinamese children. However, the authors are concerned about the ethnic self-identity of Surinamese children in the Netherlands, as the value these children place on their own ethnic group is not strong. This is partly the result of the negative attitude the Dutch display towards Surinamese, rather than of lack of appreciation for their own Surinamese culture.

292 **Education: the way up for Surinamese children in the Netherlands?**
Willem Koot, Petrien Uniken Venema. In: *Lost illusions: Caribbean minorities in Britain and the Netherlands.* Edited by Malcolm Cross, Han Entzinger. London: Routledge, 1988, p. 185-203. bibliog.

The authors discuss the factors causing the lower achievement in schools of Surinamese children as compared with that of Dutch children. The schools are not equipped to accomodate Surinamese pupils, the biggest problem being the discrepancy in language skills. The teachers' attitudes also play an important part as they have stereotypical, negative expectations of the achievements of this particular group of pupils. Moreover, the learning material is not adapted to the ethnic and cultural backgrounds of the Surinamese.

293 **Het Nederlands van Hindostaanse basisschoolkinderen.** (The Dutch of Hindustani primary school pupils.)
R. M. Marhé. *Oso*, vol. 6, no. 2 (Dec. 1987), p. 185-200. bibliog.

A linguistic analysis of the written Dutch of British Indian schoolchildren in the Netherlands. Their writing contains systematic deviations from the standard language, which cannot all be explained by referring to their mother tongue, Sarnami.

294 **Hindoestaanse gezinnen in Nederland.** (Hindustani families in the Netherlands.)
G. Mungra. Leiden, The Netherlands: Centrum voor Onderzoek van Maatschappelijke Tegenstellingen, Faculteit der Sociale Wetenschappen Rijksuniversiteit Leiden, 1990. 382p. bibliog.

An extensive study of the approximately 70,000 Surinamese Hindus living in the Netherlands in which the author examines their position in Dutch society. Topics receiving special emphasis are religion, marriage, family, language and education, employment, and the media. Mungra distinguishes three family types: traditional families; 'intermediate' ones; and modern families, and argues that a strong correlation between family type and the level of participation in Dutch society exists. This book, originally a dissertation (Rijksuniversiteit Leiden, the Netherlands, 1990), includes summaries in English and Sarnami, an extensive bibliography, and a glossary.

295 **Caribbean migration to the Netherlands: a journey to disappointment?**
Gert Jan Oostindie. In: *Lost illusions: Caribbean minorities in Britain and the Netherlands*. Edited by Malcolm Cross, Han Entzinger. London: Routledge, 1988, p. 54-72. bibliog.

An introductory article on Surinamese and Antillean migrants to the Netherlands in the 20th century. The author argues that all parties concerned were disappointed. The proverbial 'Dutch tolerance' has vanished, now that racial discrimination has become commonplace and the immigrants are ascribed second-class citizenship on racial grounds.

296 **Kondreman in Bakrakondre: Surinamers in Nederland 1667-1954.**
(Countrymen in the land of the whites: Surinamese in The Netherlands 1667-1954.)
Gert Jan Oostindie. In: *In het land van de overheerser II. Antillianen en Surinamers in Nederland, 1634/1667-1954*. Dordrecht, The Netherlands: Foris, 1986, p. 3-313. bibliog. (Verhandelingen van het Koninklijk Instituut voor Taal-, Land- en Volkenkunde, 100).

A history of the Surinamese in the Netherlands from 1667 to 1954, the year of Suriname's autonomy. Until well into the 19th century the majority of these migrants were slaves accompanying their masters. Since the turn of the century more Surinamese came to the Netherlands, in particular to receive an education. Before the Second World War the first Surinamese unions were founded and after the war these organizations played an important role in the growth of Surinamese nationalism.

297 **Dromen kost geen geld. Onderzoek naar remigratiemotieven van Hindostaans-Surinaamse potentiële remigranten.** (Dreams do not cost any money. An inquiry into the motives for remigration of potential British Indian-Surinamese remigrants.)
Radj Ramcharan. Amsterdam: Wetenschapswinkel van de Universiteit van Amsterdam, 1988. 112p. bibliog. (Deelrapport II Project Remigratie Surinamers).

This inquiry into the motives for the return migration of British Indians is based on interviews with twenty-five persons. The structure of this report is similar to Edward Headley's *Suriname is mijn moeder en iedere moeder koestert haar kind* (q.v.). The author focuses on the reasons for emigration, on the differences between life in Suriname and in the Netherlands, on ethnicity, and on return migration.

298 **Mobilization of ethnicity in Dutch politics.**
Jan Rath. In: *Lost illusions: Caribbean minorities in Britain and the Netherlands.* Edited by Malcolm Cross, Han Entzinger. London: Routledge, 1988, p. 267-84. bibliog.

Ethnicity is very important for the incorporation of the Surinamese into the political structure in the Netherlands. This is a new phenomenon in Dutch politics and most political parties seem prepared to respond to demands for an ethnic dimension to their policies. The author questions, however, whether the relative success of this ethnic mobilization within political parties will lead to the political emancipation of ethnic minorities.

299 **On the way up? Surinamese and Antilleans in the Dutch labour market.**
Theo J. M. Reubsaet. In: *Lost illusions: Caribbean minorities in Britain and the Netherlands.* Edited by Malcolm Cross, Han Entzinger. London: Routledge, 1988, p. 106-25. bibliog.

An analysis of the position of Caribbean migrants in the labour market in the Netherlands. According to the author, many interrelated factors are responsible for their adverse situation, such as their recent immigration, poor level of training, as well as discrimination on the part of employers. Reubsaet concludes that most Surinamese migrants are likely to remain at the lower levels of the labour market and moreover, that the second generation may well continue this pattern.

300 **The Surinamese in the Netherlands.**
Theo J. M. Reubsaet. *New Community*, vol. 2 (1984), p. 301-8.

An article analysing the situation of the Surinamese immigrants in the Netherlands in three sectors: housing, employment, and education. It discusses the policy adopted by the Dutch government with regard to these migrants. This paper is based on the findings of research projects carried out by the Institute of Applied Sociology at the Katholieke Universiteit Nijmegen, the Netherlands.

301 **'And leisure time is mine': the Creole youth of Amsterdam in social welfare, vocational education and leisure time.**
Livio Sansone. Amsterdam: Gemeente Amsterdam, Afdeling Bestuursinformatie, 1984. 130p. bibliog.
An examination of the second generation of Surinamese Creoles in the Netherlands, in which the author aims to detect the relationship between ethnic identity and work or school as experienced by the lower-class Surinamese youth in Amsterdam. Sansone first provides a general picture of the way in which Surinamese youth spends its leisure time and of the their methods of coping with education, training opportunities, and social assistance. He also focuses on how these young people deal with ethnicity within their own social circles and in society at large.

302 **Waar ik gelukkig ben, daar wil ik nu wonen. Onderzoek naar de achtergronden van de Surinaamse remigratie 1970-1986.** (Where I am happy, there I want to live now. An inquiry into the causes of Surinamese return migration 1970-1986.)
John Schüster. Amsterdam: Wetenschapswinkel van de Universiteit van Amsterdam, 1988. 141p. bibliog. (Deelrapport IV Project Remigratie Surinamers).
This study examines the migration histories of thirty Surinamese who returned to the Netherlands after repatriating to Suriname. This report demonstrates that in the decision to migrate the tradition to migrate is more important than political and economic pressures. Reasons to return to Suriname are often of a personal nature. The remigration to the Netherlands has political, economic, social, and psychological reasons. This report includes a one-page summary in English and fifteen tables.

303 **Etnische relaties in het basisonderwijs. 'Witte' en 'zwarte' scholen in de grote steden. With a summary in English.** (Ethnic relations in primary education. 'White' and 'black' schools in the big cities.)
Joop Teunissen. PhD dissertation, Rijksuniversiteit Utrecht, The Netherlands, 1988. 198p. bibliog.
The report of research into the ethnic relations in primary education in Dutch cities like Amsterdam, Utrecht, The Hague, and Rotterdam. In popular speech, schools with a large percentage of immigrant pupils, mainly from Turkey, Morocco, and Suriname, are called 'black' schools and those with a small percentage 'white' schools. This project concentrates on the pupils and teachers in both types. The author argues that the variation in ethnic composition of the student population is of significant importance for the social position of immigrant pupils. Their position is unfavourable in schools where they form a minority. In educational situations where Dutch children are a minority the social position of immigrants becomes 'normal'.

304 **Informal supportive networks. Quasi-kin groups, religion and social order among Surinam Creoles in the Netherlands.**
Wilhelmina van Wetering. *Netherlands Journal of Sociology*, vol. 23, no. 2 (1987), p. 92 101. bibliog.
The author argues that the involvement in lucrative but illegal activities by many of the younger Creole immigrants in Amsterdam explains the attachment to traditional institutions such as orthodox and popular religions, and kinship groups.

305 **Ritual laundering of black money among Surinam Creoles in the Netherlands.**
Wilhelmina van Wetering. In: *Religion and Development: towards an integrated approach*. Edited by Philip Quarles van Ufford, Matthew Schoffeleers. Amsterdam: Free University Press, 1988, p. 247-64. bibliog. (Antropologische Studies VU, 11).
A case study of a mourning ritual in a Surinamese Creole community in Amsterdam. The author participated in and describes a string of death rites which combined the *Winti* religion with orthodox Christian elements.

306 **Glucose-6-phosphate dehydrogenate deficiency in ethnic minorities in the Netherlands.**
B. H. M. Wolf, R. B. H. Schutgens, N. J. D. Nagelkerke, R. S. Weening. *Tropical and Geographical Medicine*, vol. 40, no. 4 (Oct. 1988), p. 322-30. bibliog.
The authors studied the distribution of glucose-6-phosphate dehydrogenase (G-6-PD) deficiency in ethnic minorities, including Surinamese, in the Netherlands in a random sample of 668 healthy pregnant women and 754 healthy full-term babies. The overall prevalence of G-6-PD deficiency was found to be 6.6% in males and 5.2% in females.

307 **Zwarte studenten aan de Rijksuniversiteit Groningen. Een verkennend onderzoek naar etnocentrisme en racisme aan de Groningse universiteit.**
(Black students at the Rijksuniversiteit Groningen. An investigation into ethnocentrism and racism at the Rijksuniversiteit Groningen.)
Jannetta H. van der Zee. Groningen, The Netherlands: Andragogisch Instituut, Rijksuniversiteit Groningen, 1988. 131p. bibliog.
Interviews with twelve students form the basis of this report, the purpose of which is to establish the kind of obstacles black students find in their way while attending the Rijksuniversiteit Groningen. The author links these obstacles to ethnocentrism and racism as it exists in Dutch society and in its educational system.

Women's Studies

308 **Women and violent crime in Suriname.**
J. M. M. Binda. In: *Crime and punishment in the Caribbean.* Edited by Rosemary Brana-Shute, Gary Brana-Shute. Gainesville, Florida: Center for Latin American Studies, University of Florida 1980, p. 124-40.

Presents data on fifteen murders committed by female offenders, based on prisoner's registers from 1965 to 1978 at the House of Detention in Paramaribo and the Central Penitentiary in the Bomapolder. The author gives a description of the circumstances of the homicides in order to provide additional information about the motives for the crimes.

309 **Mothers in uniform: the children's police of Suriname.**
Gary Brana-Shute. *Urban Anthropology,* vol. 10, no. 1 (1982), p. 71-85.

An examination of the roles played by professional policewomen in the administration of justice in Paramaribo. The author argues that certain strong cultural stereotypes which restrict and circumscribe their professional behaviour condition the duties of these women. In professional life their activities are reminiscent of female roles in the household.

310 **Women, clubs and politics: the case of a lower-class neighborhood in Paramaribo, Suriname.**
Rosemary Brana-Shute. *Urban Anthropology,* vol.5, no. 2 (1976), p.157-85. bibliog.

Lower-class Creole women are more cohesively bound together than men through kinship, sexual division of labour, residence, and ideology. This essay describes social clubs arising out of these contacts. The urban neighbourhood organizations link the domestic realm with the public sector and members can get access to services unavailable to them as individuals. Sometimes a political element is added when the club assumes an additional role as broker between a neighbourhood and a national political party headquarters.

311 **Wi uma wi sisa: tien jaar Surinaamse vrouwen in beweging.** (We women, we sisters: ten years Surinamese women's movement.) Gharietje Choenni. *Sarnami Akademie*, vol. 1, no. 2 (1988), p. 7-33; vol.2, no. 1 (1989), p. 41-52.

The author briefly outlines the history of the Surinamese women's movement in the Netherlands. She analyses the social and the economic position of these women before sketching the development of women's projects and organizations. The most expansive growth took place between 1975 and 1980, thereafter a period of stabilization ensued. In the second part of the article the author provides a typology of Surinamese women's groups and analyses the effect of these groups on the position of Surinamese women.

312 **The great escape: the migration of female indentured servants from British India to Surinam, 1873-1916.** Pieter C. Emmer. In: *Abolition and its aftermath: the historical context, 1790-1916.* Edited by David Richardson. London: Frank Cass, 1985, p. 245-66.

The author argues that the passage to Suriname amounted to a step forwards for female indentured labourers from India. They were able to improve their material conditions as well as their personal lives as they could attain more personal freedom in Suriname than in caste-dominated India.

313 **Maroon women as ancestors, priests and mediums in Surinam.** Silvia Wilhelmina de Groot. *Slavery & Abolition*, vol. 7, no. 2 (1986), p. 160-74. map.

A study of the various roles of Maroon women whose prime responsibilities are such traditional ones as the cultivation and preparation of food, child care, and the making of clothes. Matrilineal, exogamous, and polygamous institutions determine a woman's place. Women do not play an active role in the clan, village or regional administration, yet their advice and opinions are taken into consideration. They are able to exert influence through their matrilineal status. In this matrilineal society in which ancestors are worshipped, the woman's position as clan mother is prominent. In the whole of the religious concept women have specific places as priestesses, mediums, and medicine women. The article is based on oral sources, archival records, and secondary literature.

314 **Female indentured labor in Suriname: for better or for worse?** Rosemarijn Hoefte. *Boletín de Estudios Latinoamericanos y del Caribe*, no. 42 (June1987), p. 55-70. bibliog.

A study of indentured British Indian and Javanese women during the late 19th and early 20th centuries, focusing on their recruitment; work and wages; their personal lives at the estates; and on their situation after their contracts had expired. The author questions whether bonded migration improved the lives of these women. Central to her analysis is that the oppression of women was multi-dimensional and had a tripartite source: gender, race, and class. In *Boletín de Estudios Latinoamericanos y del Caribe*, no. 43 (Dec.1987) Hoefte and P. C. Emmer engage in a debate on the position of indentured women in Suriname.

315 **Surinaamse vrouwen in slavernij.** (Surinamese women in slavery.) Wilhelmus S. M. Hoogbergen, Marjo de Theye. In: *Vrouwen in de Nederlandse koloniën*. Edited by Jeske Reijs, Els Kloek, Ulla Jansz, Annemarie de Wildt, Suzanne van Norden, Mirjam de Baar. Nijmegen, The Netherlands: SUN, 1986, p. 126-51. map. (Jaarboek voor Vrouwengeschiedenis, 7).

An inventory of what is known about female slaves in Suriname between the 17th and mid-19th centuries. The authors look at the work, the social and economic relations, the family life, and the religious role of these women. A summary in English is included at the end of the volume.

316 **Mati en lesbiennes; homosexualiteit en etnische identiteit by Creools-Surinaamse vrouwen in Nederland.** (Mati and lesbians; homosexuality and ethnic identity among Creole-Surinamese women in the Netherlands.) Maria José Janssens, Wilhelmina van Wetering. *Sociologische Gids*, vol. 32, no. 5/6 (1985), p. 394-415. bibliog.

Homosexuality among (lower class) Creole women is a relatively accepted phenomenon in Suriname. The authors examine homosexuality, which often includes religious aspects, among Creole female migrants in the Netherlands. They also study the meaning of *mati* (friendship among women) and how this concept is similar to or differs from lesbianism.

317 **Female initiation among the Maroni River Caribs.** Peter Kloos. *American Anthropologist*, vol.71, no. 5 (1969), p. 898-904.

A description of the initiation rite for girls among the Maroni River Caribs, which takes place about a week after the menarche and a discussion of its symbolism, which is almost completely concerned with the economic role of women. The author argues, backed by cross-cultural comparative research, that the Caribs practise female initiation because their women play an important economic role and because they tend to remain in the group in which they were born. This essay is also published in *You and others. Readings in introductory anthropology*, edited by A. Kimball Romney, P. L. De Vore (Cambridge, Massachusetts: Winthrop, 1973).

318 **Misi Hartmann, een leven als zendelinge in de kolonie Suriname.** (Misi Hartmann, a life as a missionary in the colony of Suriname.) Maria Lenders. In: *Vrouwen in de Nederlandse koloniën*. Edited by Jeske Reijs, Els Kloek, Ulla Jansz, Annemarie de Wildt, Suzanne van Norden, Mirjam de Baar. Nijmegen, The Netherlands: SUN, 1986, p. 172-91 map. (Jaarboek voor Vrouwengeschiedenis, 7).

An article on Maria Hartmann-Lobach, a Moravian Sister who lived in Suriname from 1826 until her death in 1853. She worked in Paramaribo, at plantations, and among the Maroons. Maria Hartmann's experiences are preserved in her diaries, letters, and reports which were published in part by the Moravian Brethren. A short summary in English is printed at the end of the volume.

319 **Tropische tribaden: een verhandeling over homosexualiteit en homosexuele vrouwen in Suriname.** (Tropical tribades: a treatise on homosexuality and homosexual women in Suriname.)
Rudolf A. J. van Lier.   Dordrecht, The Netherlands: Foris, 1986. 84p. bibliog. (Koninklijk Instituut voor Taal-, Land- en Volkenkunde Caribbean Series, 4).

A study based on the life stories of five lesbian Creole women which were recorded during the years 1947-49. Homosexuality is a common occurrence in the Creole lower classes and is generally accepted by this group. This fact makes Suriname an important area for the study of homosexuality. In the introduction, the author elaborates on the present ideas on sexuality and homosexuality in the academic world.

320 **Hoe je het draait of keert, het is je land: onderzoek naar de mogelijkheden en problemen m.b.t. remigratie van Surinaamse alleenstaande vrouwen.** (Whatever way you turn it, it is your country. An inquiry into the possibilities and problems concerning the remigration of Surinamese single women.)
Urmy Macnack, Hesther Tims.   Amsterdam: Wetenschapswinkel van de Universiteit van Amsterdam, 1988. 198p. bibliog. (Deelrapport III Project Remigratie Surinamers).

A report on the migration to the Netherlands, the living conditions there, and the possible return migration of single Creole women between twenty and fifty-five years of age. Most women were satisfied with their lives in Suriname and want to return to their homeland mainly for personal reasons.

321 **Veelwijverij en andere losbandige praktijken. Bevolkingspolitiek tegenover plantageslavinnen in de negentiende eeuw.** (Polygyny and other licentious practices. Birthrate policies for Surinamese slaves in the nineteenth century.)
Marja Oomens.   In: *Vrouwen in de Nederlandse koloniën.* Edited by Jeske Reijs, Els Kloek, Ulla Jansz, Annemarie de Wildt, Suzanne van Norden, Mirjam de Baar. Nijmegen, The Netherlands: SUN, 1986. p. 152-71. map. (Jaarboek voor Vrouwengeschiedenis, 7).

The demographic policy of the Surinamese planters in the 19th century was based on two principles. The first one was introduction of monogamy and the second, the improvement of care for mothers and infants. The author questions, however, whether these improvements could genuinely be called a birthrate policy on the part of the planters. A summary in English is included.

322 Co-wives and calabashes.
Sally Price. Ann Arbor, Michigan: University of Michigan Press, 1984, 224p. map. bibliog.

A very important study of the status of Saramaka women. They live in a polygynous and matrilineal society which is reflected in both its social structure and in its art. Through a detailed examination of women's artistic expression, this book explores the ways in which cultural ideas about the sexes influence the artistic life of women and analyses the complementary contributions that the most important artistic media make to their social life. Price especially emphasizes marriage as she considers it to be the one institution bringing together the art and social aspects of life in Maroon villages. This volume draws upon a variety of resources such as popular songs, decorative arts, and clothing. It is the winner of the Hamilton Prize 1982.

323 Van de West naar het Westen: Surinaamse studentes in Nederland, 1918-1940. (From the West Indies to the West: Surinamese female students in the Netherlands, 1918–1940.)
Dineke Stam. In: *Geleerde vrouwen*. Edited by Tineke van Loosbroek, Ulla Jansz, Annemarie de Wildt, Mirjam de Baar, Francisca de Haan, Fia Dieteren. Nijmegen, The Netherlands: SUN, 1988, p. 213-26. (Jaarboek voor Vrouwengeschiedenis, 9).

An article describing the first 20th-century Surinamese women who attended a university or college in the Netherlands. As there exist virtually no published sources on this topic, the author chose to sketch the lives of four women. Her information is based on interviews and egodocuments such as diaries. The four women portrayed are: the medical doctors Mathilde Nassy and Ine Bruijning; the biologist Betsy Lobato; and the lawyer Nettie Simons. After their studies, none of these women worked in Suriname for an extended period of time.

Languages

General

324 **Creolen en Hindustanen over Nederlands, Sarnami en Sranan: een onderzoek in Paramaribo.** (Creoles and Hindustanis on Dutch, Sarnami and Sranan: research in Paramaribo.)
Kas Deprez, Renata C. L. de Bies. *Oso*, vol. 4, no. 2 (Dec. 1985), p. 191-211. bibliog.
A report on a research project carried out among Creoles and British Indians in Paramaribo to establish their knowledge, use, and appreciation of the three languages most frequently spoken in Suriname: Sarnami, Sranan, and (Surinamese) Dutch. From the nineteen tables presented it is obvious that both ethnicity and social status determine the extent of use, the knowledge, and appreciation of a language.

325 **Taal politiek en sociale mobiliteit in Suriname, 1863-1985.** (Language policy and social mobility in Suriname, 1863-1985.)
Ch. H. Eersel. *Oso*, vol. 6, no. 2 (Dec. 1987), p. 127-36. bibliog.
A discussion of Dutch cultural policy in Suriname since 1876. This policy led to an overvaluation of the Dutch language and culture and a disdain for the native Surinamese languages and cultures. The Dutch ideal was to make Suriname, culturally speaking, an overseas province of the Netherlands, where social mobility depended on one's command of Dutch. Since the Second World War, however, the Surinamese languages and cultures have been seen in a more positive light.

326 **Taalbeleid en taalemancipatie in Suriname sinds het Statuut (1954).** (Language policy and language emancipation in Suriname since the Charter of the Kingdom [1954].)
Lila Gobardhan. *Oso*, vol. 8, no. 1 (May 1989), p. 65-76. bibliog.
An overview of language policy since 1954. Even though Suriname became autonomous in that year, the 'Dutchification' of education and culture continued. Only

with independence did the government revalue native languages such as Sranan, Sarnami, and Surinamese-Javanese.

327 **Writing systems for the interior of Surinam.**
Joseph E. Grimes. In: *Languages of the Guianas*. Edited by Joseph
E. Grimes. Norman, Oklahoma: Summer Institute of Linguistics of the
University of Oklahoma, 1972, p. 85-91.
An essay on writing systems for the Coastal Carib, Ndjuka, Saramakan, Trio, and
Wayana languages. Each system's primary requirement is its adequacy for the
language; considerations of uniformity with other writing systems such as Dutch or
Sranan should be considered only in that light.

328 **Taalattitude en taalbeheersing van Surinaamse kinderen.** (Language
attitude and competence of Surinamese school children.)
Dorian de Haan, Martha Cromwell, G. Ramnandanlal. *Oso*, vol. 6,
no. 2 (Dec. 1987), p. 165-84. bibliog.
A study of the attitude of thirty British Indian and Creole children in the Netherlands
towards Sarnami, Sranan, and Dutch. The authors also examine the command these
children have of the languages mentioned.

329 **Names with a meaning in Suriname/Sprekende namen in Suriname.**
Lou Lichtveld. *Suralco Magazine*, vol. 13, no. 1 (1981), p. 8-19. map.
Proper nouns in Suriname have very divergent origins: they come from Amerindian,
English, Portuguese, African, Creole, French, Dutch, German, and Asiatic sources.
The order of this list gives an indication of the relative ages of the toponyms, while its
variety often reveals the varied fortunes of Suriname. In this article the author
emphasizes toponyms of Amerindian, European, and Maroon origin. The essay is
written in English and in Dutch.

330 **Plantation names/Plantage namen.**
Lou Lichtveld. *Suralco Magazine*, vol. 13, no. 2 (1981), p. 6-13.
An article in English and in Dutch on the significance of plantation names which reveal
great linguistic 'landslides'. All ethnic groups who lived in Suriname in the past or still
live there today have left their mark on the toponyms.

Amerindian languages

331 **Arhwaka lokonong djang. Arowakse taalkursus en woordenboek.** (The
Arawak language. Arawak language course and dictionary.)
P. van Baarle, M. A. Sabajo, A. L. Sabajo, L. L. Sabajo, G. van der
Stap. Amsterdam; Haarlem, The Netherlands: Instituut voor
Algemene Taalwetenschap, Universiteit van Amsterdam en Sociaal-
culturele Vereniging Ikysohie, 1989. 268p. (Publikaties van het
Instituut voor Algemene Taalwetenschap, 55).

The first primer on the Arawak language, which comprises an introduction to the
spelling, followed by ten lessons, songs and stories and a final section which consists of
an Arawak-Dutch and Dutch-Arawak dictionary.

332 **The Carib language: phonology, morphology, texts and word index.**
B. J. Hoff. The Hague: Martinus Nijhoff, 1968. 440p. map.
(Verhandelingen van het Koninklijk Instituut voor Taal-, Land- en
Volkenkunde, 55).

The author describes the phonology and the morphology of the Carib language based
on material collected during fieldwork at three locations in Suriname in the late 1950s.
The introduction provides historical and demographic information on the Caribs, and
includes an overview of previous studies, a summary of the author's methods, and a
description of his six principal informants. The descriptive section of the monograph is
followed by approximately 100 pages of texts and translations. There is a word index,
with some 4,000 Carib-English entries.

333 **The languages of the Indians of Surinam and the comparative study of
the Carib and Arawak languages.**
B. J. Hoff. *Bijdragen tot de Taal-, Land- en Volkenkunde*, vol. 111,
no. 4 (1955), p. 325-55. bibliog.

A survey of the nature and the quantity of the material that has been collected on the
Amerindian languages of Suriname and other cognate languages during the period
1782-1955. The author also discusses the way in which these data have been used for
comparative linguistic studies inspired by North American linguistic methods. Most of
these studies have appeared in the *International Journal of American languages*. The
bibliography lists 182 entries.

334 **A Wayana grammar.**
Walter S. Jackson. In: *Languages of the Guianas*. Edited by
Joseph E. Grimes. Norman, Oklahoma: Summer Institute of
Linguistics of the University of Oklahoma, 1972, p. 47-77.

This grammar of the Wayana language goes beyond an earlier study by C. H. de Goeje
called *Grammaire de l'Oayana* (Amsterdam, 1946). The author fills the gaps in De
Goeje's sketch of the person distinctions. He distinguishes between transitive
inflections with subject and object focus, and between the use of transitive subject
focus inflections with intransitive motion verb stems and the use of intransitive
inflection for other intransitive verb stems. He bases part of the variation in the form

of inflectional morphemes on six morphophonemic stem classes. Jackson separates inflection from the recent past from that of the distant past, and keeps the pluralizers of nouns distinct from the pluralizers of the noun possessives. The vowel distinctions are recorded phonemically rather than using De Goeje's allophonic notation.

335 Trio phonology.
Morgan W. Jones. In: *Languages of the Guianas*. Edited by Joseph E. Grimes. Norman, Oklahoma: Summer Institute of Linguistics of the University of Oklahoma, 1972, p. 42-46.
A discussion of several vowel phonemes and fifteen clusters of two vowels in the Trio language, which is closely related to Wayana.

336 Carib phonology.
Edward T. Peasgood. In: *Languages of the Guianas*. Edited by Joseph E. Grimes. Norman, Oklahoma: Summer Institute of Linguistics of the University of Oklahoma, 1972, p. 35-41.
A study based on fieldwork carried out in the late 1960s among inhabitants of Bigi Poika. The people studied there speak the western dialect, used by about 2,400 persons in Suriname at the time. Attention is given to feet (units of speech), syllables, and phonemes.

337 European influence on the Arawak language of Guiana.
Thomas E. Penard, Arthur P. Penard. *De West-Indische Gids*, vol. 8, no. 9 (Aug. 1926), p. 165-76. bibliog.
The authors list a number of Arawak words which were influenced by European languages such as *baka* from the Spanish for cow (*vaca*) and *sepi* from the Dutch for soap (*zeep*). In most cases such words are used for cultural elements introduced by Europeans for which the Amerindians had no equivalent terms. Often they adopted these foreign words outright or formed hybrid combinations. The sources from which they drew were Spanish, Portuguese, English, and Dutch.

338 Surinam Arawak as compared with different dialects of Island Carib.
Douglas C. Taylor. *Bijdragen tot de Taal-, Land- en Volkenkunde*, vol. 118, no. 3 (1962), p. 362-73.
The author compares Arawak with a few likely cognate words in Goahiro and, more especially Island-Carib, the latter of which was first recorded toward the middle of the 17th century.

339 Waphishana phonology.
Frances V. Tracy. In: *Languages of the Guianas*. Edited by Joseph E. Grimes. Norman, Oklahoma: Summer Institute of Linguistics of the University of Oklahoma, 1972, p. 78-84.
A paper presenting a phonemic analysis of Wapishana, an Arawak language spoken by 4,000 to 9,000 people. This study goes beyond a strict taxonomy and tends toward an eventual systematic phonology. The section on morphophonemics is not comprehensive, but points toward the full complexity of the morphophonemic phenomena.

Creole languages

340 **Genesis and development of the equative copula in Sranan.**
Jacques Arends. In: *Substrata versus universals in creole genesis. Papers from the Amsterdam Creole Workshop, April 1985.* Edited by Pieter Muysken, Norval S. H. Smith. Amsterdam, Philadelphia: John Benjamins, 1986, p. 103-27. bibliog. (Creole Language Library, 1).
This paper traces the historical development and differentiation of the equative copula in Sranan Tongo (also known as Sranan) between about 1750 and 1950. Further, the author, on the basis of the historical evidence, tries to clarify some problems of synchronic syntax in this area. Finally, he discusses how universals, i.e. features shared by (all) languages, in combination with European vocabulary, and also how substrata, i.e. aspects of the native language influencing the European vocabulary, affect the development of Sranan Tongo.

341 **Notes on older texts in the Surinamese Creoles.**
Peter Bakker. In: *Amsterdam Creole Studies X.* Edited by Peter Bakker, Norval Smith. Amsterdam: Universiteit van Amsterdam. 1989, p. 33-39. bibliog. (Publikaties van het Instituut voor Algemene Taalwetenschap, 56).
A discussion of manuscripts concerning Creole languages in Suriname made by the Moravian Brethren from the 1770s onwards. The article is a gold mine for anyone undertaking a diachronic study of these languages.

342 **Reduplications in Saramaccan.**
Peter Bakker. In: *Studies in Saramaccan language structure.* Edited by Mervyn C. Alleyne. Amsterdam: Centre for Caribbean Studies, 1987, p. 17-40. bibliog.
A useful study of reduplication, a feature which has been recorded in several Creole languages, but which has only been treated superficially. Reduplication involves the repetition of a syllable or morpheme to indicate syntactic or semantic changes, for example in Saramaccan *denge* means mobile, while *dengedenge* means unstable. This phenomenon is often placed within the context of an alleged limited or non-existent morphology in Creole languages.

343 **A brief note on predicate cleft in Saramaccan.**
Henk van den Berg. In: *Studies in Saramaccan language structure.* Edited by Mervyn C. Alleyne. Amsterdam: Centre for Caribbean Studies, 1987, p. 103-12. bibliog.
A study of predicate cleft in a few Caribbean Creole languages and in Sarmaccan in particular. The author examines the theory of verb movement and reviews the literature on this subject.

344 **Creoles and West African languages: a case of mistaken identity?**
Derek Bickerton.   In: *Substrata versus universals in Creole genesis.*
Edited by Pieter Muysken, Norval S. H. Smith. Amsterdam,
Philadelphia: John Benjamins, 1986, p. 25-40, bibliog. (Creole
Language Library, 1).

The author shows that if one seeks to determine what rules of grammar have given rise
to superficially similar structures in Caribbean Creole and West African languages, one
finds that the rules that generate Creoles often turn out to be quite different from those
that generate West African languages. Bickerton examines the rules governing WH-
movement and empty categories (ECs) in Yoruba, Vata, Haitian, and Saramaccan.
The latter two are the languages most often cited as among the most heavily African
influenced of the Creoles.

345 **How the 'older heads' talk: a Jamaican Maroon spirit possession
language and its relationship to the Creoles of Suriname and Sierra
Leone.**
Kenneth M. Bilby.   *Nieuwe West-Indische Gids/New West Indian
Guide*, vol. 57, no. 1/2 (1983), p. 37-88. bibliog.

This paper focuses on the 'middle language', the 'deep' Creole spoken by those who
are conceptually situated in between the living and the most ancient ancestors. The
author detects certain features in this spirit possession language which point to a
relationship with the Creole languages of Suriname and Sierra Leone. Bilby addresses
a number of historical questions raised by these parallels. In 'The epithetic vowel in the
Jamaican Maroon Spirit Possession Language compared with that in the Surinam
Creoles' in: *Amsterdam Creole Studies VII,* edited by Pieter Muysken, Norval S. H.
Smith (Amsterdam: Universiteit van Amsterdam, 1984), Norval Smith offers
additional evidence of a relationship between the spirit possession language of the
eastern Jamaican Maroons and the Surinamese Maroons supplementary to that
provided by other researchers. The author does not provide new linguistic material,
but draws new conclusions based on earlier research.

346 **The Creole base: looking for the pure Creole.**
Francis Byrne.   *Oso* , vol. 3, no. 1 (May 1984), p. 17-29. bibliog.

Provides an explanation of the fact that previous studies concentrating on the
grammatical dynamics of Creole have failed to unlock some grammatical secrets. In
addition, Byrne argues that there does exists differential or imperfect creolization.
Saramaccan may come closest of any of the Creole languages ever studied in being an
example of a pure Creole. Finally, the author examines a few of the characteristics of
pure Creole.

347 **Grammatical relations in a radical Creole: verb complementation in
Saramaccan.**
Francis Byrne.   Amsterdam, Philadelphia: John Benjamins, 1987.
293p. bibliog. (Creole Language Library, 3).

A description of aspects of predicate complementation and verb-serialization in
Saramaccan. Retention of West African syntactic structures and vocabulary was long
regarded as an important characteristic of Saramaccan. The author shows that the
verb-serializing construction, in which verbs assume the functions of adverbs and

prepositions etc. and traditionally believed to be the strongest evidence for the retention of African structures, is noticeably different from its West African models. Byrne concludes that during the pidginization preceding the emergence of Saramaccan, all conjugational devices as well as most of the independent grammatical formatives of all its antecedent languages were lost.

348 **Some aspects of the syntax of fu in Saramaccan.**
Francis Byrne. In: *Amsterdam Creole Studies VIII.* Edited by Pieter Muysken, Norval S. H. Smith. Amsterdam: Universiteit van Amsterdam, 1985, p. 1-25. bibliog. (Publikaties van het Instituut voor Algemene Taalwetenschap, 48).

An article on *fu* in Saramaccan to determine its basic properties and the categorial status of its various functions. *Fu* is derived from the English 'for' and functions as a verb, preceding sentences whose outcome is not quite certain. The author also evaluates the claims and analyses of other experts in the context of Saramaccan. Beppy Wijnen and Mervyn C. Alleyne also discuss some aspects of the use of *fu* in the article 'A note on *fu* in Saramaccan' in *Studies in Saramaccan language structure*, edited by Mervyn C. Alleyne (Amsterdam: Centre for Caribbean Studies, 1987).

349 **Some notes on Sranan.**
Frederic G. Cassidy. *Oso,* vol. 3, no. 1 (May 1984), p. 115-20.

A short article based on the author's examination of Henrik Focke's *Neger-Engelsch Woordenboek* of 1855, which records Sranan Tongo nearly 200 years after its establishment. The author sheds some light on the linguistic developments and lexical sources of Sranan. Cassidy concludes that Sranan is a conservative Creole which still shows the effects of African structures, even though non-African lexical elements have been absorbed as well.

350 **Kongo elements in Saramacca Tongo.**
Jan Daeleman. *Journal of African Languages,* vol. 11, no. 1 (1972), p. 1-44.

Several lexical items in Saramaccan suggest an African origin. The number of possible cognates in KiKóongo, a Bantu language, seems considerable, although other possible Bantu or African origins, have been only partly investigated. The author compares 1,695 items in Saramaccan with possible Kongo cognates. In 'KiKóongo and Saramaccan: a reappraisal' in *Bijdragen tot de Taal-, Land- en Volkenkunde,* vol. 131, no. 4 (1975) Richard Price gives an extensive commentary on Daeleman's article. Price attempts to place Daeleman's data in a broader perspective, to include the socio-historical implications of such a linguistic analysis.

351 **Relative clause structure in four Creole languages.**
Gail Raimi Dreyfuss. PhD dissertation, University of Michigan, Ann Arbor, 1977. 220p. bibliog. (Available from University Microfilms International, Ann Arbor, Michigan, order no. 78-4686).

The purpose of this thesis is to evaluate the various claims about the sources of change in Creole languages. The author analyses data to discover the rules governing the process of relative clause formation in Haitian Creole, Tok Pisin, Sango, and Sranan Tongo. The data used in this analysis consist of texts recorded by various investigators in each of these languages. Most of the information on Sranan is taken from John E. Reinecke, *Bibliography of pidgin and Creole languages* (Honolulu: University Press of Hawaii, 1975).

352   **Seven notes in Afaka script.**
Cornelis N. Dubelaar, Andre Pakosie.   *Nieuwe West-Indische Gids/New West Indian Guide*, vol. 62, nos. 3/4 (1988), p. 146-64.
A summary of the literature on the Afaka script of the Ndjuka Maroons, a syllabic script which was created in the first decades of the 20th century. The article includes seven notes in Afaka script, their English translation, and commentaries by the authors. An earlier study by Justus Wilhelm Gonggrijp entitled 'The evolution of the Djuka-script' published in the *Nieuwe West-Indische Gids/New West Indian Guide*, vol. 40 (1960/61) reviews the evolution of the Afaka script and presents five figures as well as four notes written by different individuals to show the sound value of this script.

353   **The English words in Sranan.**
Johannes Julius Marius Echteld.   Groningen, The Netherlands: J. B. Wolters, 1961. 219p. bibliog.
A dissertation (Universiteit van Amsterdam, 1961) investigating the extent to which English has contributed to the vocabulary and the word-structure of Sranan Tongo. Following an historical introduction to Sranan, the author discusses its pronunciation and spelling. In the last three chapters he focuses on the main characteristics of Sranan, its phonetic interpretation, and lexical interference.

354   **Role structure in Saramaccan verbs.**
Naomi Glock.   In: *Languages of the Guianas*. Edited by Joseph E. Grimes. Norman, Oklahoma: Summer Institute of Linguistics of the University of Oklahoma, 1972, p. 28-34.
An essay considering the various possiblities of role structure in Saramaccan predicates. No one role is present in the role structure of every predicate, and the role structure varies from predicate to predicate. Every verbal predicate in Saramaccan has either an agent (the initiator of an action) or a patient (the recipient of the effect of an action), which facilitates research. Other roles that are considered include location; direction; instrument; association; benefactive; manner; and range. Mervyn C. Alleyne has also written an essay dealing with a number of related themes concerning the structure of the verb phrase in Saramaccan. 'Predicate structures in Saramaccan' in *Studies in Saramaccan language structure*, edited by Mervyn C. Alleyne. (Amsterdam: Centre for Caribbean Studies, 1987, p. 71-87) introduces passive structures; lexical categories; verbal features; and aspectual categories.

355   **Structure of the Saramaccan folktale.**
Naomi Glock, Stephen H. Levinsohn.   In: *Discourse studies on Djuka and Saramaccan*. Edited by Stephen H. Levinsohn. Paramaribo: Instituut voor Taalwetenschap/Summer Institute of Linguistics, 1981, p. 31-55. bibliog. (Languages of the Guianas, III).
The authors consider four Saramaccan folk tales and demonstrate the value of recognizing both an underlying deep structure and a surface structure in them. Deep structure (or plot) may be defined in terms of hiatus features, such as changes in

spatio-temporal settings and participant focus. In a surface structure the narrator often uses a variety of devices to hide the divisions which correspond to these changes.

356 **Woordregister Nederlands-Saramakaans met context en idioom.** (Dutch-Saramaccan index with context and idiom.)
A. H. P. de Groot. Paramaribo: [no publisher], 1977. 377p.

Presents a Dutch-Saramaccan vocabulary which was researched during a four-year residence at Lombé, Brokopondo district. A second volume is entitled *Woordregister Saramakaans-Nederlands* (Paramaribo, 1981), and provides a Saramaccan-Dutch vocabulary.

357 **The 1830 Defence of Sranan: William Greenfield's gift to the Creole-speaking world.**
John W. Harris. *Oso*, vol. 4, no. 2 (Dec. 1985), p. 213-20. bibliog.

An article on the importance of William Greenfield, a scholar of both biblical and living languages. In 1830 he published *A defense of the Surinam Negro-English version of the New Testament founded on the history of the Negro-English version, a view of the situation, population and history of Surinam, a philological analysis of the language, and a careful examination of the version; in reply to animadversions of an anonymous writer in the Edinburgh Instructor*. Greenfield shows that Negro-English 'is not merely broken English or broken Dutch', but a language in its own right. He provides textual and lexical data to support his thesis. He thus demonstrates that Negro-English does have a grammar and that there is nothing about it which is not true of other languages.

358 **On the provenience of the Portuguese in Saramacca Tongo.**
Melville J. Herskovits. *West-Indische Gids*, vol. 12 (1930/31), p. 545-57.

The Saramaccan language contains a great number of Portuguese words. The author rejects the explanation that runaway slaves had learned these expressions from their Jewish masters who originally came from Brazil. Herskovits argues instead that the slaves had learned Portuguese in Africa from (slave) traders, thus constituting another African element in the civilization of the Maroons.

359 **Elements de vocabulaire de la langue Boni (Aluku Tongo).** (Elements in the vocabulary of the Boni language [Aluku Tongo].)
Jean Hurault. In: *Amsterdam Creole studies VI-Special issue*. Amsterdam: Institute for General Linguistics, University of Amsterdam, 1983, 41p. (Publikaties van het Instituut voor Algemene Taalwetenschap, 39).

In 1952 the author, while engaged in anthropological research in French Guiana on the Aluku Maroons, prepared a vocabulary of Aluku Tongo. Even though it remained unpublished for thirty years, scholars consider the vocabulary a standard work, especially considering that nothing comparable is available. This vocabulary comprises lexical material on Aluku Tongo as well as on the two secret (cult or religious) languages Papa and Kumenti.

360 **Sources of Ndjuka African vocabulary.**
George L. Huttar. *Nieuwe West-Indische Gids/New West Indian Guide*, vol. 59, no. 1/2 (1985), p. 45-71. bibliog.
In this paper the author addresses the question concerning the provenance of particular lexical items in Ndjuka. More specifically, he looks at those items that appear to be of European (English, Dutch, Portuguese, French) or Amerindian (Carib, Arawak) origin, thus leaving out those that he considers reasonable candidates for being of African origin.

361 **Notes on Djuka phonology.**
George L. Huttar, Mary L. Huttar. In: *Languages of the Guianas*. Edited by Joseph E. Grimes. Norman, Oklahoma: Summer Institute of Linguistics of the University of Oklahoma, 1972, p. 1-11.
The authors describe the segmental phoneme system of Ndjuka in sections on consonants and vowels. The structure of syllables and feet is also studied, along with the relationships among suprasegmental phenomena. Ndjuka morphophonemics is discussed only for a narrowly defined set of cases of vowel elision and a limited number of instances of tone sandhi. In the same volume a comparative word list for Ndjuka by George Huttar provides a sample of the Ndjuka lexicon. The authors also list corresponding forms in Sranan and Saramaccan. Entries are numbered consecutively and are arranged in alphabetical order by the English glosses.

362 **Serial verbs in the Creole languages.**
Bert Jansen, Hilda Koopman, Pieter Muysken. In: *Amsterdam Creole Studies II*. Edited by Pieter Muysken. Amsterdam: Universiteit van Amsterdam, 1978, p. 125-59. bibliog. (Publikaties van het Instituut voor Algemene Taalwetenschap, 20).
This paper tries to answer two central questions. First, what is the relationship between the serial verb constructions in the Creole and West African languages? Second, what is the syntactic structure of the serial verbs in the Creole languages? The authors also present the result of a survey of a number of Creole languages with regard to verb serialization. On the basis of Sranan Tongo data, the authors discuss the structure of serial verbs in detail.

363 **Stative verb formation in Saramaccan.**
Peter Kahrel. In: *Studies in Saramaccan language structure*. Edited by Mervyn C. Alleyne. Amsterdam: Centre for Caribbean Studies, 1987, p. 53-70. bibliog.
Following a brief outline of functional grammar, the author presents some features of derived stative verbs and discusses their interaction with predicate operators. In the final section of this essay, Kahrel looks at the relationship between transitive and intransitive predicates as well as 'passive' constructions in Saramaccan.

364 **Morphophonemic change in Saramaccan pronominal forms.**
Silvia Kouwenberg.   In: *Studies in Saramaccan language structure* .
Edited by Mervyn C. Alleyne. Amsterdam: Centre for Caribbean
Studies, 1987, p. 1-16. bibliog.

A presentation of data on the morphophonology of personal pronouns. This
particularly characteristic feature of Saramaccan involves a degree of variation hitherto
unsuspected and only paralleled perhaps by Haitian morphophonemics.

365 **Early Creole lexicography: a study of C. L. Schumann's manuscript
dictionary of Sranan.**
André A. Kramp.   PhD dissertation, Rijksuniversiteit Leiden, The
Netherlands, 1983. 378p. bibliog.

An historical lexicological study based on the third edition of C. L. Schumann's
manuscript dictionary, *Neger-Englisches Wörter-Buch*, from 1783, which is considered
a monument of early Creole language description. The dissertation is divided into
three chapters comprising an introduction, the edition of the manuscript, and a
commentary. In the first chapter the author gives useful information about the original
dictionary and its author, as well as his lexicographical technique, and phonological
and syntactic developments. This thesis includes summaries in Dutch and in Sranan
Tongo.

366 **Prepositions and postpositions in Saramaccan.**
Pieter Muysken.   In: *Studies in Saramaccan language structure*. Edited
by Mervyn C. Alleyne. Amsterdam: Centre for Caribbean Studies,
1987, p. 89-101.

A description and discussion of the neglected category of prepositions and
postpositions in Saramaccan.

367 **Paragraph in Djuka deliberative discourse.**
James F. Park.   In: *Discourse studies on Djuka and Saramaccan.*
Edited by Stephen H. Levinsohn. Paramaribo: Instituut voor
Taalwetenschap/Summer Institute of Linguistics, 1981, p. 1-30. bibliog.
(Languages of the Guianas, III).

An analysis of the paragraph types found in selected Ndjuka deliberative discourse
texts. The underlying theoretical approach is basically tagmemic, focusing on the
hierarchy of meaningful utterances from the paragraph, down to words and
morphemes. The author argues for the importance of recognizing and distinguishing
both the nature of the speech act involved in an utterance and the deep structure
relationships encoded in that utterance. He describes the types of rhetorical
underlining employed by Ndjuka speakers to mark the climax of a paragraph.

368 **Saramaka onomastics: an Afro-American naming system.**
Richard Price, Sally Price.   *Ethnology*, vol. 11, no. 4 (1972), p. 341-
67. bibliog.

A description and analysis of personal names and the naming system among the
Saramaka Maroons. Furthermore, the authors try to define some shared features of

Afro-American naming systems. In the process, they confront some methodological issues of general import to Afro-Americanists.

369   **Secret play languages in Saramaka: linguistic disguise in a Caribbean Creole.**
       Richard Price, Sally Price.   In: *Speech-play: research and resources for the study of linguistic creativity.* Edited by Barbara Kirshenblatt-Gimlett. Philadelphia: University of Pennsylvania Press, 1976, p. 37-50. bibliog.
A description and analysis of several play languages spoken by the Saramaka Maroons. which they call *akoopína*, secret play language(s). *Akoopína* reflect fundamental Saramaka values regarding creativity, play, and performance which influence a much wider range of linguistic contexts, from greetings and riddles to the rhetoric of ritual.

370   **The historical background of Surinam's Negro English.**
       L. L. E. Rens.   Amsterdam: North-Holland Publishing Company, 1953. 155p. bibliog.
An examination of the historical and social background of the creation and development of Sranan Tongo. The author contends that there exists a fundamental difference regarding the creation, evolution, and position of Sranan Tongo on the one hand, and pidgin English on the other.

371   **The phonological structure of stems in Saramaccan.**
       S. Catherine Rountree.   In: *Languages of the Guianas.* Edited by Joseph E. Grimes. Norman, Oklahoma: Summer Institute of Linguistics of the University of Oklahoma, 1972, p. 22-27. bibliog.
A paper dealing with the phonological properties of simple and compound word stems in Saramaccan.

372   **Saramaccan personal narrative.**
       S. Catherine Rountree.   In: *Discourse studies on Djuka and Saramaccan.* Edited by Stephen H. Levinsohn. Paramaribo: Instituut voor Taalwetenschap/Summer Institute of Linguistics, 1981, p. 56-84. bibliog. (Languages of the Guianas, III).
An essay showing how a narrative in Saramaccan develops not only chronologically, but also logically. The argument or purpose of a story is traced by means of suffixes. The main thrust of this paper is a discussion of all the major and most of the minor sentence introducers for all Saramaccan discourse types.

373 **Saramaccan for beginners (a pedagogical grammar of the Saramaccan language).**
S. Catherine Rountree, Naomi Glock. Paramaribo: Instituut voor Taalwetenschap/Summer Institute of Linguistics, 1982. 2nd ed. 197p. (Languages of the Guianas, V).
A basic Saramaccan grammar comprising fourteen units. Each unit consists of a dialogue or narrative and drills. The exercises cover pronunciation and intonation, structure, and vocabulary.

374 **Adjectives and comparatives in Sranan.**
Mark Sebba. In: *Amsterdam Creole Studies IV*. Edited by Norval S. H. Smith. Amsterdam: Universiteit van Amsterdam, 1982, p. 1-22. bibliog. (Publikaties van het Instituut voor Algemene Taalwetenschap, 34).
An examination of the comparative construction in Sranan Tongo and the question of whether the words *moro* and *psa*, which are used in comparative constructions, are verbs or belong to some other category. The author discusses the nature of Sranan adjectives and the mysterious verb 'to be'. In a second article in the same volume entitled 'Metathesis, epenthesis and liquids in Suriname Creole', Sebba focuses on the question whether clusters of consonants and liquids were present in the forerunner(s) of Sranan and Saramaccan, and what the permitted consonant clusters were. The author draws on other Creole languages for evidence and looks for pointers toward a proto-Atlantic Creole phonology.

375 **A note on two secret languages of Surinam.**
Mark Sebba. In: *Amsterdam Creole Studies IV*. Edited by Norval S. H. Smith. Amsterdam: Universiteit van Amsterdam, 1982, p. 38-43. (Publikaties van het Instituut voor Algemene Taalwetenschap, 34).
A discussion of lexical items in Papa and Kumenti, two secret languages spoken among the Alukus. The author focuses on the origin, composition, and phonology of these languages. The article 'A further note on two secret languages of Surinam' by Norval Smith in: *Amsterdam Creole Studies V*, edited by Smith, Pieter Muysken (Amsterdam: Universiteit van Amsterdam, 1983) is intended as a supplement to this essay by Sebba. Smith also discusses Kumenti and Papa, and pleads for a deeper investigation of the lexicons of African cult languages in Suriname.

376 **The syntax of serial verbs: an investigation into serialisation in Sranan and other languages.**
Mark Sebba. Amsterdam, Philadelphia: John Benjamins, 1987. 227p. bibliog.
The author examines in detail the serial constructions of Sranan Tongo. He provides a working definition of a 'serial verb', and lists, classifies, and analyses the various types of serial constructions found in Sranan. Sebba also offers a new analysis for serial verbs as a phrase construction phenomenon. Finally, he compares his analysis to serial verbs in other languages and finds remarkable similarities.

377 **The genesis of the Creole languages of Suriname.**
Norval S. H. Smith. PhD dissertation, University of Amsterdam,
1987. 494p.
In this doctoral thesis, Smith hypothesizes on the origin of the Creole languages in
Suriname: Sranan, Saramaccan, Matawai, Ndjuka, Paramakan, Aluku, and Kwinti.
Using the techniques of historical phonology he has identified the English and
Portuguese-based words in Surinamese Creoles as ultimately deriving from West
African English and Portuguese Creole. The book is divided into two parts. In the first
one, the author outlines the theoretical framework and gives a summary of the
phonological evidence. The second part is the most important and discusses the
development of English and Portuguese consonants and vowels in Surinamese Creoles.

378 **On the liquefying of /d/ in the Surinam Creole languages.**
Norval S. H. Smith. In: *Amsterdam Creole Studies II* . Edited by
Pieter Muysken. Amsterdam: Universiteit van Amsterdam, 1978,
p. 115-23. bibliog. (Publikaties van het Instituut voor Algemene
Taalwetenschap, 20).
The author describes the tendency in the earliest period of Creole English to change
the phoneme /d/ to /r/ when flanked by the same vowels. This tendency was carried
out to its completion only with words such as 'seed' or 'weed' in English, yet the rule
was never carried out across the board. In a follow-up article, 'On the liquefying of /d/
in the Surinam Creole languages again' in: *Amsterdam Creole Studies IV* edited by
Smith (Amsterdam: Universiteit van Amsterdam, 1978), Smith attempts to give a more
satisfactory account of the phenomenon of liquefaction of /d/. It proved to be
misleading to base conclusions solely on examples from the English-based vocabulary
of the Creole languages of Suriname. The author now extends the vocabulary to
Portuguese and Dutch-based words. Moreover, he seeks an African explanation.

379 **Some nasal phenomena in the Creole languages of Surinam.**
Norval S. H. Smith. In: *Amsterdam Creole Studies III*. Edited by
Pieter Muysken, Norval S. H. Smith. Amsterdam: Universiteit van
Amsterdam, 1980, p. 14-24. bibliog. (Publikaties van het Instituut voor
Algemene Taalwetenschap, 31).
An article on the mixture of African, Portuguese, English, and Dutch elements in the
phonology of the Creole languages of Suriname. The author focuses on certain
historical processes involving nasality. In his essay 'The development of Nasal-Stop
clusters in Surinam Creoles' in: *Amsterdam Creole Studies IV* edited by Smith
(Amsterdam: Universiteit van Amsterdam, 1982), he examines another aspect of the
phonological development of the Creole languages: the fate of several clusters in words
derived from English and Portuguese.

380 **Vowel epithesis in the Surinam Creoles.**
Norval S. H. Smith. In: *Amsterdam Creole Studies I.* Edited by Pieter
Muysken. Amsterdam: Universiteit van Amsterdam, 1977, p. 1-30.
bibliog. (Publikaties van het Instituut voor Algemene Taalwetenschap,
19).
An article examining the older English vocabulary in Sranan Tongo, Saramaccan, and
Aluku. The author concentrates on the nature of the epithetic or final vowel added to

the vocabulary of English origin. In an essay called 'The development of liquids in the Surinam Creoles' in the same volume, Smith brings together the relevant data concerning the history of the development of the liquids in various languages of Suriname. He merely provides an interpretation of these data to be disproved by other students if possible.

381 **Vowel harmony in two languages of Surinam.**
Norval S. H. Smith. *Spektator*, vol. 4, no. 6 (1975), p. 315-20. bibliog.
The main purpose of this article is to demonstrate that Saramaccan, uniquely among Creole languages, possesses a feature typical of African languages, namely vowel harmony. The author also shows that this feature was once present in Sranan Tongo.

382 **The development of the liquids in Kwinti.**
Norval S. H. Smith, George L. Huttar. In: *Amsterdam Creole Studies VII.* Edited by Pieter Muysken, Norval S. H. Smith. Amsterdam: Universiteit van Amsterdam, 1984, p. 21-30. bibliog. (Publikaties van het Instituut voor Algemene Taalwetenschap, 44).
The authors make a preliminary attempt to draw conclusions regarding the historical development of the liquids in Kwinti. The data base employed is small only containing a word-list of 170 items. Yet, it is evident that Kwinti differs from all other Creole languages in Suriname as far as the phonological development of the liquids are concerned.

383 **Sranantongo: Surinaamse taal. Een korte inleiding tot het Sranantongo met uitgebreide woordenlijst.** (Sranan Tongo: Surinamese language. A brief introduction to Sranan Tongo with an extensive vocabulary.)
Max Sordam, H. Ch. Eersel. Baarn, The Netherlands: Bosch & Keuning, 1985. 383p.
Presents a Sranan-Dutch and Dutch-Sranan vocabulary with flora and fauna listed separately. This volume also includes an introduction to Sranan and a grammatical overview with exercises. A second revised edition by the same author, appeared in 1989, entitled *Surinaams woordenboek, Sranantongo*.

384 **Historical and linguistic evidence in favour of the relexification theory in the formation of Creoles.**
Jan Voorhoeve. *Language in Society*, vol. 2 (1973), p. 133-45. bibliog.
An examination of Saramaccan, Sranan Tongo, and Ndjuka and their Creole origins. Saramaccan and Sranan are compared on basic vocabulary and other linguistic features, and analysed in conjunction with historical evidence, while Ndjuka seems to have developed from an 18th-century English pidgin. The author concludes that both 'normal' genetic developments and relexification may have similar results and that comparative evidence alone is not a sufficient basis for historical conclusions. In the article 'Notes on the origins of Sranan' published in *Amsterdam Creole Studies IV*, edited by Norval S. H. Smith (Amsterdam: Universiteit van Amsterdam, 1982) Douglas-Val Ziegler plays 'devil's advocate' in regard to the relexification theory of Creole origins as applied to Sranan.

385 **Spelling difficulties in Sranan.**
Jan Voorhoeve. *Bible Translator*, vol. 12, no. 1 (1961), p. 21-31.
In the 1950s, the Netherlands Bible Society had to take the initiative in the regulation
of spelling in Sranan Tongo, for it wished to produce a Sranan translation of the Bible.
The government had aimed at cultural and linguistic unity via the Dutch language and
thus had not concerned itself with Sranan. The author relates how various religious and
nationalist groups in Suriname, with their widely diverging methods of spelling, were
able to reach agreement.

386 **Sranan syntax.**
Jan Voorhoeve. Amsterdam: North-Holland Publishing Company,
1962. 91p.
A book on the grammatical structure of Sranan Tongo, the mother tongue of a large
proportion of the Creoles, and which serves as a means of communication with and
between other sections of the population. This study concentrates on the language of
young Creole workmen from Paramaribo. Some texts were recorded and later written
down and analysed. On the basis of this material experiments were carried out.

387 **Het ontstaan en de geschiedenis van het Sranan.** (The origin and the
development of Sranan.)
Herman Chr. Wekker. In: *Cultuur in beweging. Creolisering en
Afro-Caraïbische cultuur, weergave van het gelijknamige symposium
georganiseerd door Studium Generale Rotterdam, Erasmus Universiteit
Rotterdam, 1988.* Edited by Michiel Baud, Marianne C. Ketting.
Rotterdam, The Netherlands: Erasmus Universiteit, 1989, p. 37-44.
An introduction to the origins of Sranan Tongo, its development, and the
characteristics of its structure. The author concludes that pidgin elements have long
been present, yet slowly, but surely the structure of the language has changed. It
certainly is not a language which was formed within one generation of pidgin-speaking
slaves.

388 **'Sa' en 'o' in het Sranan.** ('Sa' and 'o' in Sranan.)
Wendela Wendelaar, Geert Koefoed. *Oso*, vol. 7, no. 1 (May 1988),
p. 63-75. bibliog.
In Sranan, both *sa* and *o* indicate the future tense, although they cannot be used
interchangeably. The authors focus on two questions: first, what is the difference in
meaning between *sa* and *o*?; and second, why and in what ways do linguists disagree on
the use and meaning of these two words?

389 **A sketch of Sranan Tongo.**
John Wilner. In: *Papers on Sranan Tongo.* Edited by Wilem Pet.
Paramaribo: Instituut voor Taalwetenschap/Summer Institute of
Linguistics, 1984, p. 8-123. bibliog. (Languages of the Guianas, VII).
An outline of the structure of Sranan Tongo as illustrated by nine texts in the
appendix. This essay is intended for a general audience, linguistic terminology,
therefore, has been kept to a minimum. A partial listing of publications in and about
Sranan can be found in the bibliography. Prior to this essay, in a brief article, Marilyn
Nickel discusses abbreviated forms in spoken Sranan. A characteristic of spoken

Sranan as opposed to written Sranan is the use of frequently abbreviated forms. These abbreviations occur not only in fast speech but in normal speech as well. The author attempts to account for the abbreviated forms in spoken Sranan by an ordered set of rules.

390   **Woordenlijst Sranan Nederlands English met een lijst van planten- en dierennamen.** (Sranan-Dutch-English vocabulary with a list of plant and animal names.)
Paramaribo: Vaco, 1981. 203p.
This volume includes Sranan-Dutch, Dutch-Sranan and Sranan-English vocabularies, a key to pronunciation, and a listing of botanical and zoological names.

391   **Woordenlijst van het Sranan-tongo/Glossary of the Suriname vernacular.**
Paramaribo: Bureau Volkslectuur, 1961. 102p.
A Sranan-Dutch-English dictionary, including separate lists of botanical and geographical names.

Sarnami

392   **Hindi woordenboek (Hindi-Nederlands).** (Hindi dictionary [Hindi-Dutch].)
J. H. Adhin.   Paramaribo: Vidya Pustak-Sadan, 1953. 194p.
A Hindi-Dutch dictionary originally intended for individuals with a knowledge of Hindi who want to improve their command of the Dutch language.

393   **Sarnami: a living language.**
Theo Damsteegt.   In: *Language transplanted: the development of overseas Hindi.* Edited by Richard K. Barz, Jeff Siegel. Wiesbaden, FRG: Otto Harrassowitz, 1988, p. 95-120.
A discussion of the development of Sarnami and some of its morphological characteristics. The article is based on literary prose and non-literary texts from the Netherlands and Suriname. Tape-recorded conversations and interviews supplement the texts used. The author compares his findings to data on the other varieties and dialects of overseas Hindi.

394   **Sarnami verbs in – I(Y)A-.**
Theo Damsteegt.   In: *Deyadharma: studies in memory of Dr. D. C. Sircar.* Edited by G. Bhattacharya. Delhi: Sri Satguru, 1986, p. 129-36.
The author presents an alphabetical list of Sarnami verbs containing the element -ta- or -iya-. From this list it is clear that the -i(y)a- verb in Sarnami is a living category of verbs, which even comprises denominatives from Sranan loanwords.

395 **Ká hál. Leerboek Sarnami, Surinaams Hindostaans.** (What is
happening? Sarnami, Surinamese Hindustani textbook.)
Theo Damsteegt, Jit Narain. The Hague: Nederlands Bibliotheek en
Lektuur Centrum, 1987. 154p. bibliog.

A grammar consisting of thirty-two lessons and an appendix in which the solutions to
the assignments are provided, thus making this volume suitable for self-study. Also
included is a Sarnami-Dutch and Dutch-Sarnami word list.

396 **Soeroe se soeroe kar: an audio-visual course in Sarnami Hindustani for
beginners.**
Annie B. Huiskamp. Paramaribo: Summer Institute of Linguistics,
1978, 1980. 2 vols. (Languages of the Guianas, II and IV).

This two-volume course in Sarnami is based on *First things first*, an English audio-
visual course. The first part consists of twenty lessons, each one beginning with a set of
phonology drills. These are followed by dialogues and texts. Repetition drills and
pattern drills conclude each lesson. The second part consists of lessons twenty-one
through thirty-six. Both volumes include a word index, grammatical comments, a
grammatical index, and English translations of the dialogue of each lesson and of the
word index.

397 **Distinctive features in Sarnami Hindustani.**
George L. Huttar, Judith A. Eslick. *Phonetica*, no. 25 (1972), p. 108-
18. bibliog.

The authors describe the systematic phonemes of Sarnami in terms of their distinctive
features. They suggest the necessity of a distinction between primary phonetic (such as
consonantal and vocalic) features and primary phonemic (such as syllabic) features.
Finally, Huttar and Eslick briefly describe marginal phonemes of Sarnami, reflecting
characteristics of the Hindi spoken in India. The article includes abstracts in German
and in French.

398 **Het ontstaan van het Sarnami.** (The origin of Sarnami.)
Sita Kishna. In: *De talen van Suriname: achtergronden en
ontwikkelingen.* Edited by Eddy Charry, Geert Koefoed, Pieter
Muysken, Sita Kishna. Muiderberg, The Netherlands: Dick Coutinho,
1983, p. 67-92. map. bibliog.

A number of Hindi dialects from India form the basis of Sarnami. In this article the
author provides information on the history of Sarnami, therefore placing this language
in an historical as well as in an historical-linguistic context.

399 **The recipient state construction in Sarnami.**
Sita Kishna. In: *Perspectives on Functional Grammar.* Edited by Teun
Hoekstra, Harry van der Hulst, Michael Moortgat. Dordrecht, The
Netherlands: Foris, 1981, p. 135-56. bibliog.

A description of the so-called dative construction or dative-subject construction in
Sarnami within the framework of the theory of functional grammar. The paper is
divided into three parts. The first one discusses the subject function in Sarnami. Part
two focuses on the recipient state construction, in which the author analyses the

construction from the point of view of functional grammar. The final section contains a summary and some conclusions.

400 **Sarnami byakaran. Een elementaire grammatica van het Sarnami.**
(Sarnami grammar. A basic grammar of Sarnami.)
R. M. Marhé.   Leidschendam, The Netherlands: Stichting voor
Surinamers, 1985. 165p. maps. bibliog.

A popular Sarnami grammar including a short introduction to the British Indians and their language and culture. The appendices contain folk-tales in Sarnami with translations in Dutch as well as a summary of the eleventh and twelfth chapters of the *Bhagavad Gita*.

401 **Sarnami Hindi: een eenvoudige handleiding.** (Sarnami Hindi: a simple
primer.)
Utrecht, The Netherlands: Stichting Landelijke Federatie van
Welzijnsstichtingen, 1977. 66p.

An introduction to the grammar of Sarnami.

Surinamese-Javanese

402 **Het Surinaams-Javaans: een introduktie.** (Surinamese-Javanese: an
introduction.)
Hein Vruggink.   *Oso*, vol. 4, no. 1 (May 1985), p. 53-62. bibliog.

An introduction to the Surinamese-Javanese language. The author briefly describes the history of the Javanese in Suriname and then compares Surinamese-Javanese to Indonesian Javanese. He looks at the influence of Sranan, Dutch, and Bahasa Indonesia and finally discusses the (endangered) position of Surinamese-Javanese. In the same issue, Vruggink also studies the spelling of Surinamese-Javanese.

403 **Styles of speech in Suriname-Javanese.**
Clare Selgin Wolfowitz.   PhD dissertation, Johns Hopkins University,
Baltimore, Maryland, 1983. 320p. bibliog. (Available from University
Microfilms International, Ann Arbor, Michigan, order no. 84-14304).

An analysis of the style system of spoken Surinamese-Javanese against the background of the Javanese system of lexical variation and the existing universalistic models of politeness coding. Surinamese-Javanese is seen as encoding a speaker's choice between two mutually contrastive politeness styles: close and distant politeness. A mediating option is identified as the respect style, containing elements of closeness as well as distance. This detailed description also includes such purely linguistic phenomena as intonation patterns, lexical variation, pronominal substitution, and phonological patterning.

Chinese

404 **De Hakka's van Suriname. Aspecten van het verbale systeem van hun taal.** (The Hakka's of Suriname. Aspects of the verbal system of their language.)
Helen Chang, H. Ch. Eersel, William L. Man A Hing.   *Oso*, vol. 7, no. 1 (May 1988), p. 77-96. map.

The authors discuss the language(s) spoken by the Hakka's or Han-Chinese. Hakka is the dialect most frequently spoken by the descendants of Chinese contractants in Suriname. The Hakka spoken in Suriname differs from the Hakka used in China. Helen Chang describes the spelling and the grammar of the Surinamese forms of Hakka.

Surinamese-Dutch

405 **Woordenboek van het Surinaams-Nederlands.** (Dictionary of Surinamese-Dutch.)
Johannes van Donselaar.   Muiderberg, The Netherlands: Dick Coutinho, 1989. 482p. bibliog.

This dictionary is a significantly revised and updated version of the 1976-77 edition of the same name (q.v.). Surinamese-Dutch is a variant of Dutch which developed in Suriname among the Dutch colonists. This language varies in all linguistic aspects from the Dutch used in the Netherlands. The number of entries increased from 1,400 in the original edition to 6,600. The book is divided into several chapters, which discuss the nature of Surinamese-Dutch; its spelling and pronunciation; and the methods used to compile the list.

406 **Woordenboek van het Surinaams-Nederlands: een geannoteerde lijst van Surinaams-Nederlandse woorden en uitdrukkingen.** (Dictionary of Surinamese-Dutch: an annotated list of Surinamese-Dutch words and expressions.)
Johannes van Donselaar.   Utrecht, The Netherlands: Instituut A. W. de Groot voor Algemene Taalwetenschap van de Rijksuniversiteit te Utrecht, 1976. 232p. bibliog.

The Dutch spoken by the inhabitants of Suriname differs from the Dutch spoken in the Netherlands, the main differences being found in vocabulary, grammar, syntax, and pronunciation. The author collected 1,400 words and expressions which are used by the Surinamese, but not by the inhabitants of the Netherlands. He traces the etymology of these words and gives quotations in which the words are used.

407   **Het Nederlands in Suriname.** (The Dutch language in Suriname.)
Eva Essed-Fruin.   *Ons Erfdeel*, vol. 33, no. 1 (1990), p. 52-61. map.
An introduction to the Dutch language as it is spoken in Suriname which differs from European Dutch in pronunciation, grammar, and vocabulary. The author identifies some problems which the Dutch language encounters in Suriname, but she is cautiously optimistic about the future of Surinamese-Dutch.

Religion

Afro-Surinamese religions

408 **Tori foe da bigin foe Anake: verslag van een messianistische beweging.**
(Story of the beginning of Anake: report of a missionary movement.)
Isaak Albitrouw, edited and introduced by Miriam Sterman, based on
a translation and transcription by Roelien van Es-Redmond.   Utrecht,
The Netherlands: Centrum voor Caraïbische Studies, Rijksuniversiteit
Utrecht, 1978. 147p. maps. bibliog. (Bronnen voor de Studie van
Bosneger Samenlevingen, 2).

Jan Voorhoeve discovered the manuscript *Tori vo dem begin vo Anakee en mora fara*
(Story of the beginning of Anake and more) in the archives of the Moravian Brethren
in Paramaribo. The author is Isaak Albitrouw, a Ndjuka who around the turn of the
century became a teacher and an evangelist. He describes a messianistic movement in
the Saramaka village of Sofieboeka (or Dombikondre as it is also known) whose
religious leader was Paulus Anake. In the introduction of this volume, Sterman
expands on the missionary activities of the Moravians among the Maroons and on both
Anake and Albitrouw. The book contains both the original manuscript in Sranan
Tongo and the Dutch translation.

409 **Bush prophetic movements: religions of despair?**
Chris de Beet, H. U. E. Thoden van Velzen.   *Bijdragen tot de Taal-,
Land- en Volkenkunde*, vol. 133, no. 1 (1977), p. 100-35. map. bibliog.

An article refuting the theory of J. Voorhoeve and H. C. van Renselaar as expounded
in their article 'Messianism and nationalism in Suriname' (q.v.). De Beet and Thoden
van Velzen argue two points. Firstly, Voorhoeve and Van Renselaar have overlooked
evidence of prophetic movements before 1880 or even prior to 1863. Secondly, for the
period after 1880, they have overestimated the prosperity of the Creoles and
disregarded the affluence of the Maroons. De Beet and Thoden van Velzen show that
these religious movements arose at a time when the Maroons were economically better
off than the Creoles.

111

410 **Perseverance of African beliefs in the religious ideas of the Bosnegers in Surinam.**
Bozena Ewa Bekier. *Hemispheres*, no. 1 (1985), p. 93-108. bibliog.
An introduction to the religious ideas of the Maroons. The author describes the causes and conditions which accounted for the fact that the present-day religion of the Surinamese Maroons has not evolved as much as the African beliefs of other slave groups in the Americas.

411 **Bonuman: een studie van zeven religieuze specialisten in Suriname.**
(Bonuman: a study of seven religious specialists in Suriname.)
Rudolf A. J. van Lier. Leiden, The Netherlands: Instituut voor Culturele Antropologie en Sociologie der Niet-Westerse volken, 1983. 132p.
A presentation and analysis of seven short biographies of Creole religious specialists. Although the author collected the material in 1949 in Paramaribo and the district of Para, it has retained its relevance to the present day. Van Lier looks at the social background of each specialist in order to determine how he became a *bonuman* and analyses the *bonuman's* relation to Christianity. Van Lier places this religious culture in its historical context.

412 **About the original religion of the Creoles in Suriname/ Iets over de oorspronkelijke godsdienst der Creolen in Suriname.**
J. Schoffelmeer. *Mededelingen van het Surinaams Museum*, no. 38 (Dec.1982), p. 6-48; no. 39 (April 1983), p. 4-65. bibliog.
A two-part article in English and Dutch exploring the conceptualization of a number of terms and factors of Afro-American religion. The author focuses on phenomena such as the polytheistic religion *Winti*, *kra* (soul), *djodjo* (guardian spirit) and *bonoe* (minister), and he reviews extant literature. The fieldwork for these essays was conducted north of Para.

413 **De macht van de fodoe-winti. Fodoe-rituelen in de winti-kultus in Suriname en Nederland.** (The power of *fodoe-winti*. *Fodoe* rituals in the *winti* cult in Suriname and the Netherlands.)
Henri J. M. Stephen. Amsterdam: Karnak, 1986. 205p.
A popular description of *fodoe* rituals, which form an important part of the *Winti* cult. The author, a psychiatric nurse, focuses on the use of black magic, symbolism, music and dance, herbs, and stones. He also discusses the social and psychological aspects of *Winti*. The book contains photographs, line drawings, and a glossary.

414 **The *obiaman* and his influence in the Moravian parish.**
Jan Voorhoeve. *Bijdragen tot de Taal-, Land- en Volkenkunde*, vol. 139, no. 4 (1983), p. 411-20.
A translation of a report on the *Winti* religion by Voorhoeve, drawn up during the years 1956-61. It was written specifically to inform the Ecclesiastical Council of the Moravian Brethren, who viewed the *Winti* religion as undesirable and 'heathen'. Voorhoeve attempts to give a more subtly shaded opinion of the different practices of this religion. His study focuses on the *obiaman*, who is prone to possession by the *obia*

winti (a god from the *Winti* pantheon) whereupon he may give patients suffering from mysterious maladies directions as to their cure.

415 Messianism and nationalism in Surinam.
Jan Voorhoeve, H. C. van Renselaar. *Bijdragen tot de Taal-, Land- en Volkenkunde*, vol. 118, no. 2 (1962), p. 193-216.

A comparison of several well-known messianic movements, such as those of Colin and Paulus Anake. The authors focus on the emergence and form of these movements, how they relate to social conditions, and the historical changes which they have undergone. This insight is evaluated in terms of a more recent cultural-nationalistic movement in Suriname which, although it has no specific religious content, is nevertheless comparable in various other aspects.

416 Evolving culture: a cross-cultural study of Suriname, West-Africa and the Caribbean.
Charles J. Wooding. Washington, DC : University Press of America, 1981. 329p. maps. bibliog.

A comprehensive and systematic description of the traditional religion *Winti*, aiming to trace the African origin of its gods. This analysis is based on a study of the gods' names as well as the terminology and institutions that have been preserved. The Surinamese data pertaining to the social and religious structure are compared with data from other Afro-American societies, thus demonstrating that the process of change has resulted in different types of structures. *Winti* is not found all over Suriname in exactly the same form. The volume includes a comparison of Sranan Tongo and West African words as well as a Sranan glossary.

417 The Winti-cult in the Para-district.
Charles J. Wooding. *Caribbean Studies*, vol. 12, no. 1 (April 1972), p. 51-78. bibliog.

An introduction to the *Winti* cult, a religion practised mainly by the Creole lower strata. In this cult the world of the gods is divided into a number of 'societies of gods' or acting creatures, who take possession of favoured human beings and punish others who do not heed them. The author discusses such themes as cult beliefs, magic and curing practices, worship and healing, and analyses the economic, sociological, and psychological effects of *Winti*.

Christian religions

418 **Surinam/Berbice: Christliche Kolonisten unter Indianern, Buschnegern und Sklaven 1735/38.** (Suriname/Berbice: Christian colonists among Indians, Bush Negroes and slaves 1735/38.)
Hartmut Beck. In: *Brüder in vielen Völkern: 250 Jahre Mission der Brüdergemeine.* Edited by Hartmut Beck. Erlangen, FRG: Verlag der Ev.-Luth. Mission, 1981, p. 72-89. map. bibliog.

A short history of the Moravian Brethren in Suriname during the 18th and 19th centuries. In 1735 the first missionaries were sent there. They, however, were not successful and three years later new groups arrived. The Moravians were soon active among the Amerindians and, after several failures, also among the Maroons and the slaves.

419 **Peerke Donders. Schering en inslag van zijn leven.** (Peerke Donders. The order of his life.)
J. L. F. Dankelman. Hilversum, The Netherlands: Gooi en Sticht, 1982. 283p. map. bibliog.

A modern 'hagiography' of Petrus (Peerke) Donders (1809-87). For forty-five years he worked as a missionary in Suriname, and then as a nurse at Batavia, a government hospital for lepers. In 1982, Pope John Paul II beatified Donders. This book is based on *45 jaar onder de tropenzon* by N. Gevers (Heerlen, The Netherlands: Joh. Roosenboom, 1946).

420 **Onderweg van afhankelijkheid naar zelfstandigheid: 250 jaar Hernhutterzending in Suriname 1735-1985.** (On the way from dependence to independence: 250 years Moravian Mission in Suriname 1735-1985.)
Edited by Jos Fontaine. Zutphen, The Netherlands: De Walburg Pers; Paramaribo: Evangelische Broedergemeente in Suriname/C. Kersten, 1985. 143p. maps.

A richly illustrated popular history of the influential Moravian Brethren in Suriname. In 1732 the first missionaries were sent to the Danish West Indies from whence they travelled to Suriname in 1735. Four years later the first missionaries got the order to work among the Amerindians. These first activities were not successful. Missionary work among Paramaribo slaves commenced in 1754, while the Maroons were not approached until 1765. Twenty years later the Moravians worked the plantations on a regular basis. In the 20th century the Moravians have also focused their activities on the Asian population groups.

421 **The Dutch Reformed Church and negro slavery in colonial America.**
Gerald Francis de Jong. *American Society of Church History*, vol. 40, no. 4 (1971), p. 423-36.

An examination of the attitude of the Dutch Reformed Church toward the slave trade and the use of slave labour in the American colonies. The author argues that the Church in the Americas showed little concern about slavery as an evil system. For example, the Reverend Johannes Basseliers, who served the Church in Suriname from 1668 to 1684, acquired a large sugar plantation which he worked with slave labour. Critics like Jan Willem Kals, whose life is described in a biography by J. M. van der Linde (q.v.), were largely voices crying in the wilderness.

422 **Secularisatie en zending in Suriname. Over het secularisatie proces in verband met het zendingswerk van de Evangelische Broedergemeente in Suriname.** (Secularization and mission in Suriname. On the process of secularization in connection with the missionary activities of the Moravian Brethren in Suriname.)
J. van Raalte. Wageningen, The Netherlands: H. Veenman, 1973. 276p. bibliog.
A discussion of the term 'secularization' as well as of secularization in the history of Suriname. The author studies the connection between this process and the missionary activities of the Moravian Brethren. The book includes a summary in German.

423 **Historische foto's van de R. K. Gemeente in Suriname.** (Historic photographs of the Roman Catholic community in Suriname.)
A. C. Schalken. Paramaribo: Leo Victor, 1983. 211p. maps.
This collection of photographs is not intended as a comprehensive illustrated history of the Roman Catholic community as photographs of many important events never existed or were destroyed or lost. This collection covers the period from the 1820s to 1982.

424 **Mission in the micro world of the southern Caribbean.**
J. M. W. Schalkwijk. *International Review of Mission*, vol. 60, no. 238 (April 1971), p. 196-205.
An overview of missionary activities in the pluralist societies of Trinidad, Guyana, and Suriname. The churches in this region have to serve people of entirely different religions, cultures, and languages.

425 **The Christian churches of Surinam.**
Joop Vernooij. *Exchange*, vol. 10, no. 29 (Sept. 1981), p. 16-31. maps. bibliog.
An analysis of the Christian churches before and after independence. When Suriname came under the authority of the colonists from the province of Zeeland, Reformed Protestantism was incorporated as the religion of the State. At present, due to the growth of the population, Christians no longer outnumber the adherents to other religions, nor is Christianity culturally dominant anymore.

426 **Indianen en kerken in Suriname; identiteit en autonomie in het binnenland.** (Amerindians and churches in Suriname; identity and autonomy in the interior.)
Joop Vernooij. Paramaribo: Stichting Wetenschappelijke Informatie, 1989. 178p. bibliog.
An historical study of the Christian churches – Moravian Brethren, Roman Catholic, and American religious sects – on the Amerindians in Suriname. The author stresses

two themes: the identity and the autonomy of the Amerindians. This publication includes an extensive introduction to the Surinamese Amerindians.

427 **Nieuwe religieuze bewegingen.** (New religious movements.)
   Joop Vernooij. *SWI Forum*, vol. 3, no. 2 (Dec. 1986-Jan. 1987),
   p. 24-46. bibliog.

A sketch of the history and the growth of religious movements in Suriname. In recent decades in particular, evangelization campaigns have gained in popularity and publicity. The author concludes that the presence of the established churches has largely determined the functioning of the new movements and sects.

428 **Cornelius Winst Blyd: the first negro presbyter in Surinam.**
   A. P. Vrede. *Journal of Negro History*, vol. 8, no. 4 (Oct. 1923),
   p. 448-53.

A brief biography of Cornelis Winst Blyd, the first black presbyter in Suriname. He was born of slave parents in 1860, and received his education at one of the Moravian mission boarding schools for boys. Later he attended a preparatory boarding school for teachers. In 1899 the Moravian Brethren appointed him as sub-preacher. Three years later Blyd was ordained to the order of deacon. He died in 1921.

Jewish religion

429 **An eighteenth-century prayer of the Jews of Surinam.**
   Z. Loker, R. Cohen. In: *The Jewish nation in Surinam.* Edited by
   R. Cohen. Amsterdam: S. Emmering, 1982, p. 74-87. bibliog.

An article based on an incomplete ten-page manuscript in Hebrew. The text contains verses from Psalms, Proverbs, Exodus, and Samuel II, as well as two quotations from Jeremiah and Isaiah. Parts of the travellers' prayer are also included. The manuscript serves as proof of the vitality of the Jewish Hebraic tradition in Suriname. The text is printed in English and in Hebrew.

Social Services, Health, and Welfare

430 **Voedingstoestand van de bosnegers van Suriname (1972-1977).**
(Nutritional status of the Maroons of Suriname [1972-1977].)
Huig den Butter.   PhD dissertation, Universiteit van Amsterdam,
1988. 235p. bibliog.

The author assesses the status of nutrition among the Maroons in Suriname. This dissertation is both a supplement to previously conducted studies, as well as an assessment of the nutritional status of populations for whom no previous data have been collected. The thesis includes a summary in English.

431 **Age, stature and weight in Surinam conscripts.**
A. B. Droogleever Fortuyn.   Amsterdam: Koninklijk Instituut voor
de Tropen, 1952. 126p. bibliog. (Mededeling C1, Afdeling Culturele en
Physische Antropologie, 44).

The author studied a total of 2,454 Surinamese conscripts with regard to their age, stature, weight, and the relations between the three. The author started collecting data in 1945, working backwards to previous years. The conscripts were divided into five groups: European, British Indian, Javanese, Chinese, and Amerindian. The results are recorded in several tables.

432 **Abnormal hemoglobins in Surinam I. Frequency among the different
ethnic groups.**
Wim Piet Gijzel, Shanti D. Adhin, Indradj Oemrawsingh.   *Surinaams
Medisch Bulletin*, vol. 2, no. 1 (Jan. 1978), p. 1-8. bibliog.

Following a review of the literature, this paper describes the results of a research project on abnormal haemoglobins in Suriname. Firstly, the authors present the outcome of a screening of the three major ethnic groups: British Indians, Creoles, and Javanese. Secondly, the preliminary results of a survey among pregnant women attending the government hospitals for delivery are mentioned. The sickle cell gene is most frequently found in Creole populations. Other abnormal haemoglobins encountered are HbC and HbE.

433 **Skinfold thickness, body measurements and age changes in Trio and Wajana Indians of Surinam.**
E. V. Glanville, R. A. Geerdink. *American Journal of Physical Anthropology*, vol. 32 (1970), p. 455-62. bibliog.

A comparison of 737 subjects of the Trio and Wayana tribes. The two tribes differ significantly in several measurements. The Wayana are heavier but tend to be shorter in stature than Trio Amerindians. The former also have longer and broader heads, even though the cephalic index of the two population groups is similar. Finally, they also differ in hair texture.

434 **De gezondheidszorg in Suriname.** (Health care in Suriname.)
Geert-Jaap Hallewas. PhD dissertation, Rijksuniversiteit Groningen, The Netherlands, 1981. 335p. maps. bibliog.

A dissertation based on fieldwork conducted in 1977 and on the experiences of the author during a four-year period when he was a physician at the hospital in Albina. He studies two problems in particular: he reviews the structure and historical development of health care in Suriname; and examines the differences in effectiveness and efficiency in health care over time and in different districts. A separate volume includes statistics on demography, financial aspects, medical personnel, and hospitals. The thesis includes summaries in English and Sranan.

435 **Optic atrophy in Suriname.**
Fred Hendrikse. PhD dissertation, Catholic University Nijmegen, The Netherlands, 1980. 191p. maps. bibliog. (Available from University Microfilms International, Ann Arbor, Michigan, order no. 80-70055).

From 1974 to 1977 the author conducted a retrospective case record study and a field study of the occurrence, forms, and aetiology of optic atrophy in Suriname, where the disease is quite common. The author found that bilateral unexplained optic atrophy is more common in Creoles and Maroons than in British Indians. It is only sporadically observed in the other population groups. Its incidence is highest in the Para and Saramacca districts, and is found as often in males as in females. This dissertation contains summaries in English, Dutch, French, and Spanish.

436 **Malaria in Surinam, a sero-epidemiological study.**
Hugo Jan van der Kaay. Meppel, The Netherlands: Krips Repro, 1975. 91p. maps. bibliog.

A dissertation (Rijksuniversiteit Leiden, the Netherlands, 1975) describing the results of the use of the so-called IHA (indirect haemagglutination) test in comparison with examination for spleen enlargement and the presence of parasitaemia. The IHA test carried out under field conditions produced equally reliable data as IHA tests carried out in a laboratory. The IHA test, therefore, can provide information supplementary to the parasitological examination for malaria and has the advantage that the results can be available within days after the blood samples have been taken.

437 **Report on a case of porphyria in Surinam.**
   G. G. Kletter, A. I. van de L'Isle. *Surinaams Medisch Bulletin*, vol. 2, no. 2 (April 1978), p. 46-54. bibliog.

A case study of an adult male Amerindian ill with acute intermittent porphyria, a disease which has not been mentioned before in the medical literature of Suriname. The authors advise the use of the Watson-Schwartz test to screen acute intermittent porphyria and discuss the treatment of the patient.

438 **Search for health among the Maroni River Caribs. Etiology and medical care in a 20th century Amerindian group in Surinam.**
   Peter Kloos. *Bijdragen tot de Taal-, Land- en Volkenkunde*, vol. 126, no. 1 (1970), p. 115-41. bibliog.

The article describes medical care in the 1960s in the Carib villages of Christiaankondre and Langamankondre. The data on which it is based were collected during fieldwork carried out during the period 1966-68. The author discusses such topics as shamanism, etiology, health, traditional methods of curing, and presents a survey of contemporary cases of illness.

439 **Ziektepreventie in een Karibendorp in Suriname.** (Preventive medicine in a Carib village in Suriname.)
   Anja Krumeich. *Bijdragen tot de Taal-, Land- en Volkenkunde*, vol. 145, no. 1 (1989), p. 72-86. bibliog.

A study of preventive medicine among the 300 inhabitants of the Carib village of Bigi Poika (also known as Akarani). The author discusses their religious-medical system, nutrition, and hygiene, and concludes that there exist clear similarities between the Carib and the Western view on health and preventive medicine.

440 **Ascaris lumbricoides and Trichuris trichura in rural Surinam.**
   Edwin van der Kuyp. *Surinaams Medisch Bulletin*, vol. 2, no. 2 (April 1978), p. 54-78. bibliog.

A presentation of the results of a mass anti-helminthiasis campaign in rural Suriname during the years 1956 to 1972 to eradicate the incidence of parastic worms. Of the more than 100,000 persons screened, 30.5 per cent was found to suffer from Ascaris and 6.7 per cent from Trichuris. The highest rates were found in (sub)urban areas, and among Amerindians, Maroons, and Creoles. More women than men and more children than adults were afflicted.

441 **Availability of milk and milk products in Suriname.**
   Edwin van der Kuyp. *Surinaams Medisch Bulletin*, vol. 4, no. 4 (Oct. 1982), p. 136-48.

A study of the consumption of dairy products in Suriname, where in general rather small quantities of milk and milk products are consumed. Consumption is greater in Paramaribo than in rural districts. Among the groups examined, the Javanese were found to consume the least.

442 **Bed occupancy in the Academic Hospital in Surinam in 1970-1979.**
Edwin van der Kuyp. *Surinaams Medisch Bulletin*, vol. 5, no. 3 (July 1981), p. 85-110.

The Academic Hospital Paramaribo is a general teaching hospital and contains 370 beds. This study determines which categories of patients occupy a large proportion of the beds in this hospital. The article includes fifteen tables.

443 **Contribution to the study of the malarial epidemiology in Surinam.**
Edwin van der Kuyp. Utrecht, The Netherlands: Vijlbrief, 1950. 146p. maps. bibliog.

An analysis of the Surinamese *Mosquitos*. Various surveyors have found sixteen species of Anophelines in Suriname, but only the species of the group *Nyssorhynchus* are of real importance in the transmission of malaria. Coastal malaria is transmitted by one or more species of the *Albimanus* series. Although *Aquasalis* is thought to be the most important vector of malaria in coastal areas in the Americas, this has not been proved after the analysis of the *Albimanus* series in Suriname. This dissertation (Universiteit van Amsterdam, 1950) begins with an account of the epidemiology of malaria in Suriname and includes summaries in Spanish and Dutch.

444 **Hookworm in rural Surinam.**
Edwin van der Kuyp. *Surinaams Medisch Bulletin*, vol. 2, no. 1 (Jan. 1978), p.16-39. bibliog.

A survey of the incidence of hookworm in rural Suriname. From 1956 to 1972 mass anti-helminthiasis campaigns were held, involving more than 100,000 persons. Examination of faeces revealed that the overall hookworm rate was 34.1 per cent. This rate was higher in rural areas than in (sub)urban regions. It was highest among Amerindians and Maroons, higher among males than among females, and higher among adults than among children.

445 **Surinaamse medische en paramedische kroniek, tijdvak 1494-1899.**
(Surinamese medical and paramedical chronicle, period 1494-1899.)
Edwin van der Kuyp. *Surinaams Medisch Bulletin*, vol. 9, no. 2 (March 1985), p. 1-67.

A chronological listing of all the important dates in the history of medicine of Suriname. This special issue of the *Surinaams Medisch Bulletin* contains a bibliography comprising fifty-two publications as well as a subject index.

446 **Blood group frequencies in the Netherlands, Curaçao, Surinam and New Guinea: a study in population genetics.**
Lourens Evert Nijenhuis. Amsterdam: Drukkerij Aemstelstad, 1961. 188p. maps. bibliog.

In the first chapter of this study the author summarizes the main theoretical considerations of the various blood group systems and briefly outlines the advantages of the use of blood group frequencies as anthropological markers. He gives details of the statistical methods used to analyse the results of the tests. Chapter three deals with the populations of Suriname and Curaçao. In Suriname five Afro-Surinamese populations from different parts of the country were examined. The blood group frequencies of the five differ appreciably from each other, and the author concludes that genetic drift must have played an important part in these populations. Very marked differences were also observed between four Amerindian groups from three Carib villages and a region near the southern border.

447 **Wucherias in Suriname.**
B. F. J. Oostburg. Leiden, The Netherlands: Universitaire Pers, 1974. 249p. maps. bibliog. (Acta Leidensia. Edita cura et sumptibus. Scholae medicinae tropicae. Mededelingen uit het Instituut voor Tropische Geneeskunde te Leiden, XLI).
From 1969 to 1971 the first mass filaria survey was conducted in Suriname. Approximately one-third of the population, or 120,745 individuals, were examined for this parasitic worm; in Paramaribo almost eighty per cent of the inhabitants was screened. The researchers found a drop in the percentage of persons with microfilaremia and elephantiasis when they compared their results to earlier, smaller, surveys. The author discusses the results of the mass examination in all districts. The volume includes ninety-five tables.

448 **Medical entomological aspects of the malaria problem in Surinam.**
Roy S. Panday. *Surinaams Medisch Bulletin*, vol. 3, no. 2 (March 1979), p. 52-58. map. bibliog.
The *Anopheles darlingi* mosquito is considered to be the primary vector of *Plasmodium falciparum* in Suriname. *Anopheles nuneztovari* might be a secondary vector. The breeding sites of *Anopheles darlingi* were found in low-lying areas with deep sunny swamps. The *Anopheles nuneztovari* population at Brownsweg has the same X-chromosome arrangement as the Brazilian non-vector population. Therefore, its role in malaria transmission remains obscure.

449 **Epidemiological observations in Bush Negroes and Amerindians in Surinam.**
J. D. G. Schaad. *Tropical and Geographical Medicine*, vol. 12 (1960), p. 38-46. map. bibliog.
During an expedition in 1952, undertaken in collaboration with the Public Health Office, a large number of Maroons and Amerindians were medically examined. In this article the author publishes data on the results of histoplasmin and tuberculin tests performed, and discusses the occurrence of respiratory diseases, typhoid, typhus fevers, serological syphilis reactions, splenic enlargement, and filariasis.

450 **Integration of antimalaria activities into basic health services in Suriname.**
K. Schaapveld. Dordrecht, The Netherlands: IGC Printing, 1984. 95p.
The author argues that basic health services are able to execute the present antimalaria programme at least as effectively and more economically than a specialized organization. Schaapveld maintains, however, that the existing programme will not lead to malaria eradication and therefore the eradication terminology should no longer be used, and proposes to change to a control programme. Moreover, regular residual spraying should be discontinued as no noticeable effect on the incidence of malaria can be detected. Epidemiologically, the most important conclusion is that no clear

periodicity in malaria incidence can be demonstrated, as other experts have often suggested.

451 **Anaemia in the Caribbean: its prevalence and causes.**
W. K. Simmons. *Cajanus*, vol. 18, no. 4 (1985), p. 216-36.

This article presents the available data on the prevalence of nutritional anaemia in the English-speaking Caribbean and Suriname. It is shown that pre-school children, and pregnant and lactating women are the groups affected most. The most common cause of anaemia is a deficiency of iron, probably caused by an inadequate intake accompanied by low absorbtion.

452 **Health of white settlers in Surinam.**
N. H. Swellengrebel, Edwin van der Kuyp. Amsterdam: Colonial Institute, 1940. 118p. maps. (Special Publication, LIII, Department of Tropical Hygiene, 16).

The authors address the question whether an attempt at European colonization is justifiable on hygiene grounds, and if it is, on what terms should these plans be executed. They examine health conditions during the 1930s as well as the history of previous European settlements in Suriname, starting with the Portuguese Jewish colonization in the 17th century. Although dated, this book provides a useful overview of the medical history of European settlers in Suriname.

453 **Een fysisch-anthropologisch onderzoek van de gebitten van vier Surinaamse bevolkingsgroepen.** (A physical anthropological study of the dentition of four Surinamese population groups.)
Peter Paul Taverne. PhD dissertation, Rijksuniversiteit Groningen, The Netherlands, 1980. 205p. bibliog.

In 1971, data were collected to conduct an anthropological study of the dentition of Creoles, Amerindians, Javanese, and British Indians. These data included dental casts as well as information regarding the diet and the health status of the individuals studied. The author uses this information to describe the condition of and the symmetry within the dentition and to analyse differences caused by race, gender, and age. This thesis includes a summary in English.

454 **Intestinal parasites in Amerindians of the interior of Surinam.**
W. J. Terpstra. PhD dissertation, Rijksuniversiteit Leiden, The Netherlands, 1972. 120p. map. bibliog.

The main objective of this study was to examine human stool specimens for *Isospora homines* and dogs' stools for similar sporocysts. This cross-secctional survey was conducted among four groups of Amerindians in 1965. The author obtained evidence against the hypothesis that the sporocysts found in humans and dogs were identical. It was presumed that in the Amerindian situation, in which contact between dogs and hummans is intensive, cross-infections were inevitable. The study aimed to detect as many parasites species as possible.

Politics

General

455 **Jagernath Lachmon: een politieke biografie.** (Jagernath Lachmon: a
political biography.)
Evert Azimullah.   Paramaribo: Vaco Press, 1987. 314p. bibliog.
A biography, at times verging on hagiography, of one of the most influential politicians
ever in Suriname. Lachmon (b. 1916) has been a leader in the VHP (*Vooruitstrevende
Hervormings Partij*, Progressive Reformational Party) since the Second World War.

456 **Movimientos populares y partidos políticos en Surinam.** (Popular
movements and political parties in Suriname.)
Arthur J. Ten Berge, Glenn B. Sankatsing.   *Revista Mexicana de
Sociología*, vol. 43, no. 2 (April-June 1981), p. 679-90.
The authors discuss popular movements and political parties in the history of
Suriname. In the first section, they focus attention on these movements during the
period prior to the Second World War, in particular on the escape of the Maroons to
the interior and the political activities of Anton de Kom. The second part treats the
social and political developments since 1945. In the final section, the authors call for
radical change in the then existing democratic structure with its electoral fraud,
corruption, and nepotism.

457 **Surinam's road from self-government to sovereignty.**
Maarten Bos.   *Netherlands Yearbook of International Law* , vol. 7
(1976), p. 131-55.
Following a brief political history, the author focuses on the constitutional
developments since 1972. In that year a Royal Commission was created to prepare
alternatives to the then existing constitutional relationship between the Netherlands,
Suriname, and the Netherlands Antilles. Once independence for Suriname was agreed
upon the major issues receiving attention were development cooperation, nationality,

123

and immigration. The author concludes that Suriname's achievement of sovereignty was prepared in an orderly manner. An off-print of this article is published in *Mededelingen Stichting Surinaamse Musea* 25/26 (1978).

458 **Onafhankelijkheid en parlementair stelsel in Suriname. Hoofdlijnen voor een nieuw en democratisch staatsbestel.** (Independence and parliamentary system in Suriname. Outline for a new and democratic government.)
Hugo K. Fernandes Mendes. Zwolle, The Netherlands: W. E. J. Tjeenk Willink, 1989. 326p. bibliog.

The central themes of this dissertation (Rijksuniversiteit Leiden, the Netherlands, 1989) are the origins, development, and functioning of the parliamentary system. The author pays detailed attention to the way in which independence was attained as well as to the constitution of 1975. He analyses the workings of the parliamentary system to shed light on its malfunctioning in order to formulate a number of principles for a new organization of the State. In two appendices the texts of the constitutions of 1975 and 1987 are published. This thesis is based on government papers and reports, archival sources, and secondary literature. It includes a summary in English.

459 **The politics of Surinam and the Netherlands Antilles.**
Albert J. Gastmann. Rio Piedras, Puerto Rico: Institute of Caribbean Studies, University of Puerto Rico, 1968. 185p. bibliog. (Caribbean Monograph Series, 3).

Based on his dissertation (Columbia University, New York, 1964. Available from University Microfilms International, Ann Arbor, Michigan, order no. 67-16028), the author analyses the political and constitutional development of the relationship between the Netherlands, the Netherlands Antilles, and Suriname. The author discusses why, in 1954 the two Caribbean territories chose to accept a union guaranteeing self-government with an equal constitutional status with the Netherlands rather than demand complete independence. He considers parliamentary democracy as an important factor contributing to the successful implementation of the *Charter of the Kingdom of the Netherlands*.

460 **The decolonization of Suriname.**
Ruben S. Gowricharn. *Caraibisch Forum*, vol. 1, no. 1 (1980), p. 18-34.

A Marxist analysis of the decolonization of Suriname. The author argues that the initiative to both the writing of the *Charter of the Kingdom* and the granting of independence came from the Dutch. Due to the slow development of the forces of production after the collapse of slavery, an independent class which was economically dominant could not develop. Moreover, the Dutch state was unwilling to create the conditions necessary for the development of the economy. Surinamese nationalism was too weak to force a breakthrough, according to Gowricharn, therefore, the impetus for decolonization could not have come from the Surinamese themselves.

461 **Staatsvorming en politieke cultuur in Suriname na de Tweede
Wereldoorlog.** (Formation of the State and political culture in Suriname
since the Second World War.)
Waldo Heilbron. *SWI Forum*, vol. 5, no. 2 (Dec. 1988), p. 59-88.
bibliog.

The central theme of this essay is the influence of 'foreign' institutions on the
administrative structure in post-war Suriname. The author argues that foreign
economic and political influences have caused such problems as corruption and the
establishment of the spoils system, and nepotism.

462 **Surinam and the Antilles: a new perspective.**
Embert Hendrickson. *The World Today* (June 1984), p. 261-68.

The author examines the politics, political parties, and leadership of Suriname and the
Netherlands Antilles in the period 1954-83. In Suriname, the racial chasm between the
two largest ethnic groups, British Indians and Creoles, characterized the political scene
up to 1980. An exception was the period 1958-67, when Creole leader J. Pengel and his
British Indian counterpart J. Lachmon forged an alliance. After the 1980 military
coup, D. Bouterse soon emerged as the dominant figure. The author severely
questions the political outlook for Bouterse, who lacks any significant popular base,
and whose main political ideology is said to be staying in power, while bloody purges
of the opposition have tarnished his image.

463 **Een gewezen wingewest: Suriname voor en na de staatsgreep.** (A former
colony: Suriname before and after the *coup d'état.*)
Rudie Kagie. Bussum, The Netherlands: Het Wereldvenster, 1980.
222p.

An analysis of the causes of the military *coup d'état* of 1980. The author, a well-known
journalist, describes the first five years of independence, which did not bring the
prosperity the Surinamese had hoped for. The population did not really profit from the
injection of Dfl. 3.2 billion in development aid and the military régime raised their
expectations by promising to turn things around fast.

464 **The impact of political events on a research project.**
André J. F. Köbben. In: *Adaptation of migrants from the Caribbean
in the European and American metropolis.* Edited by Humphrey E.
Lamur, Johan Dirk Speckmann. Amsterdam: Department of
Anthropology and Non-Western Sociology of the University of
Amsterdam; Leiden, The Netherlands: Department of Caribbean
Studies, Royal Institute of Linguistics and Anthropology, 1975,
p. 184-90.

The author shares his experiences concerning politically sensitive fieldwork conducted
in a charged atmosphere. In this short paper, Köbben discusses the impact of the
approach of independence on a project researching the causes and consequences of
Surinamese migration to the Netherlands.

465 **Anders maakt het leven je dood. De dreigende verdwijning van de Staat Suriname.** (Otherwise life kills you. The imminent disappearance of the State of Suriname.)
Rudi F. Kross.   Groningen, Purmerend, The Netherlands: Muuses, 1987. 144p.

Journalist Kross sketches the background to the current developments in Suriname. He formed part of the administration during the early years of the military régime, but became disillusioned with the administrative and economic chaos as well as the violation of human rights. This book is a passionate plea for change and cooperation in order to save the country.

466 **Onvoltooid verleden. De dekolonisatie van Suriname en de Nederlandse Antillen.** (Unfinished past. The decolonization of Suriname and the Netherlands Antilles.)
Kees Lagerberg.   Tilburg, The Netherlands: Instituut voor Ontwikkelingsvraagstukken, Katholieke Universiteit Brabant, 1989. 265p. maps. bibliog. (Monografie, 40).

The author questions whether Suriname and the Dutch Antillean islands are viable as autonomous states. He studies geographical and political factors to determine whether decolonization has a chance. In the first chapter he discusses the colonization of the Dutch Caribbean. The second one focuses on the decolonization of Suriname. Following a treatise on the Dutch Caribbean islands, the concluding chapter emphasizes the interdependence between the Netherlands and its (former) territories in the Caribbean.

467 **Insurrection and redemocratization in Suriname?: the ascendancy of the 'third path'.**
Scott B. MacDonald.   *Journal of Interamerican Studies and World Affairs*, vol. 30, no. 1 (1988), p. 105-32. bibliog.

This article casually examines Suriname's redemocratization and is based solely on secondary sources in English. The author suggests that the rebel insurgency led by Ronnie Brunswijk helped push the return to democratic government, but the major impetus came from civilian political groups that remained within the political system and who promoted a peaceful transition of power. According to the author, the political parties have provided a 'third path' from authoritarianism and near civil war.

468 **Post-koloniale staat, militair regime en herdemocratisering in Suriname.** (Post-colonial state, military régime and redemocratization in Suriname.)
Jack Menke.   *SWI Forum*, vol. 5, no. 1 (June 1988), p. 9-46. bibliog.

An analysis of the formation of the State in Suriname during the period 1975-88. The author pays attention to internal factors such as class structure and ethnicity as well as to external forces. Menke emphasizes the period of the military régime, the process of redemocratization, and the prospects of the elected government. The final pages of this essay are devoted to Suriname's position in the world. The author suggests that strengthening bilateral relations with other Latin American and Caribbean countries might be Suriname's best option.

469 **The Surinamese society in transition: a test-case on constituencies in values and goals in a Caribbean society.**
Betty Sedoc-Dahlberg. In: *Politics, public administration and rural development in the Caribbean.* Edited by Hans F. Illy. Munich, Cologne, FRG; London: Weltforum Verlag, 1983, p. 137-69. bibliog.
An analysis of the process of social change after two years of revolution. The author offers a fragmentary historical overview of the parliamentary democratic system and the patterns of reaction among the population relevant to politics, policymaking, and decision making.

470 **De Brunswijk-opstand: antropologische kanttekeningen bij de Surinaamse burgeroorlog.** (The Brunswijk rebellion: anthropological notes to the civil war in Suriname.)
H. U. E. Thoden van Velzen. *De Sociologische Gids*, vol. 35, no. 3 (May-June 1988), p. 212-36. bibliog.
An anthropological analysis of the guerrilla forces in the interior of Suriname. The author discusses the origins of the 'Jungle Commando' led by Ronnie Brunswijk, focuses on the question why large segments of the Maroon population became involved in the struggle against the National Army and analyses the religious context, in particular the influence of the main cults on the war.

Ethnicity and pluralism

471 **The development of pluralism in Surinam.**
M. H. Alers. *Plural Societies*, vol. 4, no. 3 (autumn 1973), p. 53-65. bibliog.
The author states that no genuine patriotism or national pride can exist in a pluralist society. As every population group in Suriname promotes its own interests, and each group has a different position in society, the basis for national integration is very small.

472 **Hindoestanen in de politiek. Een vergelijkende studie van hun posities in Trinidad, Guyana en Suriname.** (Hindustanis in politics. Comparative research into their positions in Trinidad, Guyana and Suriname.)
Chandersen E. S. Choenni. Rotterdam, The Netherlands: Futile, 1982. 150p. bibliog.
An analysis of the role played by ethnicity in the political processes in Suriname, Trinidad, and Guyana. The author argues that the British Indians form an exclusive population group due to historical, economic, social, cultural, and racial reasons.

Politics. Ethnicity and pluralism

473 **Anti-consociationalism and independence in Surinam.**
Edward Dew. *Boletín de Estudios Latinoamericanos y del Caribe*,
no. 21 (Dec. 1976), p. 3-15.
Following the model of political scientist Arend Lijphart, the author examines the
working of the consociational régime in Suriname. This is a government representing
the political leaders of the principal ethnic groups, which best serves the stability of the
plural society because it overcomes racial divisions. Dew argues that between 1949
and 1973 consociationalism proved to be successful in Suriname. Since 1973, however,
anti-consociationalism caused major tensions between Creoles and British Indians,
particularly during the heated debates on independence. Eventually, consociationalism
within the two mass parties contributed to the return of the former social equilibrium
in the country.

474 **Apanjaht and revolution in Caribbean politics: the case of Suriname.**
Edward Dew. In: *The Caribbean after Grenada. Revolution, conflict,
and democracy.* Edited by Scott B. MacDonald, Harald M. Sandstrom,
Paul B. Goodwin, Jr. New York; Westport, Connecticut; London:
Praeger, 1988, p. 127-37.
A brief analysis of Surinamese politics, which is based on pluralism and *apanjaht* or the
practice of voting for ones own race. For twenty years, until the *coup d'état* of 1980,
apanjaht consociationalism functioned successfully. The author compares developments
in Suriname with those in other Caribbean countries, notably Guyana, Trinidad, and
Grenada.

475 **The difficult flowering of Surinam; ethnicity and politics in a plural
society.**
Edward Dew. The Hague: Martinus Nijhoff, 1978. 234p. bibliog.
This political history of Suriname focuses on the emergence of the Creole, British
Indian, and Javanese political parties in the 1940s and traces their interrelations up to
1975. Dew demonstrates that ethnic politics in this plural society did not degenerate
into dictatorship or anarchism because the political leaders were aware of the necessity
of consociational, or cross cultural, governing coalitions. Besides offering a thorough
political analysis, this study also contains extensive and detailed information on the
contemporary history of Suriname. This in particular marks Dew's book as a most
valuable contribution to Surinamese politics.

476 **Ethnic fragmentation and politics: the case of Surinam.**
Peter Dodge. *Political Science Quarterly*, vol. 81, no. 4 (Dec. 1966),
p. 593-601.
Using the example of Suriname the author suggests that ethnic pluralism, rather than
the destruction of societal integration, may under some circumstances lead to the
establishment of a political consensus. This would be based upon the fragmentation of
the ethnic segments produced in the process of competition for political clientele as
well as on mutual fears of group domination.

477 **De persistentie van etniciteit in de Surinaamse politiek; enkele sociaal-historische notities.** (The persistence of ethnicity in Surinamese politics; some social-historical notes.)
Harold Jap A Joe. *SWI Forum*, vol. 5, no. 1 (June 1988), p. 47-58. bibliog.
Ethnicity and social stratification are the two explanatory factors in this analysis of Surinamese political development during the period 1948-88. The election results of 1987 show that ethnicity remains the dominant political factor and that the existing social stratification has not been altered.

478 **Democracy in plural societies: a comparative exploration.**
Arend Lijphart. New Haven, Connecticut; London: Yale University Press, 1977. 248p. bibliog.
In this comparative study, the author analyses and advocates consociational democracy, that is a government by a grand coalition of the political leaders of all of the communities into which the society is divided. He proposes this type of government for Third World countries in particular since sharp ethnic and other cleavages plague so many of them. Lijphart discusses political developments in Lebanon, Malaysia, Suriname, and the Netherlands Antilles to demonstrate that the consociational model offers more hope for democracy than other models.

The military régime

479 **De Decembermoorden in Suriname. Verslag van een ooggetuige. Met een nawoord van drs. H. Chin A Sen.** (The December murders in Suriname. Report by an eyewitness. With an epilogue by drs. H. Chin A Sen.)
Anonymous. Bussum, The Netherlands: Het Wereldvenster, 1983. 77p.
A gripping account of the death of Major Roy Horb, found dead in his prison cell in February 1983, and of the 'December murders' of 1982. The author accuses Desi Bouterse and Prime Minister Errol Alibux of masterminding this liquidation of fifteen members of the opposition. Trade union leader Cyrill Daal is said to have been executed by Bouterse himself. In an afterword the former Surinamese president Henk Chin A Sen briefly discusses the characteristics of the dictatorship in Suriname at that time.

480 **Back to the barracks? Five years 'revo' in Suriname.**
Gary Brana-Shute. *Journal of Interamerican Studies and World Affairs*, vol. 28, no. 1 (spring 1986), p. 93-121.
A review of the first five years of the military régime (1980-85). Central to this essay is the question whether Suriname will return to democracy with the introduction of a new constitution and free elections. The author thinks that the chance of the military returning to their barracks is slim. According to Brana-Shute, commander Desi Bouterse 'follows the ideology that keeps him in power'.

481 **Surinam: politics, economics and society.**
   Henk E. Chin, Hans Buddingh'. London, New York: Frances Pinter,
   1987. 192p. bibliog. (Marxist Regimes Series).
The authors give, at the outset, an overview of the history and political traditions of
Suriname. Having provided this essential background information, they then analyse
developments since the military *coup d' état* of 1980. The heart of the work deals with
the economy and with politics during the military régime, which was never Marxist,
even though the title of the series implies that it was. Small Leftist-revolutionary
groups did indeed see their opportunity to promote their ideas with the 'Revolution of
1980', but their influence remained weak and they never enjoyed any widespread
popular support. The authors conclude that the analyses made by the Left were
oversimplified and too rigid for a society as complex as Suriname.

482 **Suriname tar baby: the signature of terror.**
   Edward Dew. *Caribbean Review*, vol. 12, no. 1 (1983), p. 4-7; 34.
   map.
A brief analysis of political developments in the year 1982, which culminated in the
'December murders': the execution of fifteen members of the opposition. The author
argues that paranoia is the best explanation for the behaviour of Desi Bouterse and his
supporters.

483 **Suriname: de la révolution des sergents au retour de la démocratie.**
   (Suriname: from the revolution by the sergeants to the return of
   democracy.)
   Yolande van Eeuwen. *Problèmes d'Amerique Latine*, no. 91 (1st
   Trim. 1989), p. 25-46. map. bibliog.
One of the few recent publications in French on Suriname, this article gives an
overview of political developments from the Second World War to 1988, with an
emphasis on the period of the military régime (1980-87). Unfortunately, the essay is
exceedingly superficial and is riddled with errors in the spelling of the names of
politicians and political parties in particular.

484 **Suriname: military threat and the restoration of democracy.**
   Hugo K. Fernandes Mendes. *Internationale Spectator*, vol. 43, no. 11
   (Nov. 1989), p. 662-68. bibliog.
The author was an officer in the army of Suriname from 1975 to 1980 and is at present
a legal scholar. He describes the developments leading to the *coup d'état* of 1980. He
argues that when the army was created at independence, there was no concept of the
specific role a professional army should play, neither did any defence policy exist.
Combined with internal mismanagement this lack of purpose and guidance resulted in
the surprise *coup*. Even the return to democracy in 1987-88 did not lead to a clear
concept of the relation between the armed forces and society. Yet the author thinks a
new *coup* highly improbable because of the political division and the economic
deterioration which occurred during the time of the military régime. A similar article in
Dutch entitled 'Militair en samenleving in Suriname' (The Military and society in
Suriname) appeared in the same journal vol 43, no. 2 (Feb. 1989).

485 **De revolutie uitgegleden. Politieke herinneringen.** (The revolution
slipped. Political memoirs.)
Andre R. Haakmat.   Amsterdam: Jan Mets, 1987. 223p.

The political memoirs of 'superminister' Haakmat, who during the first year of the
military régime combined the functions of deputy prime minister and minister of
Foreign Affairs, Justice, Army and Police. He gives his view on the power game in
Paramaribo, which ultimately led to the 'December murders' of 1982 and guerrilla
warfare in east Suriname. He tells how he fled Suriname and reveals plans for an
(aborted) invasion by the United States.

486 **Class formation and class struggle in Suriname: the background and
development of the coup d'état.**
Sandew Hira.   In: *Crisis in the Caribbean.* Edited by Fitzroy
Ambursley, Robin Cohen. Kingston, Port-of-Spain, London:
Heinemann, 1983, p. 166-90.

In 1980, the army overthrew parliamentary democracy and took over power in
Suriname. Unlike the political developments in Grenada and Nicaragua, this *coup
d'état* did not prove to be the beginning of basic changes in society. According to the
author, the *coup* was directed against the 'comprador bourgeoisie', but failed to
mobilize the masses. Rapidly a new class emerged, which Hira coins the 'national
bourgeoisie'. This class has controlled the administration in Suriname since 1980.

487 **Interest groups and the military regime in Suriname.**
Betty Sedoc-Dahlberg.   In: *Militarization in the Non-Hispanic
Caribbean.* Edited by Alma H. Young, Dion E. Phillips. Boulder,
Colorado: Lynne Rienner, 1987, p. 90-111.

A rather chaotically organized article on interest groups, such as religious organizations,
labour federations, and the people's committees, and their relationship with the
military régime. In a useful appendix, the author outlines the most crucial events in
Suriname which took place between 1980 and 1985.

488 **De nacht van de revolutie: de staatsgreep in Suriname op 25 februari
1980.** (The night of the revolution: the *coup d'état* in Suriname on
February 25, 1980.)
Jozef Slagveer.   Paramaribo: C. Kersten, 1980. 208p.

Gives a description of the *coup d'état* of 1980 and its principal actors. This volume
includes interviews with Desi Bouterse and the other military insurgents. The second
part of the book contains the 'Abendanon report', which evaluated the situation in the
Surinamese army before the *coup* and played a central role in the preparation of the
take-over. The author was a journalist, who initially had enthusiastically supported
the *coup*, but was executed during the 'December murders' in 1982.

Constitution and the Legal System

489 Suriname: violations of human rights.
Amnesty International.   London: Amnesty International Publications, 1987. 19p. map.

A report outlining human rights violations perpetrated by the government of Suriname since July 1986, when a guerrilla army led by Ronnie Brunswijk began operating in the eastern part of the country. The report is based on testimonies obtained in interviews with Surinamese refugees in French Guiana. It also includes information which Amnesty International gathered detailing killings in other areas, arrests, detentions without charge, and incommunicado detention.

490 Human rights in Suriname. Report of a mission (Feb/March 1983).
Marc Bossuyt, J. Griffiths.   Geneva: International Commission of Jurists, [n.d.]. 12p.

The purpose of the International Commission of Jurists' mission was to enquire into the situation concerning the rule of law and the system of justice, which includes legal guarantees for ensuring the fair trial of suspects. The authors conclude that the deaths of fifteen members of the opposition during the 1982 'December murders' were neither 'minor' nor 'incidental', considering the number of victims in relation to the small size of the population and the country's peaceful social and political traditions prior to the *coup d'état* of 1980.

491 Jeugdrecht en jeugdbescherming in Suriname. (Child law and child protection in Suriname.)
Irma E. Loemban Tobing-Klein.   Utrecht, The Netherlands: Stichting Landelijke Federatie van Welzijnsstichtingen voor Surinamers, 1980. 255p. bibliog.

The author first provides an overview of the historical development of the law regarding children in Suriname, noting that the first children's laws and the foundation of the guardianship board date from the beginning of the 20th century. She then looks at the influences from other Caribbean countries – Jamaica in particular – and the Netherlands, the latter of which has had a great influence on Surinamese child law and child protection. She finally discusses some important international treaties in the field of child welfare legislation and child protection. A number of appendices contain the most important legal regulations for the protection of minors as well as a listing of institutions and recommendations. The book includes a summary in English.

492 **The constitutional status of the Netherlands Caribbean territories.**
J. H. A. Logeman. In: *Developments towards self-government in the Caribbean. A symposium held under the auspices of the Netherlands Universities Foundation for International Cooperation at The Hague, September 1954.* The Hague; Bandung, Indonesia: W. van Hoeve, 1955, p. 46-67.

An overview of the constitutional developments leading up to autonomy in 1954 by a former Colonial Minister. He discusses the then soon to be approved *Charter of the Kingdom of the Netherlands.* He also briefly compares the constitutional status of the Dutch colonies with developments in the British Caribbean.

493 **Onze grondwet: eenvoudige tekst en uitleg van de grondwet 1987.**
(Our constitution: simple text and explanation of the constitution of 1987.)
Coen Ooft. Paramaribo: De West, 1988. 62p.

An explanation of the new Surinamese constitution of 1987 by Coen Ooft, constitutional specialist par excellence.

494 **Report on the situation of human rights in Suriname.**
Organization of American States. Washington, DC: General Secretariat, Organization of American States, 1983. 46p. (Ser. L. / II. 61, Doc. 6 Rev. 1).

The first chapter of this report treats the regulatory and political system of Suriname. In the second one, the right to life and the right to personal integrity are discussed, followed by a chapter dealing with other human rights. The commission concludes that serious violations of important human rights, such as the right to life, the right to justice and due process, the right to free thought and expression, the freedom of association, and political rights have occurred in Suriname.

495 **Second report on the human rights situation in Suriname.**
Organization of American States. Washington DC: General Secretariat, Organization of American States, 1985. 69p. (OAS/Ser. L/V/II. 66, Doc. 21 Rev 1).

This report is a follow-up to the study published in 1983 by the Inter-American Commission on Human Rights, entitled *Report on the situation of human rights in Suriname* (q.v.). Following an invitation by the government of Suriname, the Commission visited that country in January 1985. In the light of information received then and of the subsequent events during that year, the Commission concluded that the Surinamese government continued to violate a number of fundamental human rights as established in the American Declaration of the Rights and Duties of Man.

496 **West Indisch Plakkaatboek onder redaktie van J. A. Schiltkamp en J. Th. de Smidt. Plakkaten, ordonnantiën en andere wetten, uitgevaardigd in Suriname, I 1667-1761; II 1761-1816.** (West Indian book of edicts edited by J. A. Schiltkamp and J. Th. de Smidt. Edicts, ordinances and other laws, promulgated in Suriname, I 1667-1761; II 1761-1816.)
J. Th. de Smidt, T. van der Lee. Amsterdam: S. Emmering, 1973. 1423p. map. bibliog. (Werken der Vereeniging tot Uitgaaf der Bronnen van het Oud-Vaderlandsche Recht, derde reeks, 21).

An indispensable book listing all edicts, decrees, and other laws issued in Suriname between 1667 and 1816. Volume one contains an introduction to the legal administration in Suriname and lists all primary and secondary sources used. Volume two includes indexes on subjects, persons, and geographical names.

497 **Strafrecht in Suriname.** (Criminal law in Suriname.)
Meindert Rutgert Wijnholt. Deventer, The Netherlands: Kluwer, 1965. 221p. bibliog.

A history of criminal law in Suriname before independence (1975). In the first chapter of this thesis (Rijksuniversiteit Groningen, the Netherlands, 1965) the author discusses the indigenous customary law of the Maroons. The second chapter deals with the history of Western criminal law in Suriname since 1667 and includes the complete text of *Criminelle en Penale Wetten ende Ordonnantien*, the oldest penal laws of 1669, and closes with the making of the penal codes of 1869 and 1916. In the third chapter, Wijnholt reviews the action of Western criminal law in a non-Western society. The last chapter discusses the general regulations of the penal code in Suriname and the articles that differ from the corresponding Dutch regulations in particular. The dissertation includes a brief summary in English.

498 **De Surinaamse huwelijkswetgeving in historisch en maatschappelijk perspectief.** (Surinamese marriage law and its historical and social background.)
Johannes Antonie Zevenbergen. Deventer, The Netherlands: Kluwer, 1980. 197p. bibliog.

A dissertation (Rijksuniversiteit Leiden, the Netherlands, 1980) tracing the history of the current marriage law of Suriname. Dutch colonial policy aimed to achieve legal uniformity in concordance with Dutch law. In 1940 Governor J. C. Kielstra legalized both Hindu and Muslim marriages. In 1973 a new marriage law was introduced, yet cohabitation or concubinage still lacked a legal basis. The author recommends that common-law marriage, which is socially accepted, is given a place in the legal system. The volume includes a summary in English.

Foreign Relations

499 **De revolutie van de sergeanten: getuigenis van mijn werk als residerend ambassadeur van Cuba.** (The revolution of the sergeants: witness account of my work as residing ambassador of Cuba.)
Osvaldo Cardenas. Nijmegen, The Netherlands: Studiecentrum voor Vredesvraagstukken, 1986. 89p. (Dosschrift, 20).

A diary by Osvaldo Cardenas, Cuban ambassador to Suriname from 1982 to 1983. This was a chaotic period, encompassing the 'December murders', when fifteen members of the opposition were killed, as well as the death of Maurice Bishop and the subsequent US invasion of Grenada which led to a break in official relations between Cuba and Suriname. The book starts with a visit three weeks after the *coup d'état* of 1980 and ends with 'the great treason' (the break in the good relations with Cuba) and a brief analysis of the developments until early 1984.

500 **Suriname na de Kamerverkiezingen van mei 1986.** (Suriname after the parliamentary elections of May 1986.)
G. Doeve. *Internationale Spectator*, vol. 39, no. 12 (Dec. 1985), p. 733-41.

An active Social-Democrat, Doeve discusses the relationship between the Netherlands and Suriname after the Dutch parliamentary elections of 1986. He questions whether the policy to isolate the military régime is effective and argues that gradual re-establishment of political and economic ties is in the long-term interest of both the Netherlands and the population in Suriname. A short summary in English is included.

501 **De bevroren ontwikkelingsrelatie tussen Nederland en Suriname.** (The frozen development relations between the Netherlands and Suriname.)
Paul van Gelder. *Internationale Spectator*, vol. 39, no. 12 (Dec. 1985), p. 742-48. bibliog.

The suspension of the agreement on bilateral development cooperation after the 'December murders' of 1982 has shown Suriname's economic dependency on the

135

Netherlands. The author argues that at this time of true decolonization in Suriname the terms of this agreement need to be fundamentally changed. A short summary in English is included.

502 **The Dutch Caribbean and its metropolis.**
Harry Hoetink.   In: *Patterns of foreign influence in the Caribbean.*
Edited by Emanuel de Kadt. London, New York, Toronto: Oxford University Press, 1972, p. 103-20.

A concise introduction to Suriname, with emphasis on the period after 1945, written before Suriname had attained its independence. The author concludes that the relationship between Suriname and the Netherlands is based on a mixture of moral motives, self-interest, and vague notions of historical solidarity.

503 **Brazil and the Caribbean.**
Mirlande Manigat.   In: *The Caribbean and world politics: cross currents and cleavages.* Edited by Jorge Heine, Leslie Manigat. New York, London: Holmes & Meier, 1988, p. 262-74. bibliog.

The Caribbean has traditionally been at the lower end of Brazilian foreign policy priorities. But in the 1980s this changed, heralding a period of close involvement associated with developments in Cuba, Guyana, and Suriname. Brazil has perceptibly increased its bilateral contacts with the latter, offering Suriname different forms of agricultural, industrial, and military assistance since the *coup d'état* of 1980. According to the author, the main Brazilian concern was to limit or even completely eliminate Cuban influence in Suriname by offering a reliable alternative.

504 **Money talks, morals vex. The Netherlands and the decolonisation of Suriname 1975-1990.**
Peter Meel.   *European Review of Latin American and Caribbean Studies,* no. 48 (June 1990), p. 75-98. bibliog.

A fine analysis of the political and economic relations between the Netherlands and Suriname during the period 1975-90. The author focuses on the 1980s, when the military régime put these relations under severe pressure. Instead of continuing the existing bilateral treaty Meel proposes the adoption of a multilateral approach.

505 **Internationalisatie van ontwikkelingshulp. Beschouwingen over politiek-economische aspecten van internationalisatie en de gevolgen voor ontwikkelingslanden.** (Internationalization of development aid. Reflections on political and economic aspects of internationalization and the consequences for developing countries.)
Edited by Jack Menke.   Paramaribo: Stichting Wetenschappelijke Informatie, 1988. 55p. bibliog.

This booklet considers new trends, in particular internationalization, in the allocation of foreign aid and the consequences for developing countries such as Suriname. Martin Schalkwijk, Fred Derby, and Jack Menke all discuss the relations between the Netherlands and Suriname since the latter country's independence in 1975. The agreement between the Kingdom of the Netherlands and the Republic of Suriname regarding development cooperation of 1975 is published in an appendix.

506   **Aid and dependence: the case of Suriname. A study in bilateral aid relations.**
Baijah Hunderson Philip Mhango.   Paramaribo: Stichting Wetenschappelijke Informatie, 1984. 168p. map. bibliog.
A case study of the bilateral aid relationship between the Netherlands and Suriname during the period 1975-82. Upon Suriname's attainment of independence in 1975 a bilateral aid agreement was signed guaranteeing Suriname an unprecedented amount of financial aid for a period of ten to fifteen years after independence. In December 1982 the Dutch unilaterally suspended this aid agreement in protest against the gross violation of human rights in Suriname. The author argues that the aid did not have tangible benefits for the receiving economy. It only strengthened the economic and political influence of the Dutch government over its former colony.

507   **A search for understanding: patterns of conflict resolution. Statements and papers relating to recent developments Guyana/Venezuela relations and Guyana/Surinam relations.**
Ministry of External Affairs.   Georgetown: Ministry of External Affairs, 1970. 34p.
In 1970, Guyana and Suriname concluded an agreement to solve the controversies concerning their frontiers. This booklet presents two communiqués of talks between the Prime Minister of Guyana, L. F. S. Burnham, and his Surinamese colleague, J. Sedney, held respectively in April and in June 1970.

508   **The border conflict between Suriñam and Guiana: a legal research.**
F. E. M. Mitrasing.   Paramaribo: C. Kersten, 1975. 36p. map.
The author gives a legal and historical analysis of the border dispute between Suriname and Guyana and concludes finally that the so-called disputed territory belongs to Suriname. This booklet is the translation of the original Dutch version *Het Surinaams-Guianees grensgeschil* (Paramaribo: C. Kersten, 1969).

509   **The Guyana/Surinam boundary dispute in international law.**
Duke E. Pollard.   In: *The Caribbean yearbook of international relations.* Edited by Leslie F. Manigat. Leiden, The Netherlands: A. W. Sijthoff; St. Augustine, Trinidad: Institute of International Relations, University of the West Indies, 1976, p. 217-52.
The author provides the historical background to and a legal analysis of the boundary dispute between Suriname and Guyana concerning the New River Triangle. He examines the merits of the respective arguments concerning the dispute through a dispassionate ascertainment of the facts and the application of generally accepted norms of international law to these facts. Pollard concludes that Suriname is precluded from contesting Guyana's entitlement to the region in question.

510   **Suriname en de Europese Gemeenschappen.** (Suriname and the European Communities.)
Marten Schalkwijk.   *SWI Forum*, vol. 4, no. 1 (June 1987), p. 9-27.

An overview of the relations between Suriname and the European Economic Community. Since its foundation the EEC has been one of the most important trading partners of Suriname. Furthermore, after the Dutch froze the bilateral aid agreement in 1982 the EEC has become the primary source of external finance.

511   **Mensenrechten en ontwikkelingshulp: testcase Suriname.** (Human rights and development aid: test case Suriname.)
Joan Philip VerLoren van Themaat.   In: *Ontwikkelingssamenwerking, hoe en waarom? Opstellen van Joan VerLoren van Themaat.* Edited by Karel Jansen, Nico Schrijver. Amsterdam: Evert Vermeer Stichting, 1989, p. 180-89.

A Social-Democrat, the author questions the intentions of the Dutch government when it cut off development aid following the 1982 'December murders' in Suriname. The article was previously published in *Socialisme en Democratie*, vol. 40, no. 6 (1983).

512   **The history of our borders/De geschiedenis van onze grens.**
Justus Ben Christiaan Wekker.   *Mededelingen Stichting Surinaams Museum*, nos 23/24 (June 1978), p. 31-43. maps.

An article in English and Dutch about the problems regarding the eastern and western borders of Suriname. The situation to the west was most serious, since 1970, part of the border area between Guyana and Suriname had been demilitarized. At present there is still no change in the *status quo*. Out at sea, the borders are also not yet clearly demarcated. An editorial note includes a listing of some literature and a layman's definition of some esoteric terms.

Economy

General

513 **The need for restructuring the economy of Suriname.**
Henk E. Chin. In: *The Caribbean Basin and the changing world economic structure.* Edited by Henk E. Chin. Groningen, The Netherlands: Wolters-Noordhoff, 1986, p. 89-114. bibliog.
This essay summarizes economic developments during three separate, politically determined, periods: autonomy (1954-75), independence (1975-80), and the military régime (1980-85). The high degree of dependence on Dutch aid and the fact that the key sector of the economy, the bauxite industry, is in foreign hands characterize the Surinamese economy since the Second World War. In the 1980s the economy experienced a crisis as Dutch aid was suspended because of human rights violations; revenues in the bauxite sector rapidly declined; and its low credit worthiness left Suriname with an acute shortage of foreign funds.

514 **The economy of Surinam.**
Hermann Joseph Dudler, Erhard Fürst, Michiel Hardon, Marie Henriette Lambert. *International Monetary Fund Staff Papers,* (Nov. 1971), p. 668-750. map.
A report by staff members of the IMF on the economy of Suriname during the 1950s and 1960s. The authors first discuss the structure of the economy and then go on to development planning and economic growth. The next sections deal with money, banking, and the tax system. The final chapters treat government finance and the balance of payments. The article includes summaries in Spanish and French.

515 **Economic circuits in a Surinam village.**
Richard Franke. *Nieuwe West-Indische Gids/New West Indian Guide*, vol. 48 (1971), p. 158-72.
The author explores ways in which the influence of the external market manifests itself in the economy of a Surinamese Creole village. He characterizes the village trade circuits and their interplay with the national market, and offers some speculations about the extent of changes in internal transaction modes.

516 **Werken onder de boom. Dynamiek en informele sector: de situatie in Groot-Paramaribo.** (Working under the tree. Dynamics and informal sector: the situation in Greater Paramaribo.)
Paul van Gelder. Dordrecht, The Netherlands: Foris, 1985. 244p. maps. bibliog. (Koninklijk Instituut voor Taal-, Land- en Volkenkunde Caribbean Series, 2).
One of the few studies on the informal economy in Suriname. The author analyses the labour market, the industrial sector, and political developments. In the last section, two case studies of car mechanics and furniture makers illustrate the character of the informal economy in Paramaribo. Van Gelder published an article on the same subject entitled 'Werken onder de boom: inkomensstrategieën in de informele sector in Groot-Paramaribo, Suriname' (Working under the tree: income strategies in the informal sector in Greater Paramaribo, Suriname) in *De Sociologische Gids*, vol. 13, no. 1 (1986).

517 **The State in primary export societies: the case of Suriname.**
Ruben S. Gowricharn. In: *Contemporary Caribbean: a sociological reader. vol. 1.* Edited by Susan Craig. Maracas, Trinidad: College Press, 1981, p. 283-309.
An introductory study of Suriname's (under)development from a Marxist point of view. The central argument is that the State in peripheral capitalist societies, and in primary export societies like Suriname in particular, cannot by itself be the main force in the development of the country, although it can display a certain measure of relative autonomy due to class struggle. The author concentrates on the period 1945-70.

518 **Economic and social progress in Latin America, 1989 report. Special section: savings, investment and growth.**
Inter-American Development Bank. Washington, DC : The author, 1989. 521p. bibliog.
A yearly survey of macroeconomic trends, development financing, key economic sectors, and economic integration and cooperation. Savings, investment, and growth are discussed in the second section. Country summaries are provided in part three. The section on Suriname includes seven graphs of economic indicators, a statistical profile, and a discussion of recent economic trends, economic policies, as well as an economic outlook. A statistical appendix with demographic and economic data concludes this volume.

519 **Staat, industrialisatie en technologische afhankelijkheid in Suriname 1969-1980.** (State, industrialization and technological dependency in Suriname 1969-1980.)

Satcha Jabbar. *SWI Forum*, vol. 5, no. 2 (Dec. 1988), p. 9-31. bibliog.

A discussion of the role of the State and of foreign capital in the industrial development of Suriname. According to the author the technological dependency on multinational corporations as well as on foreign consultants has impeded autonomous industrialization.

520 **Suriname, ontwikkelingsland in het Caraibisch gebied.** (Suriname, developing country in the Caribbean.)

Anna Maria Janssen. Amsterdam: SUA, 1986. 176p. map.

An analysis of the structural problems of Suriname. The author names the colonial history; the plantation system; the resulting ethnic diversity; and political and economic dependence as factors which have caused Suriname's underdevelopment. Janssen rejects the thesis that the military régime is to blame for the current social and economic crisis.

521 **Staat, klassen en economische structuur in Suriname 1948-1987.** (State, classes and economic structure in Suriname 1948-1987.)

Jack Menke. *SWI Forum*, vol. 5, no. 2 (Dec. 1988), p. 32-58. bibliog.

The author examines the changing role of the State in Suriname in the post-war period. He focuses on economic development as well as on social and ethnic relations. He describes a period of development (1948–69) based on favourable financial, economic, social, fiscal, and political conditions for foreign investors which was followed by an unsuccessful attempt to increase the State's economic control through the creation of joint-ventures. He notes that political independence did not curtail foreign economic influence. During the military régime the technological dependency decreased in some economic sectors. However, these changes have not led to structural transformations.

522 **Gap analysis applied to the Surinamese economy: a study of the savings, foreign exchange, and absorptive capacity constraints to the economic development of Suriname. (With a summary in Dutch).**

Baijah Hunderson Philip Mhango. PhD dissertation, Universiteit van Suriname, Paramaribo, 1980. 251p. bibliog.

The purpose of this study is to apply the extended two-gap model to the economy of Suriname, which focuses on three important constraints on development, namely savings, foreign exchange, and the absorptive capacity limit. The author discusses the concept of foreign aid as well as the controversies on the forms of aid before surveying the general nature of the gap model and expounding on its relevance to Suriname.

523 **Revenue-income elasticity of resource-rich developing countries: the case of Suriname.**

Baijah Hunderson Philip Mhango. Paramaribo: Institute of Economic and Social Research, University of Suriname, 1982. 42p. bibliog.

Like other developing countries, Suriname has a shortage of revenue to provide for public services and to safeguard public investment to the required degree. This situation has been alleviated somewhat by the inflow of appreciable amounts of foreign, primarily Dutch, financial aid. The author looks at the possibilities for increased development expenditure, financed by taxation and government savings. He bases this study on evaluation of the responsiveness of the Surinamese revenue structure to changes in the Gross Domestic Product over the period 1956-78.

524 **Caribbean countries: economic situation, regional issues and capital flows.**
The World Bank. Washington, DC: The author, 1988. 78p.
A report in three parts. The first one gives an overview of the Caribbean economies, including selected policy issues. Part two concentrates on external financing, including an analysis of Suriname. The final section deals with regional and sub-regional programmes. Two appendices provide country profiles, also of Suriname, as well as a statistical report covering the period 1977-1987. Figures of interest regarding Suriname include the growth of the GDP; the public sector savings; the balance of payments current account; and the value and volume of banana, bauxite, and alumina exports.

Economic policy and planning

525 **Development planning in Surinam in historical perspective (with special reference to the Ten Year Plan).**
J. H. Adhin, with a foreword by Joh. J. Hanrath. Leiden, The Netherlands: H. E. Stenfert Kroese, 1961. 215p. bibliog.
This dissertation analyses the economic history of Suriname from the perspective of planning. The author asks why the economic decline was not checked and why the stagnation was allowed to continue for more than a century. He argues that the *laissez-faire* theory adhered to by the Dutch government was responsible for the lack of adequate action to solve Suriname's problems. Adhin feels that the Second World War was a turning point; before the War development was automatic and unplanned, while after 1945 a planned approach to the problems was adopted. Following an introductory chapter on planning, chapters two and three present the economic developments from the 17th century to the Second World War. In the fourth chapter, the author analyses the Ten Year Plan. In the conclusion, he considers some general aspects of economic growth and development programming. In places the text closely resembles R. M. N. Panday's, *Agriculture in Suriname, 1650-1950: an inquiry into the causes of its decline* (q.v.).

526 **Government finance and planned development: fiscal surveys of Surinam and the Netherlands Antilles.**
Fuat M. Andic, Syphan Andic, foreword by Alan T. Peacock. Rio Piedras, Puerto Rico: Institute of Caribbean Studies, University of Puerto Rico, 1968. 395p. bibliog. (Caribbean Monograph Series, 5).
This study uses the economic theories of Jan Tinbergen and Henri Theil as a general frame of reference in evaluating and reviewing the fiscal systems of Suriname and the Netherlands Antilles in the light of the development policies adopted by these countries. In the chapters devoted to Suriname, the authors cover the prevailing

general economic conditions; describe the historical development of planning; survey the fiscal system; and attempt to evaluate the feasibility of the second Ten Year Plan (1966-75). They conclude that the levels of consumption and investment achieved were only possible because of external financial aid. The authors consider self-sustained growth to be out of the question.

527 **Post-colonial Surinam: continuity of polities and policies.**
Jan Breman. *Development and Change*, vol. 7, no. 3 (July 1976), p. 249-65.

An evaluation of the policies followed during the final phase of the colonial period. The economic stagnation, increasing social problems, and growing political tension made the first years of independence difficult ones. The author describes the post-independence development strategy, which was a combination of neo-colonial and populist elements. He also discusses the chances of a more socialist polity.

528 **Geldanalyse en Centrale Bankpolitiek in Suriname. Enige beschouwingen over de rol van het monetaire beleid bij de ekonomische ontwikkeling sedert 1957.** (Monetary analysis and Central Bank policy in Suriname. Some views on the role of monetary policy in the economic development since 1957.)
Anthony Richard Caram. PhD dissertation, Katholieke Hogeschool Tilburg, The Netherlands, 1981. 270p. bibliog.

An analysis of two monetary issues. First, the author traces the effects of the use of monetary financing on the development of the economy of Suriname as it disturbs the circular flow in the economy. The second issue concerns the contribution which the Central Bank of Suriname could make towards regulating monetary financing as an instrument to achieve national economic objectives. This thesis includes a summary in English.

529 **Suriname's opbouwplanning: tegenspoed of falen?** (Suriname's economic planning: misfortune or failure?)
R. Hoppe. In: *Succes en falen van overheidsbeleid.* Edited by A. Hoogerwerf. Alphen aan den Rijn, The Netherlands: Samsom, 1983, p. 192-215. bibliog.

An evaluation of economic planning for the period 1946-75. The author looks at the content of the proposed plans and whether they were implemented. He focuses on the political and administrative problems which led to the failure of many of these projects.

530 **Ontwikkelingsplanning in Suriname: een economisch-historische studie.** (Development planning in Suriname: an economic historical study.)
Aikson Martopawiro. *Sarnami Akademie*, vol. 1, no. 2 (Nov. 1988), p. 63-78.

The author discusses the goals, financing, and the results of several development plans to stimulate the economy of Suriname. He starts his analysis with the *Welvaartsfonds* (Welfare Fund) Suriname, which was set up in 1947. He then discusses respectively the Ten Year Plan; the first and second Five Year Plans; the MOP or long-range development plan; the urgency programme by the Chin-A-Sen administration (1980–82); and finally, the probable reactivation of the long-range plan.

Natural resources

531 **Gold in Suriname: the beginning and the end of a dream?/Goud in Suriname: begin en einde van een droom?**
F. C. Bubberman. *Suralco Magazine*, vol. 9, no. 3 (1977), p. 1-25.
A popular scientific article in English and Dutch on gold production in Suriname. In the first part the most important dates in the development of the Suriname gold industry from 1687 to 1977 are listed. The second section deals with gold extraction and includes data of the 'White Water Mines'. This is followed by accounts of events and stories relating to gold production. The final pages contain a glossary.

532 **Small-scale gold mining: a manual based on experience in Suriname.**
E. H. Dahlberg. London: Intermediate Technology Development Group, 1984. 51p. maps. bibliog.
The first purpose of this manual for small-scale gold mining is to show how systematic prospecting can ensure better grades and the longer life of the deposit. Secondly, it demonstrates how simple equipment, which can be made locally, can reduce the effort required and at the same time considerably improve the recovery of gold. The manual deals only with alluvial operations. One of the methods described uses mercury and therefore a chapter on mercury poisoning is added. The booklet contains twenty-six figures.

533 **Bauxite: the need to nationalize.**
Norman Girvan. *The Caribbean economies: perspectives on social, political and economic conditions.* Edited by Vincent R. McDonald. New York: MSS Information Corporation, 1972, p. 148-69. bibliog.
The author argues that the Caribbean bauxite industry needs to be nationalized and shows how this can be done. The basic reason for nationalization, according to Girvan, is to establish the preconditions for the industry to be put to the service of the material development of the population. This article tries to pull away the veil of mystery, uncertainty, and ignorance which has shrouded the nationalization issue. It is also published in *The Review of Black Political Economy*, vol. 2, no. 1 (1971).

534 **Making the rules of the game; company-country agreements in the bauxite-industry.**
Norman Girvan. *Social and Economic Studies*, vol. 20, no. 4 (Dec. 1971), p. 378-419.
This paper is part of a wider work on the political economy of the relationships between aluminium companies and bauxite-producing countries. The author hypothesizes that these relationships lead to a cumulative process of development and enrichment for the aluminium companies, and the metropolitan economies where they

are based. In short, there exists a cumulative process of underdevelopment and dependence for the bauxite countries. The narrower concern of this essay is with the laws and agreements relating to the terms under which the companies operate in host countries. Girvan shows that these companies obtain the active collaboration of the host governments to adapt the political environment in order to secure the corporations' growth and profitability.

535 **Guyana und Surinam: wirtschaftsgeographische Probleme der Rohstoffabhängigkeit bauxitexportierender Entwicklungsländer.**
(Guyana and Suriname: economic-geographical problems of the dependency on raw materials of developing countries exporting bauxite.)
Georg Scherm.   Munich: Florentz, 1982. 280p. maps. bibliog.
The author discusses the export of raw materials, which is the basis of the national economies of both Guyana and Suriname. The history of the Guianas as plantation economies based on the cultivation of sugar cane caused structural deformations which could not be overcome by exporting bauxite. The author concludes that even though the export of raw materials is the economic basis for Guyana and Suriname, it has not contributed to reduced dependency on exports or to a diversification of the economic structure by stimulating other sectors. The book contains a summary in English.

Finance, Trade, and Transport

536 **El efecto económico de la asociación de Surinam con el Mercado Común Europeo.** (The economic effect of the association of Suriname with the European Economic Community.)
Walther R. W. Donner. *Caribbean Studies*, vol. 6, no. 2 (July 1966), p. 3-16.

A discussion of the economic results of the first years of Suriname's association with the EEC. The author compares the export and import figures of the country between 1957 (the founding of the EEC), 1961 (the year of Suriname's association), and 1964. He concludes that the effect of association has been disappointing. Since 1961 exports to EEC member states had declined appreciably. The main problems were the inflationary effects on the economy of Suriname, and the tariff and agricultural policy of the EEC.

537 **Marketing vegetables in Surinam.**
C. B. Houtman, G. W. Cellarius. *De Surinaamse Landbouw*, vol. 20, no. 2 (1972), p. 34-43; vol. 21, no. 1 (1973), p. 12-20; vol. 21, no. 3 (1973), p. 89-99. maps. bibliog.

A description of the production and marketing of vegetables in Suriname is given in the first part of this article. The most important vegetables as well as the wholesale units and their weights are listed in tables. The authors also discuss assembling, transport, marketing, prices and price fluctuations, storage, finance; risks, market information, distribution, processing, and export. The second part focuses on price structure, turnover, and wholesalers' and retailers' margins. From these and other data, the authors estimate the value of all vegetables marketed at the Central Market on an average day. Finally, the authors pay attention to the total lack of market information and its repurcussions on the marketing structure in Suriname.

538 **The history of money in Suriname.**
C. de Jong. *Suralco Magazine*, vol. 2 (June 1974), p. 6-11.

The author divides the history of Surinamese money into four periods: the sugar money period (1667-1761) when raw sugar was the means of payment; the card money period (1761-1828), when playing cards containing a seal, stamp, warrant or signature were legal tender; the reformation of Surinamese money and the subsequent introduction of the Dutch monetary system (1828-1940) which used coins and banknotes; and the modern period which started in 1940, with the issue of Surinamese currency.

539 **Vlucht PY-764. De SLM vliegramp in Suriname.** (Flight PY-764. The SLM aircrash in Suriname.)
Roy Khemradj. The Hague: Warray, 1990. 126p.

A journalistic account of the Surinam Airways (SLM) plane crash which occured on 7 June, 1989 near Zanderij Airport, Paramaribo. The author describes the role of SLM and KLM (Royal Dutch Airlines) on the transatlantic route between Paramaribo and Amsterdam.

Agriculture and Fishing

General

540 **Marketing problems and agricultural extension in Nickerie (Surinam): a stimulant to an alternative strategy.**
Jan van Huis. In: *Peasants, plantations and rural communities in the Caribbean*. Edited by Malcolm Cross, Arnaud Marks. Guildford, England: Department of Sociology, University of Surrey; Leiden, The Netherlands: Department of Caribbean Studies, Royal Institute of Linguistics and Anthropology, 1979, p. 263-84.

The author describes in detail one experimental project which sought to facilitate cooperative solutions to some agricultural problems. Extension officers, who demonstrate new technologies, tried to help farmers in overcoming low profitability caused by the activities of middlemen and also, often by the State. The new approach fell short of a radical break with tradition, yet created more understanding of common interests and succeeded in raising confidence.

541 **Patronen van communicatie en hun organisatorisch verband bij de landbouwvoorlichting in Suriname.** (Communication patterns and their organizational structure in agricultural extension in Suriname.)
G. Kalshoven. Wageningen, The Netherlands: Centrum voor Landbouwpublikaties en Landbouwdocumentatie, 1977. 181p. maps. bibliog.

This dissertation (Landbouwhogeschool Wageningen, the Netherlands, 1977) is divided into two parts. The first one deals with the communication and adoption behaviour of small rice farmers in different agricultural settings. In the second part, the author discusses the communication process within the extension service itself, including organizational aspects.

148

542 **Symposium on maize and peanut, November 13-18, 1978.**
Edited by Ferdinand E. Klas. Paramaribo: Agricultural Experiment
Station Suriname, 1978, p. 216-33. map. bibliog. (Proceedings of the
Caribbean Food Crops Society, XV, 1978).
A volume containing fifteen articles on the cultivation of peanuts, maize, sugar cane,
and papaya. The book is divided into four sections covering pests, diseases, and weeds;
economic aspects; soil management; and cultivation and production.

543 **Agricultural credit to small farmers in Surinam.**
A. M. Klink, J. J. A. Nagel. *De Surinaamse Landbouw*, vol. 24,
no. 2/3 (1976), p. 55-67.
A review of the activities of the Landbouwbank (Agricultural Bank) Ltd, founded in
1972. First, a brief overview of the agricultural structure in Suriname is given. Second,
the authors present data on the impact of the Agricultural Bank on outstanding loans
and an analysis of the loans related to this kind of business. Finally, they discuss
problems which have a delaying influence on the development of small farmers.

544 **Estimating free water evaporation in Surinam.**
K. J. Lenselink, R. van der Weert. *De Surinaamse Landbouw*,
vol. 21, no. 2 (1973), p. 70-79. map. bibliog.
In the design of irrigation and drainage systems it is important to take evapotrans-
piration data into account. Free water evaporation can be estimated from standard
metereological measurements of air temperature, wind velocity, actual vapour
pressure, and relative duration of bright sunshine. The authors present the distribution
of the annual evaporation over Suriname during the period 1960-70.

545 **Agricultural cooperatives in Surinam: complex problems and policy
responses.**
Jan Kazimierz Maria Morenc. *Boletín de Estudios Latinoamericanos y
del Caribe*, no. 35 (Dec. 1985), p. 51-70. map. bibliog.
An analysis of cooperative development in Suriname, in Saramacca and Nickerie in
particular. According to the author, ethnic antagonism, reluctance of governments to
allocate resources, the failures of attempts at cooperative legislation, corruption, and a
lack of expertise seriously hampered cooperative development in Suriname until 1979.
For the period after the *coup d'état* in 1980 no significant improvements have been
recorded.

546 **Surinaamse kleine landbouw en landbouwbeleid: een structurele analyse.**
(Surinamese smallholding and agricultural policy: a structural analysis.)
Jan Kazimierz Maria Morenc. PhD dissertation, Katholieke
Universiteit Nijmegen, The Netherlands, 1988. 319p. bibliog.
This dissertation deals with the structures which determine the marginal position of
small farmers in Suriname. Anthropologist Morenc also focuses on the institutional
context in which government officials operate and which is the source of much
ineffectiveness of policy measures and inefficiency in policy implementation. The thesis
contains a summary in English.

547 **The government Land Settlement Program in Surinam.**
Kalervo Oberg.   Ithaca, New York: Comparative Studies of Cultural
Change, Department of Anthropology, Cornell University, 1965. 388p.
An evaluation of a number of settlement projects undertaken by the Surinamese
government in order to ascertain the causes for the problems encountered. These
projects were designed to provide land for smallholders but since 1957, when settlers
began to live on the first of these areas, certain difficulties became apparent:
development began to lag; productivity was below expectations; and the planned land-
use pattern was not implemented. In the introduction, the author briefly outlines the
agricultural development of Suriname since 1500.

548 **Agriculture in Surinam 1650-1950: an enquiry into the causes of its
decline.**
R. M. N. Panday.   Amsterdam: H. J. Paris, 1959. 226p. bibliog.
An investigation into the real and alleged factors causing the decline in Surinamese
agriculture. Following a boom in the sugar industry, many misfortunes occurred.
According to the author, the first genuine difficulties appeared during the financial
crisis in the money market in Amsterdam during the second half of the 18th century.
Coupled with the Napoleonic wars, the economic repercussions were enormous. The
abolition of slavery created acute labour shortages. The competition from the other
Dutch colony of Java was a third factor contributing to the agricultural problems of
Surinam. Thus scarcity of capital and labour as well as the loss of markets caused the
decline of agriculture.

549 **Social and cultural factors in production by small farmers in Suriname
of tomatoes and rice and their marketing.**
Fred Sukdeo.   Paris: UNESCO, 1981. 105p. maps. bibliog. (Division
for the Study of Development, RRD 9).
The author addresses three basic questions regarding small-scale farming. He examines
the economic, social, and cultural problems which influence production and marketing
by small farmers; the organization of these farmers; and the organization of the
production and marketing of their products. This article is also published in *Small
farmers in the Caribbean and Latin America: explorations into a programme of research
and action* (Paris: Center for Economic and Social Studies of the Third World, 1984).

Cultivation and production

550 **Botanical and agronomic characteristics of three new rice varieties from
Surinam.**
C. W. van den Boogaert.   *De Surinaamse Landbouw* , vol. 20, no. 2
(1972), p. 44-51.
In 1971, the Foundation for the Development of Mechanized Agriculture in Suriname
released three new varieties of rice called Acorni, Apani, and Awnini. Since these
varieties differ greatly from other well-known varieties, the author, a plant breeder,
records a number of botanical and agronomic traits in comparison with those of five
other varieties.

551 **Providing agricultural services in rice farming areas: Malaysian and Surinam experiences.**
G. Kalshoven. In: *Essays in rural sociology in honour of R. A. J. van Lier.* Wageningen, The Netherlands: Agricultural University, Department of Rural Sociology of the Tropics and Subtropics, 1981, p. 89-124. map. bibliog.

This essay focuses on the structure of selected rural service organizations and the modes of government intervention in rice-producing areas. Suriname and Malaysia have tried to intervene in the existing farming systems by establishing public agencies and field offices with the task of modernizing farming practices. In Suriname, the institutional approach to rural development is manifested in a network of extension offices. Extension work is combined with the provision of farming inputs. The author doubts the effectiveness of these rural institutions and suggests that the present skills of field personnel seem inadequate to tackle the more complex problems of rural development. According to the author, rural service organizations appear to function primarily as heavily subsidized units, created and maintained by the government.

552 **Irrigation and drainage requirements for large scale mechanized rice farming in Surinam.**
G. E. Kamerling, K. J. Lenselink, R. van der Weert. *De Surinaamse Landbouw,* vol. 22, no. 1 (1974), p. 1-12. bibliog.

A presentation of the results of calculations concerning the irrigation and drainage requirements for the mechanized double-cropping of lowland rice in Suriname's coastal area. Based on an assumed water management scheme and other data, the authors give a calculation procedure for the day-to-day computation of supply and discharge.

553 **The effect of climatic factors on the grain yield of wetland rice in Suriname.**
J. T. Keisers. *De Surinaamse Landbouw/Surinam Agriculture,* vol. 35, no. 1/2/3 (1987), p. 29-39. bibliog.

An analysis of the effects of climatic factors on the grain yield of wetland rice in Suriname. The climate affects the processes involved in grain yield formation as well as the yield through incidence of diseases and pests. This analysis reveals the positive effect of average daily incident solar radiation during the reproductive period of the crop. The average daily mean air temperature has a negative effect during the reproductive period.

554 **The economic transformations of smallholder rice farming in Surinam.**
Henk Luning, Prakash Sital. In: *Peasants, plantations and rural communities in the Caribbean.* Edited by Malcolm Cross, Arnaud F. Marks. Guildford, England: Department of Sociology, University of Surrey; Leiden, The Netherlands: Department of Caribbean Studies, Royal Institute of Linguistics and Anthropology, 1979, p. 193-219,

An examination of the structure of the rice industry at three different stages of development. The authors focus on British Indian farmers in Nickerie who successfully cultivate rice with high levels of technical sophistication. In contrast with Guyana, landholdings in Suriname expanded with the advent of mechanization. In the 1960s the limits of expansion were reached and migration to Paramaribo from the rural areas commenced. Even so, the authors record major increases in productivity income for all farm sizes. It seems that Nickerie has profited most from mechanization and lower labour inputs coupled with infrastructural improvements.

555 **Citrus cultuur in Suriname.** (Cultivation of citrus fruits in Suriname.)
J. A. Samson. *Nieuwe West-Indische Gids/New West Indian Guide*, vol. 55, no. 3/4 (1981), p. 109-37. bibliog.

The author reviews research on citrus cultivation before and after 1950. The main subjects covered are: rootstocks; propagation and cultivation methods; soils and fertilizers; control of pests and diseases; and post-harvest handling. In the 1960s, a large citrus enterprise was founded at Baboenhol. Due to low yields and attacks of blight, the project had to be converted into a cattle breeding station. In the 1970s, citrus production dropped so far that there was hardly enough fruit for local consumption. The article includes a summary in English.

556 **Oil palm accessions of Surinam.**
B. Schut. *De Surinaamse Landbouw*, vol. 24, no. 1 (1976), p. 42-47. bibliog.

A paper about eight accessions of oil palm in Suriname originating from both Asia and Africa. Through these accessions, the country obtained a rich genetic variability which has already been exploited in seed production programmes. In the second part of this essay, the author describes oil palm accessions at three experimental farms.

557 **Plantain growing in Suriname; a survey.**
H. J. Veltkamp. *De Surinaamse Landbouw*, vol. 25, no. 1 (1977), p. 20-35. bibliog.

A presentation of a survey to detect the most important constraints to the cultivation of plantains in Suriname. Aspects which need improvement are drainage, weed control, control of banana weevil, banana stalk borer, nematodes and cordana leaf spot, and fertilizer application.

558 **The Wageningen rice project in Surinam: a study on the development of a mechanized rice farming project in the wet tropics.**
Theodorus Petrus Maria de Wit. The Hague: Mouton, 1960. 293p. maps. bibliog.

A dissertation (Landbouwhogeschool Wageningen, the Netherlands, 1960) discussing the problems which presented themselves during the development of the Wageningen mechanized rice project. The project was financed by the Dutch government and since 1949 a polder of about 6,000 hectares has been brought into cultivation. The Wageningen settlement includes a rice mill, a power station, and a central pumping station. The project was completed in 1958, by which time it had expanded to become one of the largest undertakings in Suriname.

Pests, diseases, and weeds

559 **Some aspects of the biology of the paddy bug, Oebalus poecilus (dall) in Surinam.**
P. van Halteren. *De Surinaamse Landbouw*, vol. 20, no. 2 (1972), p. 23-33. bibliog.

The paddy bug *Oebalus poecilus* is a common insect in the rice fields of the coastal plain of the Guianas and other Latin American countries. Although the first record dates from 1788, little information is available and it is often inaccurate. This article contains data on the biology, damage caused by, and control of this pest.

560 **Investigations on 'Hartrot' of coconut and oil palms in Suriname.**
Pieter Kastelein. PhD dissertation, Rijksuniversiteit Utrecht, The Netherlands, 1987. 130p. bibliog.

The aim of the investigations described here are fivefold. Firstly, to fill some of the gaps in the knowledge of the aetiology of 'Hartrot'. Secondly, to attempt to prove the pathogenecity of *Phytomonas* which cause 'Hartot'. Thirdly, to elucidate the role of weeds in the incidence of disease. Fourthly, to obtain information on the spread of the disease, and finally, to achieve an integrated control of 'Hartrot'.

561 **Host-induced changes of the virulence of eggplant mosaic virus (EMV).**
Ferdinand E. Klas. *De Surinaamse Landbouw*, vol. 24, no. 1 (1976), p. 19-29. bibliog.

A study of the eggplant mosaic virus (EMV) and the different types of symptoms which may appear. Experiments were conducted in order to ascertain whether these symptoms are caused by one and the same virus. The results indicate that it is the same virus that evokes different types of symptoms. The virulence as well as the type of symptoms seem to be host-induced as are changes in the antigenic properties and the thermal inactivation point. Klas found that the greatest increase of virulence is induced by tomato plants, which should therefore not be grown too close to EMV-infected eggplants.

562 **Timing of the control of yellow sigatoka (*Mycosphaerella musicola* leach) of banana: a system analytical approach.**
Ferdinand E. Klas, Robert H. Power. *De Surinaamse Landbouw/Surinam Agriculture*, vol. 36, no. 1/2/3 (1988), p. 19-24. bibliog.

The authors have developed a weather-based simulation model with which to time air spray cycles in order to control the yellow sigatoka disease of bananas which plagues the Caribbean.

563 **Early senescence of rice and Drechslera oryzae in the Wageningen polder, Surinam.**
A. O. Klomp. Wageningen, The Netherlands: Centre for Agricultural Publishing and Documentation, 1977. 97p. maps. bibliog.
This dissertation (Landbouw Universiteit Wageningen, the Netherlands, 1977) analyses the problem of fungal diseases in the Wageningen polder in Suriname. Fungal disease is a term used locally to indicate all diseases affecting the leaves and inflorescences of rice collectively. These diseases caused appreciable losses in rice crops over several years, sometimes by as much as twenty per cent. Earlier attempts to solve the problem were not successful; application of fungicides was too expensive; breeding resistant cultivars was possible but the level of resistance achieved was seldom sufficient and the longevity of the resistance obtained was disappointingly short. Early senescence of rice in the Wageningen polder can be prevented by good tillage and balanced application of nitrogen.

564 **Tentative list of plant parasitic nematodes in Surinam, with descriptions of two new species of Hemicycliophorinae.**
P. W. Th. Maas. Paramaribo: Landbouwproefstation Suriname, 1970. 9p. bibliog. (Bulletin, 87).
This list of nematodes and their habitats in Suriname is based on reports published between 1959 and 1965, and on the study of permanent mounts of the nematode collection of the Agricultural Experiment Station in Paramaribo.

565 **Moko, a new bacterial disease on banana and plantain in Surinam.**
Robert Henri Power. *De Surinaamse Landbouw*, vol. 24, no. 2/3 (1976), p. 85-92. map. bibliog.
A paper focusing on the first discovery of an outbreak of Moko-disease in Suriname. The author emphasizes pathogenicity, symptomatology, and the distribution of the disease. The causal agent may be transmitted when affected tissue and damaged rhizomes of healthy plants get in contact.

566 **Studies on dieback and fruitrot of Passiflora edulis f. flavicarpa in Suriname.**
Robert Henri Power. PhD dissertation, Rijksuniversiteit Utrecht, The Netherlands, 1982. 87p. bibliog.
The author re-examines the work done on dieback and fruitrot of passionfruit plants in the past. He also probes further into the cause of the disease which until then had been described as dieback and fruitrot. Finally, Power develops adequate control measures. Previously, prophylactic as well as therapeutic treatments with a great variety of fungicides had been applied but without any satisfactory results.

567 **Phloem inhabiting Phytomonas protozoa in diseased coffee, coconut palms and African oil palms.**
W. G. van Slobbe. *De Surinaamse Landbouw*, vol. 25, no. 1 (1977), p. 4-13.
The government of Suriname invited several experts to study the occurrence of a flagellate (*Phytomonas sp.*) in the phloem of diseased coconut and oil palms. The

author gives a brief historical outline of the *Phloem Necrosis* in coffee, because this was the only recorded crop at that time in which this type of organism seemed to be pathogenic. Van Slobbe also presents some results of research in palms and some hypotheses concerning the disease.

568 **Variabiltity in the occurrence of the sugar cane froghopper,** *Aeneolamia Havilatera* **(Homoptera: Cercopidae), on sugar estates in Guyana and Surinam.**
F. Wiedijk. Wageningen, The Netherlands: H. Veenman, 1982. 59p. map. bibliog. (Mededelingen Landbouwhogeschool Wageningen, Nederland, 82-7.1982).

This book studies the population dynamics of *Aeneolamia flavilatera* in relation to its environment. This research improves current control measures by way of providing reliable guidelines for the correct timing of a chemical control action. Moreover, the author suggests alternative control methods based on cultivation measures. In the introduction, he discusses the main characteristics of sugar cane cultivation as it is presently practised in Guyana and Surinam, as well as the climate that affects these cultivation areas.

Soil management

569 **Soil properties in relation to the growth and yield of oil palm (elaeis Guineensis jacq.) in Surinam.**
F. W. van Amson. Paramaribo: Landbouwproefstation Suriname, 1972. 103p. bibliog. (Bulletin, 89).

A collection of soil data in relation to the growth and yield of the oil palm. In 1959, after several failures, a private company started selection and breeding work. About four hectares were planted with the Deli-Dura and Tenera types. After seven years, growth and yield in the area of Oema were spectacular. This success resulted in the establishment of an oil palm industry on a commercial basis. The studies collected in this volume were mainly carried out on soils of the Old Coastal Plain (Oema) and of the interior (Brokobaka).

570 **En vooronderzoek naar het bekalkingseffect op terrasgronden.** (A lime experiment with a sandy loam soil of the interior.)
F. W. van Amson, R. H. Dom, A. M. San Ajong. *De Surinaamse Landbouw*, vol. 20, no. 1 (1972), p. 5-14.

A report of field experiment carried out to obtain information about the influence of different lime treatments on the pH of a sandy loam soil. Lime treatments increase production as well as the quality of the products. The results suggest that lime treatments of more than 2,500 lbs per acre will be needed to increase the pH of the topsoil. The article includes a summary in English.

571 **Soil productivity factors of the soils of the Zanderij formation in Surinam.**
H. Schroo. *De Surinaamse Landbouw*, vol. 24, no. 2/3 (1976), p. 68-84. map. bibliog.

A review of the results of soil surveys carried out on light textured soils of the Zanderij formation. This region offers good possibilities for mechanization because of the excellent drainage. To evaluate the agricultural potential of these soils, the author discusses soil production as well as soil problems. He makes recommendations for chemical and physical improvement of selected soil types.

572 **Moisture characteristics of a number of soils in the interior of Surinam.**
R. van der Weert, K. J. Lenselink. *De Surinaamse Landbouw*, vol.22, no. 1 (1974), p. 13-22. bibliog.

An article on the moisture-holding characteristics of soils in the interior of Suriname. The authors pay special attention to the amount of soil moisture available to plants, while they also try to consider the available moisture at different levels. They created moisture retention curves of a number of soil types and carried out a number of field capacity measurements. Furthermore, the paper focuses on the relationship between available moisture and texture, organic content, and bulk density of the soil.

Fishery

573 **State of exploitation and development strategies for the fishery resources in Suriname (fin-fish).**
Pierre Charlier. *De Surinaamse Landbouw/Surinam Agriculture*, vol. 36, no. 1–3 (1988), p. 1-18.

A review of fisheries in Suriname, excluding shrimp trawling. The author estimates the present landing of the various fishing methods and examines their main biological, economic, and socio-economic characteristics. He classifies the fishery resources and discusses their significance as well as the state of exploitation.

Employment, Labour, and Trade Unions

574 **Vakbeweging en arbeidsverhoudingen in Suriname. Trade unions and industrial relations: the case of Suriname (with a summary in English).**
Edward Edgar Campbell. PhD dissertation, Katholieke Universiteit Brabant, Tilburg, The Netherlands, 1987. 308p. bibliog.
The author analyses the development of the trade union movement and industrial relations from the perspective of the modernization theory. The thesis also includes a review of the literature on this subject. The author focuses on two issues: the contributions made by the trade unions in Suriname to the modernization of industrial relations, their influence on politics, the economy, and social welfare in general; and a survey of 977 union members, and their views on the contributions and influence of their unions. The dissertation includes a seven-page summary in English.

575 **Demographic aspects of Suriname's employment.**
Humphrey E. Lamur. In: *Contemporary Caribbean: a sociological reader. vol. 1.* Edited by Susan Craig. Maracas, Trinidad: College Press, 1981, p. 167-83. bibliog.
An investigation into the relationship between population growth and labour surplus in Suriname's recent past. The author argues that too much attention is being paid to external factors such as the influence of multinational corporations. He hypothesizes that the class interests of the dominant groups partly explain both the population explosion and the labour surplus.

576 **Gastarbeiders en werkloosheid in Suriname.** (Guest workers and unemployment in Suriname.)
Jeannot L'Hoëst. In: *De mensen van de houten vis, 18 opstellen over ontwikkeling.* Edited by Ruddy Doom. Ghent, Belgium: VVN, 1982, p. 363-79.
An overview of migration to and from Suriname in the late 1970s and 1980. The author examines the labour market in order to explain these migratory movements. L'Hoëst

L'Hoëst argues that this migration is a consequence of the capitalist mode of production, which strives to keep the wages as low as possible. Therefore (illegal) guest workers are welcome in a country with a high unemployment rate.

577 **Economic impacts of education and personnel management: case studies from the industrial sector in Iran and Surinam.**
Gerben van der Molen. *Development and Change*, vol. 7, no. 1 (Jan. 1976), p. 45-65.

This study has three objectives. First, it endeavours to ascertain the impact of education on the productivity, income, and careers of workers. Second, it attempts to assess how far the impact of education is conditioned by personnel management systems. Third, the author looks at the impact of different systems of personnel management on productivity, the income, and the careers of workers. The data from Suriname were collected in 1969 at Suralco, an aluminium company.

578 **Werkgelegenheid en werkgelegenheidsonderzoek in Suriname.**
(Employment and employment research in Suriname.)
Reynold Simons. *SWI Forum*, vol. 4, no. 1 (June 1987), p. 28-59.

Analyses the failure of the employment policy as conducted by the Surinamese government. The author notes that growth in the number of bureaucrats has structurally disrupted both production and the labour market. Most jobs are created as part of the political spoils system, so the success of the 'employment policy' is measured in terms of election results.

579 **Guyanese gastarbeid in Suriname.** (Guyanese guestworkers in Suriname.)
Richard Singelenberg. Utrecht, The Netherlands: Centrum voor Caraibische Studies, Instituut voor Culturele Antropologie, Rijksuniversiteit Utrecht, 1983. 106p. map. bibliog. (ICAU Mededelingen, 20).

A report on the economic importance of Guyanese migrant workers in Suriname. The author concentrates on those labourers employed in agriculture in Nickerie and at the Mariënburg plantation in the district of Commewijne. He also discusses the role of both the State and the trade unions as well as their policies concerning migrant labour.

Statistics

580 **Minderheden in Nederland, statistisch vademecum.** (Minorities in the Netherlands: statistical handbook.)
T. Ankersmit, Th. Roelandt, J. Veenman.   The Hague: Staatsuitgeverij/CBS-publikaties, 1987. 124p. bibliog.

A handbook listing statistical data of ethnic minorities living in the Netherlands. The subjects covered are demography, labour, housing, education, and health. This publication includes more than fifty tables and nine figures.

581 **Expenditures derived from budgetary surveys in Suriname.**
Edwin van der Kuyp.   *Surinaams Medisch Bulletin*, vol. 4, no. 4 (Oct. 1982), p.149-58.

A presentation of the average household expenditure in various areas of Suriname basded on three budgetary surveys which were done in 1952, 1968–69 and 1977–79. The author demonstrates that absolute expenditure on goods and services has increased substantially over time, and although the percentage of expenditure on food is the highest, it has decreased over the years; the higher the income, the lower the percentage spent on food. He notes that there is a sharp rise in money earmarked for education, recreation, transportation, and health care.

582 **De Amsterdammers in zeven bevolkingskategorieën, 1 januari 1989. Statistische gegevens per 1 januari 1989 over Surinamers, Antillianen, Turken, Marokkanen, Zuideuropeanen, overige buitenlanders en overige Nederlanders.** (The people of Amsterdam in seven population categories, 1 January 1989. Statistical data on 1 January 1989 on Surinamese, Antillians, Turks, Moroccans, Southern Europeans, other foreigners and other Dutch.)
Amsterdam: Het Amsterdamse Bureau voor Onderzoek en Statistiek, 1990. 320p. map.

An important source of information on ethnic minorities living in Amsterdam, this publication provides data on gender, age, family structure, and religion for the whole of the city as well as for the eighteen districts. This volume includes 145 tables and 4 graphs. On 1 January 1989, 52,757 persons, or 7.3 per cent of the total population of Amsterdam, were classified as Surinamese.

583 **Statistical yearbook. Annuaire statistique. Anuario estadístico.**
Paris: UNESCO, United Nations Educational, Scientific and Cultural Organization, 1989. 1051p.

A yearly publication in English, French, and Spanish. This authoritative source, with a section on Suriname, contains data on education, science and technology, libraries, book production, newspapers and other periodicals, archives; museums and related institutions, film and cinema, radio and television broadcasting, and international trade in printed matter. The Statistical Office of the United Nations in New York publishes the *Demographic yearbook*, which is the main source for worldwide demographic statistics.

584 **Venezuela, Suriname, Netherlands Antilles country profile 1989-1990.**
London: The Economist Intelligence Unit, 1989. 70p. map. bibliog.

An annual survey of the political and economic background of Suriname. There are sixteen pages and twenty-three tables of data on the population and society, currency, the economy, national accounts, employment, wages and prices, agriculture, forestry and fishing, mining, energy, manufacturing, transport and communications, finance, foreign trade, external payments and debt, and trade and investment regulations. The same publisher also puts out a quarterly analysis of the latest political and economic trends entitled *Country report Venezuela, Suriname, Netherlands Antilles* (q.v.).

Environment

Ecology

585 **Uitverkoop van de tropische natuur. Het ontwikkelingsprojekt West Suriname.** (The selling out of the tropical environment. The West Suriname development project.)
Edited by Henk van Arkel, Joke Oosterhuis. *Ekologie*, no. 7 (1979), p. 385-448. maps.
A critical analysis of the ecological effects of the 'West Suriname development project'. The authors discuss the damage to the rain forests as well as the more general consequences of Dutch development aid in Suriname, such as economic dependency, migration, and social and economic inequality. The final section considers the forms of action which are most successful in counteracting the problems mentioned in this article.

586 **Forest and forestry in Suriname/Bos en bosbouw in Suriname.**
F. C. Bubberman. *Suralco Magazine*, vol.13, no. 3 (1981), p. 1-16. map.
A popular article in Dutch and English discussing many aspects of the forest and forestry, such as forest types, production possibilities, management, and preservation.

587 **A silvicultural system for natural regeneration of tropical rain forest in Suriname.**
Nicolaüs Reitze de Graaf. PhD dissertation, Landbouwhogeschool Wageningen, The Netherlands, 1986. 250p. maps. bibliog.
Discusses the use of a polycyclic system for the economically accessible mesophytic rain forests of Suriname which involves the controlled felling of a limited quantity of timber about once every twenty years. The author feels that this is the best compromise between economic demands and ecological constraints due to nutrient-

161

poor soils which are susceptible to degradation following deforestation. In this way the nutrient store of the ecosystem, which is largely locked in the vegetation, can be preserved as much as possible. This thesis includes many tables, graphs, stereophotographs, and a summary in Dutch.

588 Lake Brokopondo: filling phase limnology of a man-made lake in the humid tropics.
Jacob van der Heide.   PhD dissertation, Vrije Universiteit te Amsterdam, 1983. 428p. maps. bibliog.

The damming of the Suriname River in 1964 created Lake Brokopondo. This thesis describes the evolution of the aquatic environment and the plankton composition in the reservoir during the filling phase. For comparison, the author reviews relevant literature on other tropical reservoirs. and presents some information on streams in Suriname.

589 Hydrobiology of the man-made Brokopondo lake. Brokopondo research report, Suriname
Jacob van der Heide, P. Leentvaar, J. Meyer.   Utrecht, The Netherlands: Natuurwetenschappelijke Studiekring voor Suriname en de Nederlandse Antillen, 1976. 95p. maps. bibliog. (Uitgave, 90).

During the period between November 1963 and June 1967 hydrobiological research was carried out in the region of the man-made Lake Brokopondo. The formation of this lake started when a large area of tropical rain forest was flooded. The research programme consisted of weekly samplings at six fixed stations, and of incidental samplings at many other points. Physico-chemical observations were restricted mainly to measurements of temperature, dissolved oxygen, acidity, electrical conductivity, and transparancy at a series of depths.

590 Vegetation structure, logging damage and silviculture in a tropical rain forest in Suriname.
Wybrand Barend John Jonkers.   PhD dissertation, Landbouwuniversiteit Wageningen, The Netherlands, 1987. 172p. maps. bibliog.

This study is part of a long-term effort to devise a forest management system for the tropical rain forests of Suriname. The author notes that the development of its resources for sustained timber production would benefit the economy and after decades of investigations a polycyclic system was formulated. The principal aims of this dissertation are to strengthen the ecological basis of this polycyclic system and to achieve reductions in silvicultural treatment costs. The author presents data from experiments in a mesophytic rain forest in the Kabo region.

591 Soils, water and nutrients in a forest ecosystem in Suriname.
Renier Laurentius Hubertus Poels.   PhD dissertation, Landbouwuniversiteit Wageningen, The Netherlands, 1987. 253p. maps. bibliog.

The author investigates whether a polycyclic silvicultural system, based on the natural regeneration of the tropical rain forest, would result in unacceptable ecological losses which may endanger the long-term productivity of these forests. The study area comprises two hydrological catchment areas; one is undisturbed, the other is treated according to the polycyclic system. Data were collected over a period of almost five years. Poels studied the hydrological cycle, the nutrient amounts, and the flows in both catchments. The results indicated that the polycyclic system did not result in unacceptable losses of nutrients from the ecosystem.

592 **Nature reserves and tourism/ Natuurreservaten en toerisme.**
J. Schulz. *Suralco Magazine*, vol. 8, no. 2. (1976), p. 1-11. map.
A popular introduction to the nature reserves of Suriname, in which the author pays special attention to the coastal reserves of Galibi and Wia-Wia, the Raleigh Falls, Voltzberg National Park, and Brownsberg. The article includes a map locating the nine nature reserves and is written in English and Dutch.

593 **Protected wildlife along the coast/ Beschermd dierenleven langs de kust.**
J. Schulz. *Suralco Magazine*, vol. 8, no. 3 (1976), p. 14-24.
A brief introduction in English and Dutch to the causes of the high biological productivity of estuarine ecosystems in Suriname. The author descibes the wealth of birds along the coast, the large number of organisms living there on which they feed and the ideal breeding and roosting sites in the tidal forest. Schulz also notes that the sand beaches provide nesting sites to sea turtles.

594 **Ecological studies on rain forest in northern Suriname.**
J. Schulz. Amsterdam: N. V. Noord-Hollandsche Uitgeversmaatschappij, 1960. 267p. maps. bibliog.
A dissertation (Rijksuniversiteit Utrecht, the Netherlands, 1959) on the environmental factors prevailing in the rain forest of the northern half of central Suriname and its regeneration. The first and second parts of the book deal with observations made in a number of different habitats on various environmental factors, such as light, humidity, evaporation, temperature, and soil. The author devotes particular attention to a comparison of the climate in a dense forest with that in clearings of different sizes. In the third part the results of phytosociological observations are discussed. The thesis includes a summary in Spanish.

595 **The influence of mechanical clearing of forest on plant growth.**
R. van der Weert, K. J. Lenselink. *De Surinaamse Landbouw*, vol. 21, no. 3 (1973), p. 100-11. bibliog.
Crop development on mechanically cleared land is normally very irregular. The authors emphasize root development because the 'rootability' of the soils determines to a large extent the soil suitability for crop growth. Especially increased mechanical impedance, caused by compaction, is a limiting factor in root development.

Housing and architecture

596 **Monumentengids van Paramaribo.** (Guide to the monuments of
Paramaribo.)
Ypie Attema. Paramaribo: Evaco; Zutphen, The Netherlands: De
Walburg Pers, 1981. 112p. maps. bibliog.
This guide is divided into five units, the first three forming a general introduction to
Paramaribo and Surinamese architecture and the last two listing the monuments of
Paramaribo. The guide includes a chronology of the most important events in the
history of Suriname from 1500 to 1975 and a glossary.

597 **Paramaribo: history rich town of wooden houses/Stad van houten huizen
en historie.**
Ypie Attema. *Suralco Magazine*, vol. 10, no. 4 (1978), p. 6-19. maps.
A richly illustrated introduction to the various architectural styles found in
Paramaribo. This article includes a brief history of Suriname and of the origins of
Paramaribo.

598 **The reluctant colonists: Netherlanders abroad in the 17th and 18th
centuries.**
Doreen Greig. Assen, Maastricht, The Netherlands: Van Gorcum,
1987. 306p. map. bibliog.
The author, an architect, describes the architecture resulting from the expansion of the
Netherlands in Asia, Africa, and the Americas during the 17th and 18th centuries. She
also analyses the diffusion of Dutch cultural institutions against the background of the
vicissitudes of the Dutch India Companies. The chapter on Suriname discusses
architecture and town planning, Jodensavanne, and the plantations. Most attention,
however, is devoted to Paramaribo.

599 **Comfort and indoor climate in Paramaribo (Surinam).**
J. H. Raat. Groningen, The Netherlands: Boekdrukkerij voorheen
gebroeders Hoitsema, 1958. 114p. bibliog.
The first chapter of this dissertation (Rijksuniversiteit Utrecht, the Netherlands, 1958)
provides an introduction to comfort studies and points to the connection between these
studies and the study of indoor climates. The author investigated the feeling of comfort
in terms of temperature and humidity of over 1,900 subjects of different races and
sexes in Paramaribo and proves that aspect has a great influence on the natural indoor
climate in the different rooms of a house in the city. With the aid of models a study
was made of the effects of aspect, outer walls, shade, size of window openings, roof
covering and ceilings, and external colours on indoor climates. In two appendices the
mathematical methods employed in formulating comfort equations are outlined.

600 **De architectuur van Suriname 1667-1930.** (The architecture of Suriname 1667-1930.)
C.L. Temminck Groll. Zutphen, The Netherlands: De Walburg Pers, 1973. 363p. maps.

An overview of urban architecture in Suriname. Over the centuries this country has been exposed to a series of influences from England, the Netherlands, France, and Germany. Creole craftsmen modified these successive European influences and adapted the foreign styles to local conditions, combining them into a harmonious style of construction. In the 19th century the colonnaded porticos of the southern part of the United States became popular in Suriname. The 'Neo'-styles of this century, however, barely left traces. The first part of the book deals with the architecture of Paramaribo and the second part examines that of the districts. The introductory texts are in English.

601 **Bouwkunst in Suriname: driehonderd jaar nationale architectuur. Geschreven en getekend door Ir. J.L. Volders.** (Architecture in Suriname: three hundred years of national architecture. Described and illustrated by J.L. Volders.)
Jean-Louis Volders. Hilversum, The Netherlands: G. van Saane, Lectura Architectonica, 1966. 152p. bibliog.

Presents drawings and descriptions of Suriname's monumental buildings as well as small commonplace houses. The text and nearly 300 illustrations present a concise view of the architecture of Paramaribo, the plantations and plantation houses, the forts of Zeelandia, Nieuw Amsterdam, and Sommelsdijck, Amerindian and Maroon housing, and interiors and furniture. Each of the ten chapters includes a summary in English.

Education

602 **Onderwijs in Suriname. Verslag van de identificatiemissie Technische Samenwerking Onderwijs 29 april-13 mei 1989.** (Education in Suriname. Report of the Technical Cooperation Education identification trip 29 April-13 May 1989.)
P. Blok, D. W. Bresters, J. A. van Kemenade, E. H. B. Puylaert. The Hague: NUFFIC, 1989. 57p. bibliog.

A set of recommendations to improve the educational system in Suriname. This volume includes an outline of the different types of education as well as twelve tables of statistical data. In 1990 a follow-up of the same name appeared, authored by Blok, Van Kemenade, and M. C. Brandsz.

603 **Language problems in Surinam. Dutch as the language of the schools.**
W. Gs. Hellinga. Amsterdam: North-Holland Publishing Company, 1955. 123p. maps. bibliog.

Questionnaires, interviews, and discussions form the basis of this study of the language problems in the schools of Suriname during the late 1940s and early 1950s. Apart from focusing on the linguistic situation, this research project also pays attention to education in general. The author stresses that educational conditions in Suriname were and are far from satisfactory because the country is heir to a colonial system which has always tried to economize on education.

604 **De koloniale onderwijspolitiek in Suriname en haar gevolgen.** (The colonial educational policy in Suriname and its consequences.)
Sjoerd Karsten. *Oso*, vol. 6, no. 2 (Dec. 1987), p. 137-46. bibliog.

A comparison of Dutch colonial educational policy in Suriname and Indonesia. The author also examines the colonial educational system in Suriname and its consequences for Suriname and Surinamese migrants living in the Netherlands.

605 **Final report of the research into illiteracy in Suriname.**
Ministry of Education and Community Development. Paramaribo:
Research Division of the Ministry of Education and Community
Development, 1980. 38p.

This report presents and interprets quantitative data on the nature and distribution of
illiteracy in Suriname; the social factors influencing this phenomenon; and the extent to
which there is a need for illiterates to learn to read and write in Dutch. The report
includes priorities for alphabetization campaigns to eliminate illiteracy and recommendations for further research.

606 **National report on progress and achievements in the framework of the**
Major Project in the field of education in Suriname.
Ministry of Education, Sciences and Culture. Paramaribo: The
author, 1987. 52p. map.

A presentation of the interim state of the various projects, as well as the way in which
they were initiated and executed within the framework of the Major Project, which
aims to provide schooling for children up to the age of fourteen, to build schools for
retarded children, to eradicate illiteracy and develop adult education, and to effect an
improvement of the quality and efficiency of the educational system in general. Due to
the social and economic problems in Suriname, the Ministry was not able to adequately
execute the plans and has established a National Reconstruction Programme to
overcome these problems. The appendices include basic social and economic data.

Literature

607 **Aphra Behn's Surinam interlude.**
Elaine Campbell.   In: *A double colonization: colonial and post-colonial women's writing*. Edited by Kirsten Holst Petersen, Anna Rutherford. Mundelstrup, Denmark: Dangaroo, 1986, p. 25-35.

In 'Mrs Behn's Oroonoko' in *Kittredge Anniversary Papers* (Boston: Ginn, 1913) Ernst Bernbaum accused Aphra Behn of having 'stolen' her *Oroonoko* materials from George Warren's *An impartial description of Suriname*. However, in this essay Campbell contends that the inspiration for *Oroonoko, or the royal slave* was derived from Behn's short residence in Suriname.

608 **In de spiegel van de poëzie.** (In the mirror of poetry.)
Maarten van Dullemen.   *Alerta*, vol. 15, no. 1 (Jan-Feb. 1989), p. 8-14.

Reflects on the influence of political events on the work of several poets in Suriname, including Dobru (*pseud.* for R. Ravales), Shrinivasi (*pseud.* for M. H. Lutchman), Michael Slory, Orlando Emanuels, Trudy Guda, and Denise de Hart.

609 **Boesi sa tek' mi baka – Let the bush receive me once again. Edgar Cairo – Surinamese writer.**
Vernie A. February.   *Oso*, vol. 3, no. 1 (May 1984), p. 39-62.

A discussion of the work of Edgar Cairo (b. 1948), one of the most prolific writers living and working in the Netherlands. He is a novelist, poet, playwright, storyteller, journalist, and performer. Cairo was born in the district of Para, and grew up in close proximity of the old Creole (slave) culture and its traditions in song, dance, drama, *anansi tori*, tales from slavery (*srafuten tori*), and *Winti*.

610 **R. Dobru: een maatschappelijke inhoud en zijn vorm.** (R. Dobru: a social content and its form.)
Michiel van Kempen. *Oso*, vol. 7, no. 1 (May 1988), p. 7-20. bibliog.

An evaluation of the work of the well-known Surinamese author R. Dobru (1935-83). Van Kempen focuses on four themes in this article: Dobru's preoccupation with the Surinamese masses; the emphasis Dobru places on being a Creole who takes pride in his cultural heritage; Dobru's nationalism; and his commitment to the revolution.

611 **De Surinaamse literatuur 1970-1985: een documentatie.** (Surinamese literature 1970-1985: documentation.)
Michiel van Kempen. Paramaribo: De Volksboekwinkel, 1987. 405p. bibliog.

A research tool divided into two parts. In section one the well-known literary critic, Van Kempen treats some preliminary aspects such as the nature of Surinamese literature and he describes trends between 1970 and 1985. The second part provides two bibliographies. The first one lists secondary literature arranged by author. The second one contains all monographs regarding Surinamese literature covering the period 1970-85.

612 **Surinaamse schrijvers en dichters met honderd schrijversprofielen en een lijst van pseudoniemen.** (Surinamese authors and poets with profiles of one hundred authors and a list with pseudonyms.)
Michiel van Kempen. Amsterdam: De Arbeiderspers, 1989. 191p.

Van Kempen outlines the Surinamese literary world. In the first chapter he describes the relationship between literature in Suriname and emigrant literature. He then looks at the development of Surinamese literature and the oral literature of Amerindians, Creoles, British Indians, and Javanese. However, this book is not a systematic guide to Surinamese literature. This volume builds upon and is an addition to *De Surinaamse literatuur 1970-1985* (q.v.) by the same author. A companion volume is the anthology selected by Van Kempen entitled *Verhalen van Surinaamse schrijvers gekozen door Michiel van Kempen* (Amsterdam: De Arbeiderspers, 1989) containing the work of twenty-eight authors.

613 **Geschreven creoolse literatuur van Suriname.** (Written Creole literature from Suriname.)
Geert Koefoed. In: *Cultuur in beweging. Creolisering en Afro-Caraïbische cultuur, weergave van het gelijknamige symposium georganiseerd door Studium Generale Rotterdam, Erasmus Universiteit Rotterdam, 1988.* Edited by Michiel Baud, Marianne C. Ketting. Rotterdam, The Netherlands: Erasmus Universiteit, 1989, p. 45-52.

A discussion of the development of written Creole literature in Suriname. The author concludes that this development has been largely autonomous. There exist differences as well as similarities with the négritude movement in the French Caribbean. The importance of Trefossa (*pseud.* for Hennie De Ziel), Michael Slory, and Edgar Cairo on the development of Surinamese literature is emphasized.

Literature

614 **Surinaamse schrijvers en dichters als taalpolitici.** (Surinamese authors and poets as language politicians.)
Geert Koefoed. *Oso*, vol. 6, no. 2 (Dec. 1987), p. 147-64.

A look at the 'language policy' of Surinamese authors whose choice to write in one of the Surinamese languages has exerted a positive influence on the appreciation of these languages. Koefoed discusses the work of Albert Helman (*pseud.* for Lou Lichtfeld), Trefossa, Michael Slory, Dobru, Shrinivasi, Edgar Cairo, Astrid Roemer, and Jit Narain.

615 **Colonialism and the author: Albert Helman's 'Hoofden van de Oayapok!'.**
Hilda van Neck Yoder. *Oso*, vol. 7, no. 1 (May 1988), p. 21-30. bibliog.

The author analyses Albert Helman's short story *Hoofden van de Oayapok!* and shows how Helman (b. 1903) uses his narrative technique to lead Western readers to define themselves not in opposition to non-Western or 'savage' people, but instead to view themselves as both 'civilized' and 'savage'. Thus Western readers are able to see themselves from a perspective beyond Western ideology.

616 **The theme of imprisonment in Bea Vianen's novels.**
Hilda van Neck Yoder. *Journal of Caribbean Studies*, vol. 2, no. 2/3 (autumn/winter 1981), p. 228-36.

A review of several novels by Bea Vianen (b. 1935), one of Suriname's most successful authors who often focuses on vulnerable persons such as children, women, intellectuals, and the poor in her work. In four novels published between 1969 and 1973 a recurring theme is the perversion of innocent children by a European system. However, Vianen stresses the ability of the individual to find solutions to his or her problems. Innate vitality and a native sense of right and wrong helps one to escape from the prison called society. In a later novel, Vianen rejects her previous conclusions, having lost her faith in the individual. The novels discussed are *Geen onderdelen* (No parts), *Sarnami, hai*, *Paradijs* (Paradise), *Ik eet, ik eet, tot ik niet meer kan* (I eat, I eat, till I can no more) and *Strafhok* (Punishment shed).

617 **Reinhart: Nederlandse literatuur en slavernij ten tijde van de Verlichting.** (Reinhart: Dutch literature and slavery during the Enlightenment.)
A. N. Paasman. Leiden, The Netherlands: Martinus Nijhoff, 1984. 277p. maps. bibliog.

Using the novel *Reinhart, of natuur en godsdienst* (1791-92) by Elisabeth Maria Post as the base for his research, the author analyses the discussion of slavery in the Dutch literary world from the times of Hugo Grotius (1625) to Isaac da Costa (1823). This study provides a detailed account of the attitudes towards slavery in fiction and non-fiction. The volume contains an eight-page summary in English.

618 **Surinaams en Nederlands. De tweedeling van de Surinaamse literatuur.** (Surinamese and Dutch. The split in Surinamese literature.)
Hugo Pos. *De Gids*, vol. 148, no. 3/4 (1985), p. 297-304.

The well-known Surinamese author Hugo Pos discusses literature written in Sranan and Surinamese-Dutch and puts it in a social and political context. He focuses on

Edgar Cairo, Albert Helman and Bea Vianen, but also pays attention to younger talents like Astrid Roemer and Rabin Gangadin.

619 **Aphra Behn, Suriname and the critics.**
Anneke Prins-s'Jacob. *Oso*, vol. 3, no. 1 (May 1984), p. 127-35. bibliog.
A study of Aphra Behn, the rather mysterious 17th-century author. Prins briefly examines three biographies of Aphra Behn which have appeared since 1968. She reports on some research done on Suriname at the time of *Oroonoko, or the royal slave*, as well as the question whether Behn ever visited Suriname. Prins argues that Behn did in fact spend some time there.

620 **Creole drum, an anthology of Creole literature in Surinam.**
Edited by Jan Voorhoeve, Ursy M. Lichtveld, with English translations by Vernie A. February. New Haven, Connecticut: Yale University Press, 1975. 308p. bibliog. (Caribbean Series, 15).
A history of the Creole literature of Suriname. The nine chapters, each preceded by a general introduction, are ordered chronologically and illustrated by a variety of texts from slave lore to fashion in literature and Afro-Surinamese nationalism up to 1975. This important anthology is of interest to general Caribbeanists as well as to Afro-Americanists.

621 **Sta op en roep haar naam . . . zwarte lesbische dichteressen over de liefde.** (Stand up and call her name. . .black lesbian poetesses about love.)
Gloria Wekker. *Lust en Gratie*, vol. 12 (1986), p. 10-35.
The author studies the love of black women for women by examining the work of five female poets, four North-American and one Surinamese: Angelina Weld Grimké, Pat Parker, Audre Lorde, Cheryl Clarke, and Astrid Roemer. She also discusses the similarities and differences in the history of Afro-Americans in the United States and in Suriname.

The Arts

Music

622 **Saramaka music and motion.**
Terry Agerkop. *Anales del Caribe*, vol. 2 (1982), p. 231-45.
The Maroons have developed an Afro-American culture based on strong stylistic forms, mainly derived from the African continent. Ritualized performance is one of the most striking characteristics in the life of the Saramaka population. There exist many ceremonies for the veneration of sacred powers and author focuses on the ritual music and dance events which constitute the core of such ceremonies. He distinguishes various structures, which are defined by a sequence of ritual events, special dresses, drum rhythms, songs, and dance movements.

623 **Some remarks on Amerindian songstyle.**
Terry Agerkop. *Latin American Indian Literatures Journal*, vol. 5, no. 2 (fall 1989), p. 31-42.
An introduction to the music of several Carib tribes in Suriname and French Guiana. The author discusses the *alemi*, *sambura warery* (drums) and *karawasi* (basket rattle) of the Kalihna, the *kalaw* (dance) and *luwe* (flute) of the Wayana, and the *poinekë* song of the Turaekare.

624 **Ritual songs and folksongs of the Hindus of Surinam.**
U. Arya. Leiden, The Netherlands: E. J. Brill, 1968. 178p. bibliog. (Orientalia Rheno-Traiectina, Nonum).
A book divided into two parts. About two-thirds of the volume is devoted to songs and their translations. In the introduction, the delivery of the songs; the prosody and rhyme; the language; and the musical instruments are discussed. The author also focuses on the functions of the songs, identifying ritual songs, songs of the life cycle and the annual cycle, caste and work songs.

625 **Les chansons et la musique de la Guyane Néerlandaise.** (The songs and music of Dutch Guiana.)
L. C. van Panhuys. *Journal de la Société des Américanistes de Paris*, vol. 9 (1912), p. 27-39.
An article on music in Suriname in which the author reviews the literature from 1770 to 1908, and discusses the music of Amerindians, the Maroons, and the Creoles. He also provides the original and translated lyrics and music to five popular songs.

626 **Four Arawak songs.**
Thomas E. Penard, Arthur P. Penard. *West-Indische Gids*, vol. 7 (1925/26), p. 491-500.
A paper on four Amerindian songs recorded in the early 20th century. In three of them the subject is love or drink. The final song deals with the departure of Amerindians to England to escape man-eaters.

Visual arts

627 **Bush Negro art: an African art in the Americas.**
Philip J. C. Dark. London: Academy Editions; New York: St. Martin's Press, 1973. 54p. map. bibliog.
A comprehensive study considering the most important facets of Maroon art within its own cultural context. In this volume, which is illustrated with fifty-two plates and sixteen diagrams, the author describes some principal forms of art mainly displayed on utensils such as combs, paddles, stools, trays, and clothes beaters. Moreover, he pays attention to materials, tools, carving techniques, designs, symbolism, origins, and the sexual division of labour. The text was previously published as number twenty-five of the series *Chapters in Art*.

628 **Africains de Guyane. La vie matérielle et l'art des Noir Réfugiés de Guyane.** (Africans of Guyana: Material life and the art of the Black Refugees of Guyana.)
Jean Hurault. The Hague, Paris: Mouton, 1970. 224p. map. bibliog. (Art in its Context. Field Reports, 4).
Geographer Hurault extensively discusses the aesthetics and the dynamism of Maroon cultures. The text is well illustrated with numerous plates and drawings. Less than half of the book, however, is devoted to this discussion of art and almost all of the rest of the text (chapters one, two, and four) has been lifted verbatim from previous publications. Even the map on page nine has not been updated and does not include Lake Brokopondo.

629 **Farawe. Acht kunstenaars van Surinaamse oorsprong.** (Faraway. Eight artists of Surinamese origin.)
Emile R. Meijer. Heusden, The Netherlands: Aldus, 1985. 96p.
A beautifully produced book containing interviews with eight Surinamese artists living and working in the Netherlands, as well as a discussion of Surinamese art in general.

The artists portrayed here are Armand Baag, Frank Creton, Eddy Goedhart, Hans Lie, Guillaume Lo A Njoe, Sam Parabirsingh, Q. Jan Telting, and Erwin de Vries. The volume includes a list of the addresses of thirty-nine Surinamese artists in the Netherlands.

630   **Pawa paw dindoe: Surinaamse houtsnijkunst.** (Pawa paw dindoe: Surinamese woodcarving.)
F. H. J. Muntslag.   Paramaribo: Evaco, 1979. 148p.

This volume provides an overview of the symbolic meaning of a number of motifs used in Maroon woodcarving. The author does not deny the African origin of these motifs but calls them Surinamese on account of the many changes they have undergone over the years. The last twenty pages contain a listing of the major types of wood used in Suriname.

631   **Saramaka woodcarving: the development of an Afroamerican art.**
Richard Price.   *Man*, vol. 5, no. 3 (Sept. 1970), p. 363-78. map. bibliog.

This article suggests the importance of a time perspective for an understanding of Maroon art. The author argues that inventiveness and change have always characterized woodcarving among the Saramakas, and that one can distinguish styles which have specific and rather limited temporal distribution. Price denies that Saramaka woodcarving is an original African art form, as it was in its infancy in 1850, which effloresced only during the early 20th century.

632   **John Gabriel Stedman's collection of 18th-century artifacts from Suriname.**
Richard Price, Sally Price.   *Nieuwe West-Indische Gids/New West Indian Guide*, vol. 53 (1979), p. 121-40. bibliog.

In J. G. Stedman's famous *Narrative of a five years expedition . . .* (q.v) of 1796, several pages are devoted to the description and depiction of the material life of the Afro-Americans and Amerindians. The authors were able to trace the history of some of the actual artifacts depicted by Stedman, some of which are located in the Rijksmuseum voor Volkenkunde in Leiden, the Netherlands, an important repository of Maroon art. The authors summarize their findings of the Afro-Surinamese portions of the Stedman collection. This article is also published in *Mededelingen Stichting Surinaams Museum*, no. 27 (April 1979).

633   **Kammbá: the ethnohistory of an Afro-American art.**
Richard Price, Sally Price.   *Antropologica*, no. 32 (1972), p. 3-27.

Documents the history of Saramaka cicatrization. The authors stress the extreme responsiveness of this art to changing social conditions and suggest that Saramaka cicatrization may even have disappeared for several generations, only to reappear as, in many respects, a new, dynamic art form. Saramaka cicatrization, like woodcarving or onomastics, provides a good illustration of how Afro-American culture represents an imaginative extrapolation of general West-African ideas.

634 **Primitive art in civilized places.**
Sally Price. *Arts in America*, vol. 74, no. 1 (Jan. 1986), p. 9-26.

An article about the exhibition 'Afro-American arts of the Suriname rain forest' which brought together some 400 objects from twenty collections in Europe, the United States, and Suriname. The author describes the reactions revealing the strength of Western expectations about the arts of the 'primitives'. Many people had become wedded to a particular image of 'primitive art', and found it hard to accept that their ideas about the culture of 'primitives' had been shattered.

635 **Afro-American art of the Suriname rain forest.**
Sally Price, Richard Price. Los Angeles: Museum of Cultural History and the University of California Press, 1980. 237p. maps. bibliog.

Arguing against widespread stereotypes about 'primitive art', the authors present the arts of the Maroons historically and from the point of view of Maroon aesthetic ideas. They give a detailed analysis of Afro-American creativity and artistic forms over time. They interpret the artistry and aesthetics of the Maroons from an ethnographic and ethnoaesthetic perspective, rather than allowing the *objets d'art* to speak largely for themselves.

636 **A critical analysis of the serpent symbol as it is relevant to the perpetuation of the Djuka art tradition.**
Doris Elrina Rogers. PhD dissertation, Pennsylvania State University, University Park, 1980. 243p. bibliog. (Available from University Microfilms International, Ann Arbor, Michigan, order no. 80-24485).

This dissertation comprises a theoretical framework for analysing the serpentine style in Ndjuka art. The method of investigation was carried out under three main categories: historical aspects, recreative aspects, and the educational implications of the serpentine style. The historical study reveals that the training of the pre-industrial artist was based on traditional cultural norms. The recreative aspects are analysed through line, illusion, cognition, intuition, continuity, and change. The educational implications show that Ndjuka art is an embodiment of spirituality, knowledge, and human representational nature.

Folklore

637 **Patterns in the stories of the Dakota Indians and the negroes of Paramaribo, Dutch Guiana.**
Robert Plant Armstrong. PhD dissertation, Northwestern University, Evanston, Illinois, 1957. 243p. bibliog. (Available from University Microfilms International, Ann Arbor, Michigan, order no. 00-23482).

The author attempts to define a method to demonstrate the phenomenon of patterning, and to describe and quantify expression in those patterns which comprise a culture. He compares several samples of stories, two of which have culture in common, and two of which have story type in common, in order to reveal significant differences

175

and similarities with respect to the cultural and generic uses of stories. The narratives used come from the Paramaribo Creoles and the Dakota Indians of the United States. The Creole stories were collected in 1929 by Melville and Francis Herskovits.

638 **Legends of Suriname.**
Petronella Breinburg. London; Port of Spain: New Beacon Books, 1971. 47p. map.

A reconstruction of five folk-tales based on the Afro-centred traditions of Suriname. The legends emphasize the persistance of African belief; the organic unity between animals – including men – and nature; and between the living and the dead. The volume is intended for children but the stories will certainly appeal to adults as well. It includes a select glossary of words and pronunciations.

639 **Surinam negro folktales.**
Cornelis Nicolaas Dubelaar. Groningen, The Netherlands: [no publisher] 1973. 66p. bibliog.

A collection of five folk-tales, *anansi tori* (spider or trickster tales), two of which are published with a simultaneous translation. A brief explanation of types and motifs accompanies each story, which are preceded by a more theoretical chapter introducing the origin of and the varieties in *anansi tori*; European and African influences; and narrative techniques.

640 **Het grote Anansiboek.** (The great Anansi book.)
Johan Ferrier, illustrations by Noni Lichtveld. 's Hertogenbosch, The Netherlands: Aldus; Helmond, The Netherlands: Uitgeverij Helmond; The Hague: Nederlands Bibliotheek en Lektuur Centrum, 1986. 144p.

A volume containing twenty-six stories about Anansi, a cunning spider who outwits animals and humans. Many of these stories are situated in Africa, the place of origin of the *anansi tori*.

641 **Aleks de Drie. Sye! Arki tori!** (Aleks de Drie. Silence! Listen to my story!)
Trudi Martinus Guda. Paramaribo: Ministerie van Onderwijs, Wetenschappen en Cultuur, 1985. 378p. bibliog.

Aleks de Drie (1902-82) was one of the most famous narrators of Creole popular stories, some of which were also broadcast on radio. Anthropologist Guda transcribes his work in this volume and brings together a selection of forty stories out of a total of approximately 140. Together with *Wan tori fu mi eygi sreti* (One story of my own) by Guda and De Drie (Paramaribo: Ministerie van Onderwijs, Wetenschappen en Cultuur, 1984) these books offer an in depth look at Creole culture.

642 **Suriname folk-lore. With transcriptions of Suriname songs and musicological analysis by Dr. M. Kolinski.**
Melville J. Herskovits, Frances S. Herskovits. New York: AMS Press, 1969. 766p. bibliog. (Columbia University Contributions to Anthropology, 27).

A classic study of the coastal Creoles and the Maroons of the upper Suriname River. The greatest portion of ethnological information and tales were gathered in Paramaribo. In part one the authors describe the culture of the Paramaribo Creoles in detail. Part two presents 148 stories, riddles, proverbs, and dreams. The third part concentrates on music, comparing the musical expression of Paramaribo Creoles, Maroons, and Haitian blacks. The book includes twenty-seven plates.

643 **Oral literature of the Trio Indians of Surinam.**
Cees Koelewijn, Peter Rivière. Dordrecht, The Netherlands: Foris, 1987. 312p. map. bibliog. (Koninklijk Instituut voor Taal-, Land- en Volkenkunde Caribbean Series, 6).

Koelewijn collected one hundred narratives comprising so-called myths, containing ultimate truths about the nature of the world; stories relating to more actual events; stories with a historical basis; and, finally, fables. A major goal of publishing this volume is to preserve something of the older generation's knowledge of traditional Trio culture. Rivière contributes an introduction to Trio society and culture as well as a concluding commentary on Trio oral literature and the degree to which the narratives reflect fundamental ideas of the Trio about the nature of their universe.

644 **Negro riddles from Surinam.**
Arthur P. Penard, Thomas E. Penard. *West-Indische Gids*, vol. 7 (1925/26), p. 411-32.

An introduction to riddles or *lai tori*, an important aspect of Creole folklore. Despite European influences, the overwhelming majority of riddles is of native origin. As a rule these are short and simple and not presented in verse or rhyme. The article includes sixty-seven riddles.

645 **Surinam folk-tales.**
Arthur P. Penard, Thomas E. Penard. *The Journal of American Folk-Lore*, vol. 30, no. 116 (April-June 1917), p. 239-50. bibliog.

The authors collected four *anansi tori* of African and European origin. The first three stories were chosen because they had not previously been recorded. The fourth one is included to show how a narrator from Suriname treats familiar themes.

646 **Popular beliefs pertaining to certain places in Surinam.**
Thomas E. Penard, Arthur P. Penard. *West-Indische Gids*, vol. 10, no. 11 (1928/29), p. 17-33.

The authors list a number of haunted places in Suriname which are said to be the abodes of supernatural beings, each with peculiar attributes and spheres of action. Some of these beings are malicious, some beneficient, and some neutral. They may choose to inhabit a river or a creek, a waterfall, a rock, a road or street corner, a bridge, a plantation; in short, any place or object that may be to their liking.

647 **Popular notions pertaining to primitive stone artifacts in Surinam.**
Thomas E. Penard, Arthur P. Penard. *Journal of American Folk-Lore*, vol. 30, no. 116 (April-June 1917), p. 251-61.

The authors made a large collection of so-called primitive stone implements found in various parts of Suriname, enabling them to record the notions and superstitions which exist regarding these implements of Amerindian origin. Many are preserved by the Amerindians and Creoles as curiosities or as amulets and charms. They ascribe mysterious properties to these stones.

648 **Let them talk: de historische ontwikkeling van de kleding van de Creoolse vrouw.** (Let them talk: the historical development of the costume of the Creole woman.)
Laddy van Putten, Janny Zantinge. *Mededelingen van het Surinaams Museum*, no. 43 (Oct. 1988), p. 16-112. bibliog.

This special edition highlights the historical development of Creole women's costume from slavery to the present. The authors discuss the so-called *kotomissie* (woman wearing traditional costume), the *angisa* headkerchief and the different ways of tying it, and jewellery. The essay includes a short summary in English and a glossary.

649 **Tiermärchen der Buschneger in Surinam.** (Animal tales of the Maroons in Suriname.)
F. Stähelin. *Hessische Blätter für Volkskunde*, vol. 8 (1909), p. 173-84.

A collection of six Maroon folktales which were recorded during the first decades of the 20th century.

Cookery

650 **Surinaams koken.** (Surinamese Cooking.)
Ilse Marie Dorff. Houten, The Netherlands: Unieboek, 1987. 3rd ed. 96p. (Van Dishoeck Kreatief Koken).

A paperback with approximately 100 recipes, including some for holidays and parties. The book includes an index in the original language and one with a Dutch translation.

651 **Surinaams kookboek. Authentieke gerechten uit een exotisch land.**
(Surinamese cookbook. Authentic recipes from an exotic country.)
Line Karimbux. Utrecht, The Netherlands: Luitingh, 1981. 146p.

Besides recipes, this paperback contains a short history of the cuisine of Suriname as well as an identification list of herbs and other ingredients.

652 **Groot Surinaams kookboek met exotische Creools, Hindoestaanse, Indonesische, Chinese en Europese gerechten.** (Great Surinamese cookery book with exotic Creole, Hindustani, Indonesian, Chinese, and European dishes.)
A. A. Starke, M. Samsin-Hewitt.   Paramaribo: Stichting Kankantrie; Utrecht, The Netherlands: Onderwijspers (OTO), 1976. 331p.

A choice of Creole, British Indian, Javanese, European, and Chinese recipes. This cookbook includes an alphabetical index and a glossary.

653 **Surinaamse gerechten.** (Surinamese dishes.)
Nel Tjon Tam Sin-Nieleveld.   The Hague: BZZTôH/Novib, 1987. 111p.

A paperback with a selection of Surinamese recipes including snacks, soups, entrées, deserts, cakes and cookies, syrups, as well as tips for pickling and food preservation.

654 **Swiet Sranan njan (oh that sweet Surinam food).**
Suralco Magazine, no. 3 (1973), p. 6-13.

A description of the different foods of Suriname: Creole, British Indian, Chinese, and Javanese.

Sports and Recreation

655 **Gullit.**
Martin van Amerongen, Gerlof Leistra.   Amsterdam: De
Arbeiderspers, 1990. 147p.
A 'biography' of star football player Ruud Gullit, who is of Surinamese descent and
the captain of the Dutch national team, which is based almost entirely on secondary
sources. It not only focuses on football, but also looks at the impact of the outspoken
Gullit on race relations in the Netherlands. The style is at times ironic.

656 **Speciale catalogus van de Nederlandse munten van 1806 tot heden met
Nederlands West Indië, Nederlands Oost Indië, Suriname, Curaçao,
Nederlandse Antillen, Aruba.** (Special catalogue of the Dutch coins
from 1806 to the present with the Dutch West Indies, the Dutch East
Indies, Suriname, Curaçao, Netherlands Antilles, Aruba.)
Johan Mevius.   Vriezenveen, The Netherlands: Mevius Numisbooks,
1989. 21st ed. 145p. bibliog.
A yearly catalogue for collectors of coins with four pages on Suriname (pre-1975) and
six pages on the Republic of Suriname (post-1975).

657 **Ontstaan en ontwikkelingen van Surinaamse voetbalverenigingen in Den
Haag.** (Origin and developments of Surinamese football clubs in The
Hague.)
S. R. Ramsahai.   *Sarnami Akademi*, vol. 2, no. 1 (1989), p. 102-18.
One of the few publications on Surinamese athletic organizations in the Netherlands,
where football clubs play an important role in the organization of youngsters in
particular. The first Surinamese football team in The Hague was founded in 1962. The
author emphasizes the importance of football in the social organization of the
Surinamese by analysing the football team of 'De Ster'.

658   **Catalogus van de postzegels van Nederland en Overzeese Rijksdelen.**
(Catalogue of the stamps of the Netherlands and overseas territories.)
The Hague: Nederlandsche Vereeniging van Postzegelhandelaren,
1988. 40th ed. 304p.
Forty-four pages in this yearly catalogue cover Surinamese stamps issued during the
period 1873-1945.

659   **Speciale catalogus van de postzegels van Nederland, Nederlands Indië,
Indonesië, Nederlands Nieuw Guinea, Curaçao, de Nederlandse
Antillen, Aruba, Suriname.** (Special catalogue of the stamps of the
Netherlands, the Dutch East Indies, Indonesia, Dutch New Guinea,
Curaçao, the Netherlands Antilles, Aruba, Suriname.)
The Hague: Nederlandsche Vereeniging van Postzegelhandelaren,
1989. 49th ed. 519p. bibliog.
A yearly guide for stamp collectors, seventy pages of which are devoted to Surinamese
stamps. A separate section lists the 'Koninkrijks-series' or Kingdom of the Netherlands
series. The guide contains an index of persons, subjects, and designers.

660   **Suriname's postage stamps.**
Suralco Magazine, no. 2 (1973), p. 16-21.
A brief description of Surinamese stamps from the first one issued in 1877 to 1968. An
update appeared in *Suralco Magazine,* vol. 15, no. 2 (1983).

Libraries and Archives

661   An annotated catalog of original source materials relating to the history of European expansion 1400-1800.
James Ford Bell Library, University of Minnesota.   Boston, Massachusetts: G. K. Hall, 1981. 493p.

The James Ford Bell Library at the University of Minnesota in Minneapolis holds the largest collection in the United States of materials on Dutch expansion of the period 1500-1800. Most of the documents are the writings of explorers, merchants, and missionaries, with a particular emphasis on mercantile aspects. The collection on Suriname is impressive and contains several unique documents and archives. This volume on European expansion is organized alphabetically with brief annotations to most items, and follows the format of the National Union Catalog. The guide does not incorporate materials held by the Department of Special Collections or other divisions of the University of Minnesota.

662   Inventaris van het archief van de Gouverneur van Suriname, afdeling Kabinet Geheim 1885-1951. (Inventory of the archive of the governor of Suriname, department of secret correspondence 1885-1951.)
J. A. A. Bervoets.   The Hague: Algemeen Rijksarchief, Tweede Afdeling, 1982. 218p.

An inventory of the archives of the Governor of Suriname, deposited at the General State Archives (Algemeen Rijksarchief) in The Hague. This listing includes an index on personal names and subjects.

663 **Inventarissen van het archief van de beheerder van het Surinaams Welvaartsfonds 1947-1960.** (Inventories of the archive of the administrator of the Surinamese Welfare Fund 1947-1960.)
J. A. A. Bervoets. The Hague: Algemeen Rijksarchief, Tweede Afdeling, 1982. 149p.

This guide includes five inventories of archives pertaining to Suriname deposited at the General State Archives in The Hague. These include the archive of the administrator of the Welfare Fund; the archive of the adminstrator of the Administration of Indian Pensions in Suriname Foundation (*Stichting Administratie van Indische Pensioenen in Suriname*); the archives of the chairman of the (Surinamese) Advisory Committee concerning Technical Assistance (*Voorzitter van de Surinaamse Adviescommissie inzake technische bijstand*); the archives of the government spokesperson (*Rijksvoorlichtingsambtenaar*) in Suriname; and the archives of the Prince Bernhard Foundation (*Prins Bernhard Stichting*). This guide includes indexes.

664 **Surinam plantations in Dutch archives.**
Peter Boomgaard. *Itinerario* , vol. 1 (1982), p. 121-26.

A listing of documentary sources on some 200 plantations. The most important collection is housed at the General State Archives in The Hague. Other collections are located in the municipal archives of Amsterdam and Rotterdam, and in Amsterdam's Economic Historical Library which all contain documentation of influential 18th and 19th-century merchant and banking houses. Finally, Boomgaard surveys some of the preliminary results of a research project started in 1979, the objective of which was to collect as much data on as many plantations as possible.

665 **Inventaris van de collectie prenten, tekeningen, kaarten en foto's van de Evangelische Broedergemeente te Zeist (ca. 1700-1982).** (Inventory of the collection of prints, drawings, maps and photographs of the Moravian Brethren in Zeist [ca. 1700-1982].)
C. M. P. F. van den Broek. Utrecht, The Netherlands: Rijksarchief, 1985. 227p. bibliog.

Following an introduction to the history of the Moravian Brethren in Zeist, the Netherlands, the compiler provides an inventory of the holdings of the Moravian Brethren in this town. The collection on Suriname includes technical drawings, maps, engravings, and photographs. The appendix contains an index of individuals appearing in the illustrations.

666 **The archives of the Nederlandsche Handel Maatschappij – NHM-Mariënburg branch, Suriname/Archief Nederlandsche Handel Maatschappij NHM afdeling Mariënburg, Suriname.**
L. H. Ferrier. *Mededelingen van het Surinaams Museum*, no. 42 (April 1986), p. 35-48.

A description of the archives of the Mariënburg plantation owned by the Netherlands Trading Company (NHM). This collection is housed at the Surinaams Museum in Paramaribo and contains sixty-nine files of correspondence to and from the Mariënburg management. The correspondence covers the period 1881-1943. In addition, there are a few files listing labourers and wages on the Slootwijk plantation in around 1950. The correspondence is in a rather good state of preservation, except for

Libraries and Archives

some of the oldest letters. An inventory has been made of the entire collection. The
paper is written in English and Dutch.

667 **Correspondence of J. H. Lance Judge in the Mixed Court of Justice in
Paramaribo, 1822-1833/Korrespondentie van J. H. Lance rechter bij het
Gemengd Gerechtshof te Paramaribo, 1822-1833.**
L. H. Ferrier. *Mededelingen van het Surinaams Museum*, no. 40
(Aug. 1983), p. 4-25.

In 1978, the Surinaams Museum in Paramaribo obtained a collection of letters by J. H.
Lance, Judge in the Mixed Court of Justice from 1822 to 1833. John Henry Lance was
born in England in 1793, he attended Eton College and pursued a career as a jurist. In
1822, the English Crown appointed him to the Mixed Court, which had to ensure that
no traffic in slaves would take place. A large collection of his private letters addressed
to his family in England gives an impression of his life in Suriname and his feelings
about slavery and the slave trade. This unique collection does not include Lance's
official correspondence. This article is published in English and Dutch.

668 **Correspondence of the NHM (Netherlands Trading Co.) 1889-1894 on
the subject 'The Immigration of Javanese' parts I and
II/Korrespondentie NHM (Nederlandsche Handel Maatschappij) 1889-
1894. Onderwerp: Immigratie van Javanen deel I en II.**
L. H. Ferrier. *Mededelingen van het Surinaams Museum*, no. 41
(Dec. 1983), p. 26-53; no. 42 (April 1986), p. 17-35.

A description of the archive of the NHM (Netherlands Trading Company) regarding
the Mariënburg plantation. This collection consists of the originals and transcriptions
of official correspondence to and from the plantation management. The essays, in
English and Dutch, deal in particular with correspondence dating from the period
1889-94. During this time negotiations concerning the importation of some one
hundred Javanese took place.

669 **Gids voor de in Amsterdam aanwezige bronnen voor de geschiedenis van
Suriname.** (Guide to the historical sources in Amsterdam pertaining to
the history of Suriname.)
R. van Gelder. The Hague: Algemeen Rijksarchief, 1985. 28p.

A guide to the historical sources in Amsterdam pertaining to the history of Suriname
during the period from 1621 to the Second World War. These collections can be found
in the Municipal Archives of the Royal Tropical Institute, and in other libraries,
museums, and institutes in the Dutch capital. The author describes three categories of
documents: written sources (except for printed material), topographical descriptions
and maps, portraits, and miscellaneous objects. In the collection of the Municipal
Archives approximately twenty collections are of particular importance for the history
of Suriname's plantations. In the various annotated lists, the author indicates the
availability of inventories as well as the codes and the call numbers of the collections.

184

670 **Inventaris van de papieren van A. van den Brandhof, stichter van de Nederlandse boerenkolonie in Suriname.** (Inventory of the personal documents of A. van den Brandhof, founder of the Dutch colonial settlement in Suriname.)
A. A. Hamburger-Wolterbeek Muller. Leiden, The Netherlands: Royal Institute of Linguistics and Anthropology, 1980. 70p. maps. bibliog.

An inventory of the archival documents, mainly concerning the period 1840-53, pertaining to European colonization, of the Saramacca River and the organization thereof. This collection is housed at the Royal Institute of Linguistics and Anthropology, Leiden, the Netherlands. The volume also includes some government documents and laws, genealogical and demographic information, a glossary, and an index of personal names.

671 **Inventaris van het archief van het Zendingsgenootschap der Evangelische Broedergemeente te Zeist (Zeister Zendingsgenootschap) 1793-1962.** (Inventory of the archive of the missionary society of the Moravian Brethren at Zeist [Zeister Zendingsgenootschap] 1793-1962.)
C. G. W. M. van Hoogstraten. Utrecht, The Netherlands: Rijksarchief Utrecht, 1985. 203p. maps. (Inventaris, 48).

Following an historical introduction, the author presents an inventory of the archive of the Moravian Brethren in the Netherlands. This listing is divided into seven categories: general documents; documents concerning special topics; involvement with overseas territories; filed documents; maps, prints, and floor plans; documentation; films and tapes. The entire third section deals with Suriname. The volume includes an index of personal names and one on geographical names.

672 **Researching slave culture at the General State Archives.**
Saskia Keller. *Itinerario*, vol. 4, no. 2 (1980), p. 64-70.

A brief discussion of the sources deposited at the General State Archives in The Hague containing information on slavery. Most records deal with one of the following three themes: Maroons; plantation disputes; and the treatment of slaves. Quantification of data is, according to the author, hardly feasible.

673 **Archieven over Suriname.** (Archives pertaining to Suriname.)
Evert van Laar. *Oso*, vol. 7, no. 2 (Dec. 1988), p. 169-74. bibliog.

Archivist Van Laar sums up the archives pertaining to the history of Suriname deposited at the General State Archives in The Hague. In the final section of this paper, he briefly discusses the location and the condition of several archives in Suriname.

674 **A survey of the archives in the Netherlands pertaining to the history of the Caribbean area.**
Evert van Laar. The Hague: Algemeen Rijksarchief, 1975. 24p. bibliog.

A supplement to M. Roessingh's *Guide to the sources in the Netherlands for the history of Latin America* (q.v.) by the keeper of the Second Section of the General State

Archives. It lists archives and collections kept in state and town archives; the Department of Foreign Affairs; the Department of Home Affairs; and the Cabinet for Surinamese and Netherlands Antillean Affairs.

675   **Libraries and special collections on Latin America and the Caribbean: a directory of European resources.**
Roger Macdonald, Carole Travis.   London; Atlantic Heights, New Jersey: Athlone Press, 1988. 2nd ed. 339p.

A directory published for the Institute of Latin American Studies at the University of London, covering research resources on Latin America and the Caribbean, with a heavy emphasis on collections in the United Kingdom. Entries include general details of the services of the libraries, together with full descriptions of the collections. Particular strengths in coverage are mentioned in the annotations. The index covers libraries and named collections by title, acronym, parent organization, and subject area.

676   **The Dutch colonial archives: a bird's eye view.**
Margot E. van Opstall.   *Itinerario*, vol.4, no. 2 (1980), p. 29-43.

Following an introduction, the author describes the organizational structure of the General State Archives. In the second section, she first examines the archives which were formed in the Netherlands and then those formed in the colonies. A similar article by the same author is published in *Comparative perspectives on slavery in New World plantation societies*, edited by Vera Rubin, Arthur Tuden (New York: New York Academy of Sciences, 1977).

677   **Guide to the sources in The Netherlands for the history of Latin America.**
M. P. H. Roessingh.   The Hague: Government Publishing Office, 1968. 232p. bibliog.

This guide provides a survey of documents, manuscripts, maps, and topographical reproductions in the Netherlands pertaining to the history of Latin America and covers the period from 1492 to 1914. The volume is subdivided according to the organization of the Dutch archives. The author first discusses the General State Archives, the most important repository, followed by municipal archives; archives of non-governmental institutions; libraries; museums; family archives; and private collections.

678   **Sources for the history of the Dutch colonies in the ecclesiastical archives of Rome (1814-1903).**
J. P. de Valk.   *Itinerario*, vol. 9, no. 1 (1985), p. 53-66. bibliog.

The author advises researchers on the history of the Catholic missions in Suriname to visit the Vatican archives and those of other ecclesiastical headquarters in Rome. These depositories also contain documents which may illuminate other aspects of colonial history. The author provides an overview of the archival material in Rome, grouped according to the various deposits and collections.

679 **Overzicht van Suriname-collecties I, II en III.** (An overview of
collections on Suriname I, II, and III.)
Hein Vruggink, A. N. Paasman. *Oso*, vol. 7, no. 2 (Dec. 1988),
p. 189-244; vol. 8, no. 1 (May 1989), p. 77-96; vol. 8, no. 2 (Dec. 1989),
p. 196-226. bibliog.

A listing of more than one hundred collections on Suriname in the Netherlands. Each
entry includes the address, the opening hours, and details about each collection which
may cover documents, journals, newspapers, books, maps, photographs, portraits,
coins, *objets d'art*, audio-visual materials, and botanical items.

Mass Media

Newspapers

680 **Onafhankelijke Suriname Weekkrant.** (Independent Weekly
Suriname.)
Voorburg, The Netherlands: Tory Media International, 1980- . weekly.

This newspaper, published in Dutch for Surinamese abroad, informs on the current
state of affairs in Suriname. It also reports on news in the Netherlands pertaining to
the Surinamese community. Previously this weekly was called *Weekkrant Suriname.*

681 **De Ware Tijd.** (The True Times.)
Paramaribo: C. Tjong Akiet, 1957- . daily.

An independent newpaper, whose editor is the well-known Leo Morpurgo. At times
during the military dictatorship the paper could not be published due to 'paper
shortages'.

682 **De West.** (The West.)
Paramaribo: 1909- . daily.

A pro-government newspaper with a circulation of approximately 10,000 (1987).

Periodicals

683 **Aisa Samachar.** (Good News.)
The Hague: Stichting voor Surinamers Den Haag, 1976- . irregular.

The Foundation for Surinamese (SVS) publishes this periodical with information for
and about Surinamese of British Indian descent. It contains news, information, and
brief essays in Dutch. Previously this periodical was called *Aisa.*

684 **Lalla Rookh.**
Utrecht, The Netherlands: De Stichting Lalla Rookh Nederland,
1975- . bimonthly.

Lalla Rookh, named after the first ship carrying British Indian contract labourers to
Suriname, is a journal in Dutch published by the Lalla Rookh Foundation (formerly
FHON). It has a circulation of 4,000 and contains information on Surinamese
population groups in the Netherlands in general and the British Indians in particular.

685 **Lobi Krant.** (Love Paper.)
Paramaribo; Nieuw Nickerie, Suriname: Lobi Foundation. 1981- .
quarterly.

A Surinamese quarterly in Dutch on sex education and family planning published by
the Lobi Foundation.

686 **Mi Doro.** (My Door.)
The Hague: Stichting Tenasu, 1977- . 10 times a year.

A periodical published in Dutch by the Tenasu Foundation. Tenasu stands for *Terug
naar Suriname* or Back to Suriname and its main function is to study possibilities for
and to solve problems concerning return migration. Each issue contains articles,
economic notices concerning Suriname, and a book list.

687 **Span'noe.** (Support Each Other.)
Utrecht, The Netherlands: Stichting Landelijke Federatie van
Welzijnsorganisaties voor Surinamers, 1974- . quarterly.

This periodical offers information for and about Surinamese living in the Netherlands.
It is published by the National Federation of Social Welfare Organizations for
Surinamese. Each issue contains several articles, book reviews, and news items, all
written in Dutch.

688 **Suralco Magazine.**
Paramaribo: Public Relations Department of the Suriname Aluminum
Company, 1969-1986. quarterly.

A nicely illustrated magazine containing articles in Dutch and in English and covering
nature, geography, and history. Its aim was 'to promote a better understanding of this
country and its people'.

Professional
Periodicals

689   Caribbean Insight.
   London: The West India Committee, 1977- . monthly
This political and economic news bulletin incorporates the *Caribbean and West Indies Chronicle.*

690   Caribbean Report.
   London: Latin American Newsletters, 1979- . weekly (50 issues per year).
A weekly information bulletin containing political and economic news on individual Caribbean countries including Suriname.

691   Country report Venezuela, Suriname, Netherlands Antilles.
   London: The Economist Intelligence Unit, 1952- . quarterly.
A quarterly analysis of political and economic trends. Each publication includes information on the political structure, economic data, graphs with economic trends, an overview and a forecast for the future. The appendix contains quarterly indicators of economic activity. The same publisher also puts out an annual survey entitled *Venezuela Suriname, Netherlands Antille country profile* (q.v.).

692   European Review of Latin American and Caribbean Studies/Revista Europea de Estudios Latino-americanos y del Caribe.
   Amsterdam: Center for Latin American Research and Documentation (CEDLA); Leiden, The Netherlands: Caribbean Department, Royal Institute of Linguistics and Anthropology, 1965- . biannual.
This journal contains articles on anthropology, archaeology, demography, economy, geography, history, political science, and sociology, as well as book reviews. Since 1985, each December issue has contained a bibliographical essay on Caribbean studies in the Netherlands, one section of which is devoted to Suriname. A cumulative index covering the period 1965-83 includes a survey of articles published in each issue, an

190

index of countries, and a listing of books reviewed. During this period thirteen essays on Suriname appeared in this journal, which prior to no. 47 (Dec. 1989) was called *Boletín de Estudios Latinoamericanos y del Caribe.*

693　**Mededelingen van het Surinaams Museum** (Communications of the Surinaams Museum.)
Paramaribo: Stichting Surinaams Museum, [1970- .]. three times per year.

A journal in Dutch and English publishing articles focusing on archaeology, history, and anthropology. In the more recent issues of the journal several archival collections in the possession of the Surinaams Museum are partly described. Unfortunately, since the 1980s issues have been published irregularly. The journal was previously called *Mededelingen Stichting Surinaams Museum, Mededelingen Surinaamse Musea,* and *Mededeling Surinaams Museum.*

694　**Nieuwe West-Indische Gids/New West Indian Guide.**
Dordrecht, The Netherlands: Foris Publications for the Stichting Nieuwe West-Indische Gids, Utrecht, The Netherlands, in collaboration with the Program in Atlantic History, Culture and Society of Johns Hopkins University, Baltimore, Maryland, 1919- . quarterly.

Originally called *De West-Indische Gids,* this is a journal covering all aspects of Caribbean interest, ranging from history to natural sciences. The majority of the articles were written in Dutch. In 1960 it merged with two other periodicals, the *Vox Guyana* from Suriname and *Christoffel* from Curaçao and became the *Nieuwe West-Indische Gids/New West Indian Guide.* In 1982 a new editorial policy was adopted: from then on the journal focused on the social sciences and the humanities, while English became the principal language of publication. An enlarged book review section and more attention to the non-Dutch speaking Caribbean completed this change.

695　**Oso, tijdschrift voor Surinaamse taalkunde, letterkunde en geschiedenis.**
(House, journal of Surinamese linguistics, literature and history.)
Nijmegen, The Netherlands: Stichting ter Bevordering van de Surinamistiek, 1982- . biannual.

The foundation for the promotion of the study of Suriname publishes this journal containing (popular) social science articles, generally in Dutch, occasionally in English, and book reviews. Each issue also contains a listing of literature on Suriname published during the previous months. During the period 1976-79 *Oso* was a quarterly published by the Wi Na Wan group.

696　**Sarnami Akademie.** (Sarnami Academy.)
The Hague: Warray, 1988- . biannual.

A periodical containing articles on (social) science and culture, often of a rather theoretical nature. It includes a listing and reviews of unpublished theses and manuscripts. The first issue was named *Srunun Akademia.*

Professional Periodicals

697   **De Surinaamse Landbouw/Surinam Agriculture.**
      Paramaribo: Landbouwproefstation, 1953- . irregular.

A professional periodical on agriculture published by the Agricultural Experiment Station. It appears irregularly, no issues being published between 1978 and 1980. Most of the articles are written in Dutch or English, the former including summaries in English.

698   **SWI Forum voor wetenschap en cultuur.** (SWI Forum for science and culture.)
      Paramaribo: Stichting Wetenschappelijke Informatie, 1984- .
      biannual.

A periodical devoted to (social) science and culture. It includes a book review section.

Reference Books

699 **Encyclopedie van Suriname.** (Encyclopaedia of Suriname.)
   Edited by C. F. A. Bruijning, Jan Voorhoeve, W. Gordijn.
   Amsterdam, Brussel: Elsevier, 1977. 716p. maps.
An indispensable research tool, including 2,250 entries written by well-known experts.
The most important ones contain short bibliographical references. The 1975
Constitution of Suriname is published in the appendix.

700 **The Cambridge Encyclopedia of Latin America and the Caribbean.**
   Edited by Simon Collier, Harold Blakemore, Thomas E. Skidmore.
   Cambridge, England: Cambridge University Press, 1985. 456p. maps.
   bibliog.
An encyclopaedia divided into six sections covering the physical environment, the
economy, the peoples, history, politics and society, and culture of Latin America and
the Caribbean. Sister Mary Noel-Menezes contributed a chapter on the history of the
Guianas. Each chapter includes a short bibliography.

701 **The Caribbean: survival, struggle and sovereignty.**
   Catherine A. Sunshine.   Washington, DC: Epica, 1988. 2nd ed. 255p.
   map. bibliog.
A good introduction to the region. In part six of this progressive survey the author
discusses 'the Caribbean in crisis', also separately covering Suriname. She briefly
reviews the country's 'old politics' and its dependency on the Netherlands; the *coup
d'état* of 1980 and the reluctant revolution; the counter-revolution and the collapse of
the military régime; and, finally, the return of civilian government. This chapter on
Suriname includes three illustrations.

Reference Books

702 **The Caribbean handbook 1990.**
Edited by Jeremy Taylor. St. John's, Antigua: FT Caribbean, 1990.
260p. maps. bibliog.
A business guide to the Caribbean divided into two parts. The first one gives a
Caribbean profile, which is mainly economic in nature. Part two provides surveys of
the Caribbean countries, each of which includes general information; key facts; a
population profile; and reviews of the economy and the business environment.

703 **Handboek Latijns-Amerika.** (Handbook Latin America.)
Utrecht, The Netherlands: Central Latinoamericana de Trabajadores,
1988. 320p. maps. bibliog.
A collection of data on countries in Latin America and the Caribbean covering
demography; social conditions; and the economic and financial situation. The section
on more important countries, including Suriname, also reviews recent political, social,
and economic developments and provides information for travellers. This handbook
includes three general maps as well as separate maps for each country discussed. It also
contains a list of Latin American, Caribbean, and other international organizations.

704 **The Latin American and Caribbean Review.**
Saffron Walden, England: World of Information, 1988. 9th ed. 199p.
A yearly directory providing key economic indicators; several essays on economic and
socio-political topics such as the war on drugs, tourism, and foreign debts; and a
country survey. Tony Thorndike authored the section on Suriname. Following a
general introduction the focus is on a country profile and a business guide to Suriname.

705 **South America, Central America and the Caribbean 1988.**
London: Europa Publications, 1987. 2nd ed. 683p. maps. bibliog.
A useful survey of the political and economic life both of the region and of the forty-
seven countries and territories within it. The volume is divided into three parts. The
first one gives a background to the region and includes a select bibliography of
periodicals. The second section lists regional organizations. The country surveys form
the third. The section on Suriname is largely written by Elizabeth Thomas-Hope and
provides an historical and an economic overview; a statistical survey; and a directory
covering governmental organizations, the press, economic institutions, and the judicial
system. The bibliography on Suriname, however, leaves much to be desired.

Bibliographies

706 **A bibliography on Caribbean migration and Caribbean immigrant communities.**
Rosemary Brana-Shute, Rosemarijn Hoefte.   Gainesville, Florida: University of Florida Libraries, Reference and Bibliographic Department in cooperation with the Center for Latin American Studies, 1983. 339p.

A selective multi-disciplinary bibliography on migration. It includes both published and unpublished sources in various languages. The entries are listed alphabetically by author, and there are six appendices including a comprehensive index based on the origin of the migrants which lists 106 entries on Suriname, and an alphabetical listing of the destination of the migrants which contains eighty-nine entries on Suriname.

707 **Bibliografía básica para la historia de las Antillas Holandesas y Suriname.** (Basic bibliography of the history of the Netherlands Antilles and Suriname.)
Raymond Th. J. Buve.   *Historiografía y Bibliografía Americanistas,* vol. 25 (1981), p. 149-85.

An annotated bibliography in Spanish in the form of an essay, covering social science research on the Netherlands Antilles and Suriname up to 1979. It is divided into three parts: general works; slavery; and the post-Emancipation period.

708 **Women in the Caribbean: a bibliography.**
Bertie A. Cohen Stuart.   Leiden, The Netherlands: Department of Caribbean Studies, Royal Institute of Linguistics and Anthropology, 1979. 161p.

An annotated survey of books and articles on women in English, French, Dutch, Spanish, Papiamento (Creole), and Portuguese. Titles in Dutch, and several in Papiamento, are translated into English. The survey is divided into seven categories: bibliographies and other works of reference; introductory works; bibliographies of individual women; a list of women's organizations; a bibliography compiled by Cohen; an author index; and an index according to categories. The main bibliography is subdivided into five subjects: family and household; cultural factors; education; economic factors; politics and law. This volume includes approximately forty titles on Suriname.

709 **Women in the Caribbean: a bibliography, part two.**
Bertie A. Cohen Stuart. Leiden, The Netherlands: Department of Caribbean Studies, Royal Institute of Linguistics and Anthropology, 1985. 246p.

A supplement to *Women in the Caribbean* (q.v.). In this edition journals have been listed separately and a new section has been added: creative arts. Titles in Dutch and Papiamento have been translated into English as before. The volume contains more than 100 items on Surinamese women.

710 **A critical survey of studies on Dutch colonial history.**
W. Ph. Coolhaas, revised by G. J. Schutte. The Hague: Martinus Nijhoff, 1980. 2nd ed. 264p. (Koninklijk Instituut voor Taal-, Land- en Volkenkunde Bibliographical Series, 4).

This volume is the second revised English edition, with many additions, of the original French text dating from 1957. The first English edition appeared in 1960 as part of the same series. The bibliography is written in the form of a continuous narrative with a separate alphabetical bibliography at the end of the book complementing the biographical data in the text. There is an index of personal names as well as a geographical index. The section on Suriname includes approximately 100 titles, mostly in Dutch.

711 **Suriname: a bibliography 1980-1989.**
Jo Derkx, Irene Rolfes. Leiden, The Netherlands: Department of Caribbean Studies, Royal Institute of Linguistics and Anthropology, 1990. 297p. (Caribbean Bibliographies).

This survey covers titles published during the period 1980-89 and contains approximately 2,000 entries on Suriname and Surinamese migrant communities. The bibliography includes monographs, articles, novels, poetry, and youth literature, as well as unpublished monographs.

712 **Lijst van geschriften van Justus Wilhelm Gonggrijp met beknopte biografie.** (List of publications by Justus Wilhelm Gonggrijp with a brief biography.)
Cornelis Nicolaas Dubelaar. *Nieuwe West-Indische Gids/New West Indian Guide*, vol. 47 (1969-70), p. 286-93. bibliog.

A short biography of J. W. Gonggrijp, an authority on silviculture. Moreover, Gonggrijp also published studies on the Afaka script of the Ndjukas and on the problems concerning Lake Brokopondo. The bibliography lists all of Gonggrijp's publications from 1907 to 1969.

713 **Bibliografie van Suriname.** (Bibliography of Suriname.)
W. Gordijn. Amsterdam: Nederlandse Stichting voor Culturele
Samenwerking met Suriname en de Nederlandse Antillen, 1972. 256p.

This selective bibliography contains 3,714 entries on publications which appeared prior to March 1972. These are divided into nine categories: general, including newspapers and journals; religion; social science, law, and economy; science; applied science; culture and the arts; language and literature; geography; and history. The bibliography includes three indexes covering subjects, authors, and corporate authors.

714 **Repertorium op de literatuur betreffende de Nederlandsche koloniën voor zover zij verspreid is in tijdschriften en mengelwerken.**
(Repertory of the literature concerning the Dutch colonies as far as it is scattered among periodicals and miscellaneous works.)
A. Hartmann. The Hague: Martinus Nijhoff, 1895. 454p.

A classic bibliography divided into two parts. The first section covers the East Indies from 1866 to 1893. The second part is on the West Indies during the period 1840-93. The subjects covered are: country and people; history; government; slavery and emancipation; immigration and colonization; agriculture and industry; communication and transport; education and religion; and language and bibliography. Eight sequels have been published, covering the period 1894-1932, all of which include subject and geographical indexes.

715 **A selective guide to the English literature on the Netherlands West Indies. With a supplement on British Guiana.**
Philip Hanson Hiss. New York: Netherlands Information Bureau, 1943. 129p.

This bibliography for the period 1492 to 1942, is divided into three sections: Curaçao, Suriname, and British Guiana. The section on Suriname is subdivided into fourteen chapters covering general works, government publications, history and archaeology, government, missions, politics, law, social conditions, economy, anthropology, geography, science, languages and literature, and the First and Second World Wars.

716 **Bibliography of printed maps of Suriname 1671-1971.**
C. Koeman. Amsterdam: Theatrum Orbis Terrarum, 1973. 156p.

A bibliography of maps containing 385 items covering the period between 1671 and 1971, the first map being drawn by C. Mogge, and listing both old and modern maps. The volume is divided into five chapters covering Suriname as a whole, regional maps, town plans of Paramaribo, Berbice, Demerara and Essequebo, and charts. Each chapter presents the maps, plans or charts in chronological order. An index of names of authors, publishers, and engravers concludes this useful research tool.

717 **Gezondheid en gezondheidszorg in Suriname: een geannoteerde bibliografie (1900-1985).** (Health and health care in Suriname: an annotated bibliography [1900-1985].)
Anja Krumeich. Amsterdam: Universiteit van Amsterdam, Vakgroep Culturele Antropologie en Niet-Westerse Sociologie Algemeen, 1988. 92p. (Uitgave, 25).

A research tool for medical-anthropological and sociological research in Suriname. The partly annotated bibliography is divided into five chapters, each covering a different subject. These five themes include general health care, medical missions and evangelization, nutrition, natal and child care, folk medicine and religion.

718 **Handbook of Latin American Studies.**
Edited by Dolores Moyano Martin (et al.). Cambridge, Massachusetts: Harvard University Press, 1936-51. Gainesville, Florida: University of Florida Press, 1952-79. Austin, Texas; London: University of Texas Press, 1980- .

The *Handbook of Latin American Studies* (HLAS) is the most important source for a Latin American and Caribbean bibliography. It is a selective and annotated guide, with evaluative and descriptive comments in English prepared by specialists. Since 1965, the work has been published in two volumes covering the social sciences (anthropology, economics, education, geography, government and politics, international relations, and sociology) and the humanities (art, folklore, history, language, literature, music, and philosophy). Since volume fifty more attention has been paid to the Dutch-speaking Caribbean. Francisco José Cardona and Maria Elena Cardona have compiled a cumulative author index covering the first three decades of publications: *Author index to HLAS, nos 1-28, 1936-1966* (Gainesville, Florida: University of Florida, 1968).

719 **Slavery: a worldwide bibliography, 1900-1982.**
Joseph C. Miller. White Plains, New York: Kraus International, 1985. 451p.

This bibliography guides students towards modern secondary literature on slavery and the slave trade anywhere in the world. All works listed are published in Western European languages and written from the perspective of a variety of academic disciplines, such as history, economy, sociology, anthropology, philosophy, and linguistics. The bibliography is divided into eleven chapters. An author index and a subject/keyword index follow the main bibliographical listing which contains 5,177 items; approximately seventy five of which cover Suriname and the Dutch slave trade. Annual supplements are published in the journal *Slavery and Abolition*.

720 **Surinamers in Nederland: een keuze uit de literatuur.** (Surinamese in the Netherlands: a choice from the literature.)
Ministerie van Welzijn, Volksgezondheid en Cultuur. Rijswijk, The Netherlands: Ministerie van WVC, hoofdafdeling documentatie en bibliotheek, 1988. 42p. (LL931).

An alphabetical listing of approximately 160 publications concerning Surinamese living in the Netherlands. The bibliography lacks registers or indexes.

721 Current annotated bibliography of Dutch expansion studies.
Jaap de Moor. *Itinerario*, vol. 12, no. 3/4 (1988), p. 3-120.
An annotated bibliography containing 271 entries on the history of Dutch expansion in the Americas, Africa, the Middle East and Asia, and Indonesia. Forty-four publications on Suriname are listed. The bibliography includes an author index as well as an index of subjects and personal names.

722 Bibliografisch overzicht van de Indianen in Suriname. Bibliographical survey of the Indians of Surinam 1700-1977.
Gerard A. Nagelkerke.   Leiden, The Netherlands: Caribbean Department, Royal Institute of Linguistics and Anthropology, 1977. 55p.
Although this bibliography is not an exhaustive survey of all the literature on Amerindians in Suriname, it does contain many published sources and manuscripts and is based largely on the collection housed at the Royal Institute of Linguistics and Anthropology in Leiden, the Netherlands. The monographs and the periodical articles are arranged alphabetically according to author. The bibliography includes an index on the main words in the title.

723 Literatuuroverzicht van Suriname tot 1940. Literatuur aanwezig in de bibliotheek van het Koninklijk Instituut voor Taal-, Land- en Volkenkunde te Leiden. (Review of the literature on Suriname until 1940. Literature deposited at the Royal Institute of Linguistics and Anthropology in Leiden.)
Gerard A. Nagelkerke.   Leiden, The Netherlands: Bibliotheek van het Koninklijk Instituut voor Taal-, Land- en Volkenkunde, 1972. 199p.
A bibliography of articles and monographs deposited at the library of the Royal Institute of Linguistics and Anthropology in Leiden, the Netherlands. The survey covers the period from the 17th century to 1940, listing 2,480 items. The bibliography is arranged alphabetically by author. The index contains the principal words in the titles and names of persons other than the author. The volume includes a list of consulted periodicals. Since the publication of this bibliography in 1972, many new works published during this period have been acquired, but so far no update has appeared.

724 Suriname: a bibliography 1940-1980.
Gerard A. Nagelkerke.   Leiden, The Netherlands: Department of Caribbean Studies, Royal Institute of Linguistics and Anthropology, 1980. 336p.
A bibliography including the most important works on Suriname published during the period 1940-80. The survey lists 2,600 monographs and articles arranged alphabetically by author. The principal subject words of the titles and names of persons other than the author are indexed. The volume includes a list of consulted periodicals.

725 **Inventory of Caribbean Studies: an overview of social scientific publications on the Caribbean by Antillean, Dutch, and Surinamese authors in the period 1945-1978/79.**
Theo M. P. Oltheten.   Leiden, The Netherlands: Department of Caribbean Studies, Royal Institute of Linguistics and Anthropology, 1979. 280p.

A survey of more than 1,900 publications relating to the Caribbean covering the period 1945-78/79. The majority of the works are on sociology, anthropology, social geography, political science, pedagogics, and psychology. Titles in Dutch have been translated into English. The bibliography is arranged alphabetically by author and includes lists of consulted bibliographies, periodicals, and an alphabetical subject index divided into four categories: Netherlands Antilles; Suriname; Antilleans and Surinamese in the Netherlands; and the Caribbean in general.

726 **The Guiana Maroons; a historical and bibliographical introduction.**
Richard Price.   Baltimore, Maryland; London: Johns Hopkins University Press, 1976. 184p.

This general introduction covers more than three centuries of Surinamese history, from the founding of the permanent colony in 1651 to the achievement of independence in 1975. In the first part, the author provides an historical framework, with special reference to the demography and sociology of the Maroons. Part two contains a bibliographical essay, which the author combines chronological and thematical approaches. In the final section, Price lists 1,330 items of ethnological and historical relevance. Whenever possible the location of sources in three repositories is supplied: one in the United States, one in Europe, and one in Suriname. The introduction is an indispensable guide for those intending to study the Guiana Maroons.

727 **Black slavery in the Americas. An interdisciplinary bibliography, 1865-1980.**
John David Smith, foreword by Stanley L. Engerman.   Westport, Connecticut; London: Greenwood Press, 1982. vols.

A bibliography on slavery counting more than 1,800 pages and recording 21,161 items in total. Under the headings Dutch Guiana and Suriname approximately 100 items are listed. This guide includes an index of subjects and authors.

728 **Caribbean music history: a selective annotated bibliography with musical supplement.**
Edited by Robert Stevenson.   *Inter-American Music Review*, vol. 4, no. 1 (fall 1981), p. 1-112. Distributed by Beverly Hills, California: Theodore Front Musical Literature.

This special issue of *Inter American Music Review* presents a selective bibliography on Caribbean music covering the period until 1975. Some of the items are not annotated at all, while others are discussed at great length. It includes eighteen items on Suriname, some rather general, others more specific. The listing is particularly helpful to a non-Dutch-reading audience as it annotates publications written in Dutch although no indexes have been included. Relevant items published between 1975 and 1980 are covered in *Inter-American Music Review*, vol. 5, no. 1 (fall 1982).

Bibliographies

729 American studies in the Netherlands: bibliography 1970-1987.
Jean Stroom. Amsterdam: Center for Latin American Research and Documentation, 1988. 220p.

An overview of almost 2,600 Dutch publications on Latin America, the Caribbean, and Amerindian studies. Fifteen per cent of the items deal with Suriname. The volume is organized alphabetically by author and includes a subject index.

730 Latinoamericanistas en Europa 1990. Registro bio-bibliográfico. (Latin Americanists in Europe 1990. Bio-bibliographical register.)
Jean Stroom. Amsterdam: Center for Latin American Research and Documentation, 1990. 240p.

This is the fifth edition of the *Directorio de Latinoamericanistas en Europa* and lists 584 students of Latin America in Europe. Each entry includes biographical as well as bibliographical data. The guide is organized alphabetically and includes indexes on the geographical origin of individuals listed and on their regional specializations. The final part lists associations of Latin Americanists in Europe.

731 Bibliographie du Négro-Anglais du Surinam, avec un appendice sur les langues creoles parlees á l'interieur du pays. (Bibliography of the Negro-English language of Suriname, with an appendix on the Creole languages spoken in the interior of the country.)
Jan Voorhoeve, Antoon Donicie. The Hague: Martinus Nijhoff, 1963. 116p. (Koninklijk Instituut voor Taal-, Land- en Volkenkunde Bibliographical Series, 6).

An annotated linguistic bibliography of Sranan. The titles are presented systematically: general studies; dictionaries; and grammatical studies. Conversation courses precede the main part of the bibliography: a listing of publications written in Sranan which are divided into religious texts, reflecting the interest of the missionaries who used the language for the evangelization of the slaves, and secular texts. The appendix contains thirty-five items concerning the Maroon languages of Suriname. The compilers provide library or archival locations and the alphabetical index includes authors, translators, and titles.

Index

The index is a single alphabetical sequence of authors (personal and corporate), titles of publications and subjects. Index entries refer both to the main items and to other works mentioned in the note to each item. They refer also to authors who have contributed to an edited volume but who are not mentioned in the annotations. Title entries are in italics. Numbers refer to bibliographic entries.

206

207

214

K

215

216

M

218

219

225

227

Map of Suriname

This map shows the more important towns and other features.

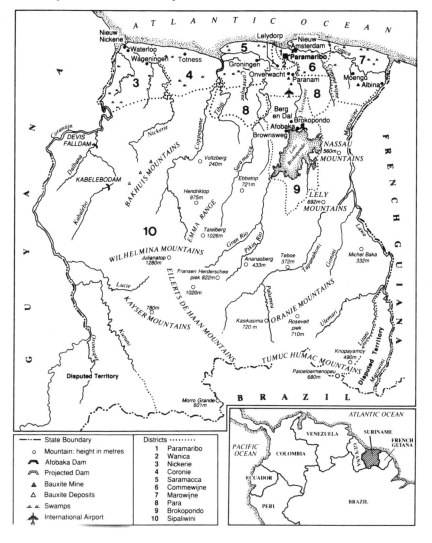